"Dominique DuBois Gilliard calls for a holy disruption of the systems and pipelines that imprison mostly black and brown people in the United States' mass-incarceration-industrial complex. *Rethinking Incarceration* exposes the ways the church has been complicit in this injustice and invites people of faith to engage in justice that is restorative. This book is historical, theological, scholarly, accessible, pastoral, and prophetic. It should be read in the seminary and university classroom, the pastor's study, and the church book club. Gilliard offers a very relevant word for one of the most central issues of our time!"

Curtiss Paul DeYoung, CEO, Minnesota Council of Churches

"An astonishing book—full of insights that draw from history, politics, social research, and Scripture. Gilliard crafts a compelling picture that links local policy and decisions and shows the impact on a national scale. This book is a thought-provoking call to the church to take a practical role in engaging with mass incarceration and its effects."

Nikki Toyama-Szeto, executive director, Evangelicals for Social Action (ESA)

"Dominique gives a thorough, honest look at the history of mass incarceration, blending advocacy and theology and driving us to respond as a community of faith. This is a must-read from a leader whose passion inspires hope."

Leroy Barber, Voices Project, board chair of Missio Alliance, author of *Embrace*

"Walking in the footsteps of Michelle Alexander and Bryan Stevenson, Dominique Gilliard lays out here the history and structure of mass incarceration in the United States, touching on all its sinister complications and biases; the equally sinister theological and scriptural moves that have accompanied it; and, most important of all, the powerful alternative vision and program that the church can—and must—now embody as it begins to dismantle this horror. A sustained, passionate, prophetic, and constructive work."

Douglas A. Campbell, professor of New Testament, Divinity School, Duke University

"This is the book I've been waiting for. Since the publication of *The New Jim Crow*, we have needed an analysis of incarceration and justice from a Christian perspective. *Rethinking Incarceration* is a powerful book that needs to circulate widely, for in it we learn not only of the issues, but how to move forward for desperately needed restorative change."

Michael O. Emerson, provost and professor, North Park University, author of *Divided by Faith*

"Dominique DuBois Gilliard's book is both hopeful and tough. The social and historical analysis is filled with hard truths. Incarceration in the United States cannot be separated from our racial history of the slavocracy in its former and contemporary forms. Gilliard writes to all who are deeply committed to embodying Christian understanding of justice, mercy, and restoration. . . . If you have ever taken time to notice the injustices that permeate our system of justice and have been brokenhearted by the abuses, racism, and privilege that doles out prison sentences to some and offers grace to others, you will be challenged by *Rethinking Incarceration*."

Phillis Isabella Sheppard, associate professor of religion, psychology, and culture, Vanderbilt University Divinity School

"This book is quick, informative, and deeply transformational. Our understanding of the human condition, notions of punishment and reform, and the nature of God are all at stake in Dominique Gilliard's theological and passionately argued work. Gilliard expertly traces our complicated relationship with prisons and mass incarceration through poignant historical analysis and compelling biblical argumentation. *Rethinking Incarceration* has the rare power to change the church in America."

Ken Wytsma, author of *The Myth of Equality: Uncovering the Roots of Injustice and Privilege*

"The church in the age of mass incarceration has too often been enslaved to a theology that makes sense of systemic oppression and human negation. Dominique Gilliard has gifted us with a robust and clarifying theology of the body and the church, pointing us in the direction of liberation, not just for the incarcerated, but also a church bound by chains of human hierarchy."

Michael McBride, National Director of PICO Network Urban Strategies and LIVE FREE Campaign

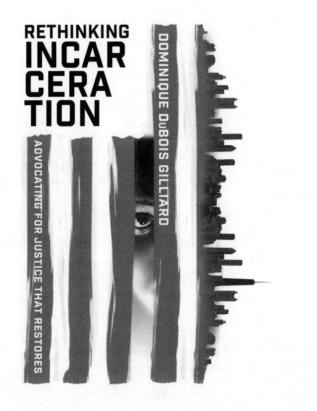

RETHINKING
INCAR
CERA
TION

DOMINIQUE DuBOIS GILLIARD

ADVOCATING FOR JUSTICE THAT RESTORES

IVP Books

An imprint of InterVarsity Press
Downers Grove, Illinois

InterVarsity Press
P.O. Box 1400, Downers Grove, IL 60515-1426
ivpress.com
email@ivpress.com

InterVarsity Press® is the book-publishing division of InterVarsity Christian Fellowship/USA®, a movement of students and faculty active on campus at hundreds of universities, colleges, and schools of nursing in the United States of America, and a member movement of the International Fellowship of Evangelical Students. For information about local and regional activities, visit intervarsity.org.

All Scripture quotations, unless otherwise indicated, are taken from The Holy Bible, New International Version®, NIV®. Copyright © 1973, 1978, 1984, 2011 by Biblica, Inc.™ Used by permission of Zondervan. All rights reserved worldwide. www.zondervan.com. The "NIV" and "New International Version" are trademarks registered in the United States Patent and Trademark Office by Biblica, Inc.™

While any stories in this book are true, some names and identifying information may have been changed to protect the privacy of individuals.

Figure 1.1: Reprinted by permission of the Prison Policy Initiative, www.prisonpolicy.org.

Cover design: David Fassett
Interior design: Daniel van Loon
Images: man: © Madison Hillhouse / EyeEm / Getty images
        Chicago skyline: ©alblec / iStockphoto

ISBN 978-0-8308-4529-3 (print)
ISBN 978-0-8308-8773-6 (digital)

Printed in the United States of America ∞

InterVarsity Press is committed to ecological stewardship and to the conservation of natural resources in all our operations. This book was printed using sustainably sourced paper.

Library of Congress Cataloging-in-Publication Data

Names: Gilliard, Dominique DuBois, 1984- author.
Title: Rethinking incarceration : advocating for justice that restores /
    Dominique DuBois Gilliard.
Description: Downers Grove : InterVarsity Press, 2018. | Includes
    bibliographical references and index.
Identifiers: LCCN 2018005769 (print) | LCCN 2018007266 (ebook) | ISBN
    9780830887736 (eBook) | ISBN 9780830845293 (pbk. : alk. paper)
Subjects: LCSH: Christianity and justice--United States. | Discrimination in
    criminal justice administration—United States. | Imprisonment—United
    States. | Jails—United States.
Classification: LCC BR115.J8 (ebook) | LCC BR115.J8 G55 2018 (print) | DDC
    261.8/336—dc23
LC record available at https://lccn.loc.gov/2018005769

P   25   24   23   22   21   20   19   18   17   16   15   14   13   12   11   10   9   8   7   6   5

Y   37   36   35   34   33   32   31   30   29   28   27   26   25   24   23   22   21   20   19   18

To parents who sacrificed, struggled,

and persevered more than I'll ever fully understand

in order to provide me with the opportunities

I've been blessed with.

And to my son Turé, whom I love

more than life itself. I vow to relentlessly fight

and toil to make this world a better place

for you to grow up in!

CONTENTS

INTRODUCTION

I MUST CONFESS THAT I STRUGGLED writing this book. Throughout the process I experienced a deep, lingering dissonance. My unrest emanated from knowing that mass incarceration is decimating communities, and yet I felt—at times—as if it is not the most urgent issue facing us today. Amid a racial nadir, it has been arduous investing my time, emotions, and heart in a project that does not explicitly name the elephant in the room. To write a book that does not explicitly address police brutality; the copious number of unarmed black, brown, and native lives lost to it; and the xenophobia spreading throughout our nation like a cancer felt disingenuous and unfaithful.

These are perilous times! I, along with much of the African American community, am living in a perpetual state of trauma resonant of this haunting line from *Hamilton*: "I imagine death so much it feels more like a memory / When is it gonna get me?"[1] I lose sleep contemplating this question. I feel paralyzed by its gravity, particularly as I pray for family members with cognitive impairments. The stress, strain, and anxiety of feeling as if there is a target on your back is debilitating. While composing this book, I repeatedly found myself paralyzed by trauma, unable to muster meaningful words. In those moments, even the most mundane tasks proved to be unbearable.

Between the World and Me is an evocative letter written by Ta-Nehisi Coates to his son about the dystopian reality of growing up black in the United States. Coates, paralleling his own experience to his son's, writes,

> The law did not protect us. And now, in your time, the law has become an excuse for stopping and frisking you, which is to say,

for furthering the assault on your body. But a society that protects some people through a safety net of schools, government-
backed home loans, and ancestral wealth but can only protect
you with a club of criminal justice has either failed at enforcing
its good intentions or has succeeded at something much darker.
However you call it, the result was our infirmity before the
criminal forces of the world. It does not matter if the agent of
those forces is white or black—what matters is our condition,
what matters is the system that makes your body breakable.[2]

As Coates explains, black bodies have historically evoked a peculiar
surveillance and a distinctive enforcement of the law. From the begin-
nings of vocational policing, where some officers functioned as slave
catchers, to the Jim Crow era, where cops rigidly enforced racial purity
boundaries, police have frequently functioned as a colonial presence
within black communities. Princeton professor Mark Lewis Taylor
writes, "The police are often the frontline for surveillance, control, and
dissemination of terror in poor communities."[3]

Within many impoverished communities of color, police are per-
ceived and experienced as an alien, occupying force. This intensifies
with each unsubstantiated stop-and-frisk, racist officer-involved text
scandal, and unarmed citizen killed—prompting a new hashtag.
Whether one affirms this perception of police or not, Scripture calls
the church to seek to understand why entire communities feel this
way. By meekly considering what has created this perception within
many stigmatized communities, the church begins to seek the interest of others first, as Philippians 2 commissions the body to do.
When the church takes this humble approach, we begin to take on the
mindset of Christ.

Let me be crystal clear: police have a difficult job, one that most
of us will never know the pressures of. I admire and respect the work
of officers who uphold their sworn duty to protect and serve, those
who patrol communities with dignity, integrity, and honor. I appre-
ciate their daily sacrifice and deeply grieve the loss of their lives in

the line of duty. These virtuous officers deserve our utmost respect, gratitude, and support.

Nevertheless, my admiration for upstanding officers cannot obscure the truth. We have systemic policing problems. While body camera, dash cams, and cell phone videos have recently exposed unethical policing practices and behavior to a broader segment of society, many of us know that these are not new realities. Furthermore, our policing problems are far more expansive than officers killing unarmed and mentally impaired citizens of color. Our policing problems—implicit bias, racial profiling, and the ethical abuse of power—are pervasive, and they cannot be reduced to a few rogue officers. Yes, bad apples must be expelled from law enforcement, but our challenges are institutional, and they are exacerbated by a lack of judicial accountability.

Policing failures are merely symptoms of problems inherent in our broader criminal justice system. Police bear a disproportionate share of the criticism for an inept system. In many ways, they have become the scapegoats of a morally bankrupt system. They are the whipping boys of a system marred by racial and class biases, breeding racial profiling and partial sentencing that has crescendoed into mass incarceration. This does not exonerate police—corrupt cops must be held accountable—but we must acknowledge that officers frequently carry more than their fair share of the blame within a system proven to be ethically and morally deficient.

Our nation's overcrowded jails, prisons, and detention centers are an indictment of our criminal justice system. It is impossible to visit these institutions and not be struck by the inhumane treatment of the people serving time and the disproportionate number of black and brown bodies confined in cages like animals. These men and women are America's latest crop of strange fruit.

THE REVELATION THAT BRED A REVOLUTION

In the groundbreaking book *The New Jim Crow* (2010), Michelle Alexander defines our prison system as a method of racially charged social control that creates "a lower caste of individuals who are permanently barred by law and custom from mainstream society."[4] While many knew our criminal justice system was flawed, virtually no one dared to ponder something this dire was transpiring in 2010. In fact, Alexander herself was initially skeptical of activists who connected mass incarceration to Jim Crow. She initially called their claims hyperbole and detrimental to the cause. However, as she formed relationships with people disenfranchised by the system, she was compelled to do more investigative research on their claims and started to see the system anew. Alexander, who was working as the director of the Racial Justice Project at the American Civil Liberties Union (ACLU) of Northern California, set the spark that has ignited a revolution.

Alexander begins her book by sharing the story of Jarvious Cotton, a disenfranchised black man. Alexander says, "Like his father, grandfather, great-grandfather, and great-great grandfather, he has been denied the right to participate in our electoral democracy."[5] Expanding the scope of her inquiry, she reveals that "today there are more African-American adults under correctional control, in prison or jail, on probation or parole, than were enslaved in 1850, a decade before the Civil War."[6] Honing in on how the War on Drugs has depleted the black community, Alexander notes that "in at least fifteen states, blacks are admitted to prison on drug charges at a rate from twenty to fifty-seven times greater than that of white men."[7] However, in spite of needed policy reforms, Alexander ultimately concludes that "all of the needed reforms have less to do with failed policies than a deeply flawed public consensus, one that is indifferent, at best, to the experience of poor people of color."[8]

As a pastor, this haunted me. It lingered, and I kept thinking, *If anyone should be leading the charge, demonstrating what a morally and ethically rooted public consensus consists of, it should be—it must be—the church!* But as someone who has ministered in some of the cities most ravaged by mass incarceration (Atlanta, Chicago, and Oakland), I lamentably confess that we have failed to do this. Furthermore, I can attest that the church—broadly speaking—is still eerily silent, seven years later.

Bryan Stevenson's *Just Mercy* picked up where *The New Jim Crow* left off, keeping mass incarceration on our national conscience. *Just Mercy* explores how mercy should inform our understanding of justice, causing us to see how our brokenness distorts what we understand and pursue as justice. Stevenson writes, "The power of just mercy is that it belongs to the undeserving. It's when mercy is least expected that it's most potent—strong enough to break the cycle of victimization and victimhood, retribution and suffering. It has the power to heal the psychic harm and injuries that lead to aggression and violence, abuse of power, mass incarceration."[9]

Rethinking Incarceration picks up on *Just Mercy*'s ethos, illuminating restorative justice as a philosophical practice that enables Christians to practically embrace mercy as we pursue justice that reflects God's heart. While it builds on both Alexander's and Stevenson's works, it is profoundly different. This book will frame mass incarceration theologically, examining the church's role in its evolution and sustainment while advocating for an alternative, christocentric way to engage our criminal justice system.

This book provides a historical analysis of mass incarceration and a biblical basis for reframing how we think, teach, and preach about justice. It offers a new lens for interpreting how God's justice is manifested in the world, and provides tangible steps for individual Christians and congregations who are interested in pursuing biblically rooted justice.

This book is unique because it is written for the church, and yet it upholds a robust historical and sociological analysis. Both Alexander and Stevenson identify the detrimental effects of the War on Drugs, but this text explores four additional pipelines feeding the prison-industrial complex: the war on immigration, mental health, private prisons, and the school-to-prison pipeline.

This book interrogates some sacred cows that generally go unquestioned in the church, troubling some of our presuppositions regarding incarcerated people, the social function of prisons, and theologies promoting an unquestioned allegiance to law and order. Many

Christians rarely question things like what it means to pledge our allegiance to anything other than God, or how neatly our faith can fit within a particular political party. Due in large part to the muddling of patriotism and Christianity, being a good citizen for many is equivalent to being a good Christian. But what happens when patriotism opposes what Scripture tells us faithfully following Christ entails? These questions profoundly inform our response to mass incarceration.

The first part of this book deals with how mass incarceration evolved and evaluates who is incarcerated. Chapter one details the history of the War on Drugs and frames the pivotal moment we are in. Chapter two traces the sociopolitical history of our criminal justice system, exploring the impact of institutional racism, sexism, and classism while connecting incarceration to a history of profiteering and privatization. Chapter three explores law and order, its political roots, evangelical base, and congruence with Scripture. Chapter four unpacks how immigration, mental health, and private prisons serve as conduits to mass incarceration. Chapter five details the history of our juvenile justice system and the school-to-prison pipeline.

The second half of the book looks at the role of the church and its theology, pointing to ways we can join the revolution to end mass incarceration. Chapter six explores the church's engagement with those behind bars, from the initial prison ministers to the growth of prison ministries, identifying what the church has done well and ways we can still improve. Chapter seven explores the role of prison chaplains and how their theology has informed prison culture, discipline, and punishment. Chapter eight interrogates Christian theology's connection to mass incarceration, specifically addressing penal substitution and the ways it has undergirded a retributive response to crime. Chapter nine lays out a biblical definition of justice and righteousness. Chapter ten elucidates the overarching nature of divine justice as restorative—bringing about healing in the face of harm and reconciliation amid conflict. Chapter eleven then reframes incarceration and highlights some of the most innovative approaches to curtailing mass incarceration.

A REVELATORY MOMENT

With most issues like mass incarceration, there is a revelatory moment when we realize how profoundly this world has trained us to think about others. This moment is a rude awakening, and the knee-jerk reaction is to deny the truth of what the Spirit is prompting within. My moment came within a group of men reentering society after being incarcerated. These men were recovering from addictions and striving to turn their lives around one day at a time.

As an urban pastor working within institutionally neglected communities, I was asked to do a number of unusual things. One of the most peculiar—and challenging—requests I have received was to teach men returning to society from prison how they should define and practice healthy sexuality.

I remember feeling intimidated by this request. I did not know these men. I had never taught a course for people reentering society, much less those reentering with addictions. And even as a seminary graduate and pastor, I had participated in very few in-depth, honest conversations about healthy sexuality within the confines of Christianity. So, how was I going to teach these men? This was a daunting task.

I was married, in my late twenties, and had never struggled with substance abuse. I had never been incarcerated, and while I had done some ministry behind bars, I had not yet learned what it meant to authentically commune with prisoners. I doubted whether God had inspired this invitation; was the organization short of staff and simply trying to fill gaps? I wondered why these men would listen to me, and what wisdom I had to offer them.

Upon beginning the course, my anxieties were relieved. The men were surprisingly eager to learn and were overjoyed to have authentic conversations about sex within a Christian setting—something they unanimously said they had never done before. These men were diligent, inquisitive, and sincere learners.

Through this class I bonded with these men in unexpected ways. We were all surprised at how much more we had in common than we initially expected. On the one hand, sexuality is something we all think about, and everyone desires intimacy. So maybe we should not have been shocked, but we all made assumptions of the other. Because of the social labels we bore—pastor and formerly incarcerated—we entered into the arrangement with suspicion.

The experience left me wondering why I held certain assumptions about prisoners and the formerly incarcerated. I began pondering the various ways those unconscious assumptions prohibited me from doing kingdom work and authentically communing with my brothers and sisters behind bars, who were trying with every fiber of their being to turn their lives around and reintegrate into society with integrity and honor. I needed to explore what needed to change within me before thinking about how I could minister to those I was asked to teach and lead.

It was not until I reached this point of clarity that God began to expand my ministry and fruitfully use me in this context. I had to realize that any time we try to do ministry with an *us*-and-*them* mentality—no matter how subtle it may be—we fail to authentically embody the gospel. Before we enter a new ministerial context, we must be responsible enough to interrogate our hearts and minds to unearth the stereotypes, prejudices, and fears that lie dormant or that we clandestinely hold.

I had to consistently ask God to reveal to me these implicit and explicit biases. As they were divulged, I had to confront the ways I had conformed to the patterns of this world. This was not easy, and at many points it was a painful blow to my ego. But we all have blind spots and biases; therefore, we all need the Spirit of God to renew our minds.

In Matthew 25, Jesus says, "I was sick and in prison and you did not look after me." Hebrews 13:3 exhorts Christians to "continue to remember those in prison as if you were together with them in prison, and those who are mistreated as if you yourselves were suffering." I could not shake these two calls and the claim they made on my life as a new creation. As I grew as a minister, these passages intensified my conviction, and God began leading me down a path I would have never anticipated for myself. In fact, some of the most profoundly revelatory moments of my faith journey have occurred as I have walked with people who have been adversely affected by our criminal justice system. Moreover, some of the most significant ways the Spirit has begun renewing my mind did not occur until I started spending time with Jesus in prison, becoming aware of his presence within those the world and much of the church believes are unredeemable.

A LOVE OFFERING

This project is a labor of love—a sacrificial offering—laid before the throne of God on behalf of my neighbor. I pray it awakens the church to the tragic realities of mass incarceration and inspires us to envision and work toward a justice system predicated on reconciliation, restoration, and reintegration. I hope this book makes clear that mass incarceration will not end via legislative tweaks and incremental reforms. Mass incarceration will be halted only by a moral awakening. Citizens nationwide must refuse to remain silent while entire communities are stigmatized, targeted, and destroyed by a system preying on the least of these.

As followers of Christ, we must ask what our faith calls us to in this unprecedented era of mass incarceration. Collectively and individually, we must contemplate what bearing witness to the gospel in this critical moment entails. Dr. King said, "The church must be reminded that it is not the master or the servant of the state, but rather the conscience of the state. It must be the guide and the critic of the state, and never its tool. If the church does not recapture its prophetic zeal, it will become an irrelevant social club without moral or spiritual authority."[10] For far too long, the church has functioned as the state's tool. Unwittingly, we have theologically legitimated mass incarceration and conceded our prophetic zeal. But we must reemerge as the moral conscience of our nation.

Toni Cade Bambara says, "The job of a writer is to make revolution irresistible."[11] I pray this book awakens readers to the urgent need for a revolution and inspires the church to play a leading role in it. United, empowered by the Spirit, and in humble solidarity with others, we can end mass incarceration, shaking the very foundations of an immoral system, as Paul and Silas did in Acts 16!

PART 1

THE ROOTS AND EVOLUTION OF MASS INCARCERATION

THE WAR ON DRUGS

DURING THE WINTER OF 2006—my senior year of undergrad studies—a tragedy occurred ten miles from my campus, changing the trajectory of my life. Kathryn Johnston, a ninety-two-year-old woman, was shot and killed by police in the living room of her Atlanta home. In what was deemed a "botched drug raid," unidentified officers stormed Johnston's home with assault weapons drawn—at 3:00 a.m.—murdering her without cause. Three officers discharged thirty-nine shots, fatally striking Johnston five times. These three officers, Jason Smith, Greg Junnier, and Arthur Tesler, then conspired to cover their transgressions.

In the court proceedings for Johnston's homicide, it was determined that the police raid was based on and legitimated by falsified paperwork. Officer Tesler had lied in an affidavit, saying that illegal drugs were being harbored in Johnston's home. Tesler swore under oath that an informant purchased crack cocaine at Johnston's house, but during the trial the informant testified that he had never been to Johnston's home.

Ultimately, all three officers pled guilty to federal charges of conspiracy to violate civil rights resulting in death. Officers Smith and Junnier also pled guilty to state charges of voluntary manslaughter and making false statements, while Smith admitted to planting bags of marijuana in Johnston's home after killing her in an attempt to justify the home invasion and murder. The three officers were sentenced to prison terms ranging from five to ten years, to be followed by three years of supervised release after their prison terms, and were ordered to split the cost of Johnston's funeral.

During the trial, Greg Junnier broke down on the witness stand, declaring, "I used to think I was a good person." Jason Smith, weeping, said, "I pray daily for Ms. Johnston. I also pray other officers in Atlanta will have the moral fortitude I didn't have."[1]

At the conclusion of the trial, US attorney David Nahmias said, "As Atlanta police narcotics officers, these three defendants repeatedly failed to follow proper procedures and then lied under oath to obtain search warrants." Nahmias concluded, "Their routine violations of the Fourth Amendment led to the death of an innocent citizen." Further, according to an article recapping the trial, "The officers regularly presented false information to obtain warrants and . . . cut corners to make more time for lucrative side jobs providing additional security to businesses, often while on duty, and receiving cash payments."[2]

Before the trial, these officers had vehemently declared their innocence. They claimed to have surveilled Johnston's home for months, identifying it as an epicenter for drug trafficking. Tesler's falsified affidavit had been the key to obtaining a no-knock warrant (a warrant that allows officers to enter private property without displaying a warrant or issuing credentials). Tesler knew that his "confirmation" of illicit activity in Johnston's home would be enough to persuade the judge to issue a no-knock warrant, particularly because her community was stigmatized as "the ghetto."[3]

No-knock search warrants are issued by judges at the request of law enforcement to acquire evidence that can be quickly destroyed. They are also granted in cases where it is believed an officer's safety is at risk while executing the warrant. No-knock warrants are predominantly issued in impoverished, governmentally neglected communities of color, marred by failing schools, a lack of economic opportunity, and drug trafficking. No-knock warrants are commonplace in these communities, and they give police the authority to conduct militarized "dynamic entry" raids. Dynamic entry raids include the use of door-breaching shotguns, battering rams, sledgehammers, Halligan bars (for smashing windows), ballistic shields, Colt submachine guns, light-mounted AR-15 rifles, Glock .40-caliber sidearms, body armor, Kevlar helmets, and potent flash-bang grenades. Under the legislative power endowed by no-knock warrants, these militarized weapons are subject to be used at an officer's discretion, without accountability.[4]

Dynamic entry raids are conducted by SWAT officers. SWAT is a specialized enforcement taskforce pioneered in Los Angeles in 1967. Kevin Sack, a *New York Times* columnist, details the rapid growth of SWAT teams, writing, "Today, almost every police agency with at least 100 officers, and about a third of all smaller ones, either has its own full-time unit or participates in a part-time or multijurisdictional team."[5] Dr. Peter B. Kraska, a criminologist at Eastern Kentucky University, writes that SWAT deployments increased "roughly fifteenfold between 1980 and 2000 as the drug war escalated."[6] According to Michelle Alexander, "The most common use of SWAT teams is to serve narcotics warrants, usually with forced, unannounced entry into the home."[7] The ACLU found that 42 percent of SWAT search warrant raids were conducted in black communities, and 12 percent in Hispanic neighborhoods.[8] This history and these statistics begin to explain the disproportionate number of black and brown bodies warehoused within our nation's prisons, jails, and detention centers.[9]

Sack writes that the Bureau of Justice Statistics illustrates that "the no-knock process often begins with unreliable informants and cursory investigations that produce affidavits signed by unquestioning low-level judges. It is not uncommon for the searches to yield only misdemeanor-level stashes, or to come up empty."[10] Not only are dynamic entry raids ineffective, they are also extremely dangerous, as evidenced in Johnston's case. The National Tactical Officers Association (NTOA) has consistently contested the overuse of dynamic entry raids, and its chairman, Robert Chabali (2012–2015), recommended that dynamic entry "never be used to serve narcotics warrants."[11] Chabali, a SWAT veteran, said, "It just makes no sense. . . . Why would you run into a gunfight? If we are going to risk our lives, we risk them for a hostage, for a citizen, for a fellow officer. You definitely don't go in and risk your life for drugs."[12]

Kathryn Johnston's murder was an affront to justice. It placed a spotlight on the Atlanta Police Department that revealed broad corruption in the narcotics unit and eventual guilty pleas. Upon learning about this corruption, I became infatuated with learning about the War on Drugs. As I researched I soon learned that Johnston's case was not an anomaly—it was merely the latest tragedy in a host of civil rights breaches caused by drug war legislation.

What I learned changed my life. It compelled me to devote my ministry to defending the dignity of poor, undereducated, disenfranchised people living within stigmatized neighborhoods. While the police misconduct exposed in Johnston's case provoked major changes throughout the APD, it inspired me to commit my life to ending mass incarceration.

As someone who grew up with numerous friends who did not have black men in their lives (fathers, brothers, uncles, and cousins), I was acutely aware that incarceration was crippling my community. I knew that many black men with the potential to be community role models were continuously being extracted from neighborhoods and transported to prison. But I did not know at the time that incarceration was also adversely affecting black women, other communities of color, and society's most vulnerable populations.

I also did not realize that while our criminal justice system was being celebrated as the most responsible way to reform and rehabilitate people serving time, mass incarceration had corrupted and perverted our system into a complex in which exploitation, profiteering, and inhumane treatment were the norm. Upon awakening to these realities, the Spirit convicted me and compelled me to become an advocate and activist for those rendered voiceless by the system. While there are no voiceless people, when powerful systems and structures go astray, they mute the voices of those who are persecuted and crushed by systemic sin and immorality.

As Christians, people called to seek the peace and prosperity of our cities, we must oppose policies like no-knock warrants, dramatic entry, and the ability for one officer's unsubstantiated claim to legitimate warfare. These polices wreak havoc on vulnerable communities, cause senseless deaths—think of Kathryn Johnston, Aiyana

Jones (a seven-year-old in Detroit), and Eurie Stamps (a sixty-eight-year-old grandfather in Framingham, Massachusetts)—and embolden police corruption.

THE WAR ON DRUGS

While SWAT teams are on the frontlines enforcing the War on Drugs, Michelle Alexander notes that "police and prosecutors did not declare the War on Drugs."[13] Drug war rhetoric has been strategically championed by presidents, congressional representatives, and senators. While officers are frequently vilified and scapegoated for the drug war, often they are simply carrying out the orders of their superiors.

Richard Nixon initially declared the War on Drugs in 1971. His administration oversaw the creation of new measures, such as mandatory sentencing and no-knock warrants, and worked tirelessly to bolster federal drug control agencies. The War on Drugs led to the creation of the Drug Enforcement Administration (DEA) in 1973. The DEA's mission was to establish a single, unified command to wage "an all-out global war on the drug menace."[14]

The War on Drugs was expanded under Ronald Reagan's presidency, and funding radically increased.[15] The Reagan administration launched an offensive on drug crimes at a time when only 2 percent of Americans felt that drug crimes were the most important issue facing the country.[16] This expansion of the drug war bred critical policy changes, increasing the penalties for drug offenses while simultaneously incentivizing drug arrests for law enforcement agencies. Reagan granted state and local law enforcement agencies the right to keep most of the cash and assets seized during drug raids and arrests.[17] Alexander says, "Suddenly, police departments were capable of increasing the size of their budgets, quite substantially, simply by taking the cash, cars, and homes of people suspected of drug use or sales."[18]

The use of mandatory minimum sentences for drug offenses also expanded under Reagan. Mandatory minimums are often cited as an important way of keeping violent criminals and drug lords off the streets, but these sentences are most often handed down against nonviolent drug offenders.[19] The Anti-Drug Abuse Act of 1986 changed drug sentencing, creating mandatory minimum sentences typically ranging from five to ten years.[20] In the rest of the developed world, a first-time drug offense is typically only met with up to six months in jail.[21]

Statistics illustrate that mandatory minimums disproportionately affect minority offenders. Until 2010, a five-year mandatory minimum was triggered for the sale of five hundred grams of powder cocaine, a drug more typically associated with white users, while the sale of *five grams* of crack, a drug more typically associated with black and Hispanic users, triggered the same sentence.[22] According to the ACLU,

> The scientifically unjustifiable 100:1 ratio meant that people faced longer sentences for offenses involving crack cocaine than for offenses involving the same amount of powder cocaine—two forms of the same drug. Most disturbingly, because the majority of people arrested for crack offenses are African American, the 100:1 ratio resulted in vast racial disparities in the average length of sentences for comparable offenses. On average, under the 100:1 regime, African Americans served virtually as much time in prison for non-violent drug offenses as whites did for violent offenses.[23]

In 2010, this gross disparity was finally addressed by Congress, but only partially. The Fair Sentencing Act (FSA) reduced the sentencing disparity from 100:1 to 18:1. Consequently, a stark racial disparity persists, because, as the ACLU concludes, "the only truly fair ratio is 1:1."[24]

Michelle Alexander explains something that makes the sentencing disparity for cocaine even more sinister. She writes,

> The CIA admitted in 1998 that guerrilla armies it actively supported in Nicaragua were smuggling illegal drugs into the United States—drugs that were making their way onto the streets of inner-city black neighborhoods in the form of crack cocaine. The CIA also admitted that, in the midst of the War on Drugs, it

blocked law enforcement efforts to investigate illegal drug net-
works that were helping to fund its covert war in Nicaragua.[25]

What does the CIA's confession convey to the black community—
particularly communities ravaged by the drug war?

Another important Reagan-era policy was the 1988 Omnibus Anti-
Abuse Act. This act precipitated a five-year mandatory sentence for
possessing as little as five grams of crack cocaine. It also broadened
the definition of drug trafficking crimes to include conspiracy to
commit those offenses.[26] The US Sentencing Commission notes that
mandatory minimums are frequently used as a coercive bargaining
chip to get defendants to acquiesce to plea bargains.[27]

During Bill Clinton's presidency, the War on Drugs was expanded
yet again. While many have depicted the War on Drugs as a Republican
initiative, the drug war was a bipartisan effort. This rhetoric of law and
order deployed by politicians won elections nationwide, from races for
local council seats to the presidency. The Clinton administration
created the Violent Crime Control and Law Enforcement Act of 1994,
which included a provision that required a life sentence in prison to
any individual convicted of committing their third drug offense, even
though only one of the three offenses was serious enough to be classified as a felony.[28] During Clinton's State of the Union address in
1994, he declared, "Three strikes and you're out!" before an applauding
audience. Between the years of 1993 and 1995, twenty-five states enacted three-strikes legislation.[29] In 1995, Georgia passed a "two strikes
and you're out" sentencing policy, which penalized offenders to life
imprisonment for their second drug offense.

Alexander writes,

> Georgia's district attorneys, who had unrestrained discretion re-
> garding when to enact this punitive penalty, decided to only
> issue it for 1 percent of white defendants facing a second drug
> conviction but chose to issue it against 16 percent of black defen-
> dants. Consequently, 98.4 percent of those serving life sentences
> under the provision were black. Additionally, The Justice Policy

Institute found that "the Clinton Administration's 'tough on crime' policies resulted in the largest increases in federal and state prison inmates of any president in American history."[30]

Under Clinton, the militarization of local police departments increased. Alexander explains,

> The Pentagon has given away military intelligence and millions of dollars in firepower to state and local agencies willing to make the rhetorical war a literal one. Almost immediately after the federal dollars began to flow, law enforcement agencies across the country began to compete for funding, equipment, and training. By the late 1990s, the overwhelming majority of state and local police forces in the country had availed themselves of the newly available resources and added a significant military component to buttress their drug-war operations.[31]

In fact, the Cato Institute, a public policy organization, notes that in 1997 alone, "the Pentagon handed over more than 1.2 million pieces of military equipment to local police departments."[32] Additionally, the *National Journal* reported that between January 1997 and October 1999 there were 3.4 million orders of Pentagon equipment—from over eleven thousand domestic police agencies across every state.[33]

The War on Drugs opened the floodgates, sanctioning law enforcement to engage in guerrilla warfare within impoverished communities coast to coast. It also criminalized addiction while most Americans barely batted an eye, leading to a great multitude of nonviolent drug addicts who needed medical interventions instead being sentenced to life in prison. We cannot incarcerate ourselves out of addiction. Addiction is a medical crisis that—when it comes to nonviolent offenders—warrants medical interventions, not incarceration. Decades later, data unequivocally illustrates that this war has been a massive failure. It has not only failed to reduce violent crime, but arrest rates—throughout its tenure—have continuously ascended even when crime rates have descended.[34]

For example, while crime rates in countries such as Finland, Germany, and the United States remained stable in the latter half of the twentieth century, incarceration in the United States quadrupled. Comparatively, it fell by 60 percent in Finland, and there was little change in Germany.[35] The drug war fostered a 1,100 percent increase in drug arrests between 1980 and 2006.[36]

In 2010 it was estimated that three-quarters of young black men in Washington, DC (and higher in the poorest neighborhoods) could expect to be incarcerated for drugs. As a result, these young men will carry criminal records for the rest of their lives—criminal records that will legalize discrimination against them.[37]

Sociologist Loïc Wacquant writes, "The rate of incarceration for African Americans has soared to levels unknown in any other society and is higher now than the total incarceration rate in the Soviet Union at the zenith of the Gulag and in South Africa at the height of the anti-apartheid struggle."[38] According to Wacquant, in order to understand the phenomena of black hyper-incarceration, we need to examine the crime-and-punishment paradigm that ultimately serves to disfranchise and control.[39]

THE INCARCERATION OF WOMEN

While analysis of the War on Drugs usually focuses on men, the number of women imprisoned during this era has also skyrocketed, growing 700 percent since 1980. The United States represents nearly one-third of the world's female prisoners. They are incarcerated primarily for nonviolent crimes, including drug and property offenses.[40] Today women represent 9 percent of the state and federal prison population.[41] Furthermore black women's arrest in particular for drug-related offenses "grew by 828 percent—triple the growth in arrest rate for white women and double that of black men" during the prime years of the drug war, the late 1980s and 1990s.[42]

In *Just Mercy*, Bryan Stevenson notes that a series of legislative changes have led to this dramatic increase in the incarceration of women. He details what he calls the "the collateral consequences of incarcerating women," explaining, "Approximately 75 to 80 percent of incarcerated women are mothers with minor children. Nearly 65 percent had minor children living with them at the time of their arrest—children who have become more vulnerable and at-risk as a result of their mother's incarceration and will remain so for the rest of their lives, even after their mothers come home."[43]

Stevenson writes,

> One of the first incarcerated women I ever met was a young mother who was serving a long prison sentence for writing checks to buy her three young children Christmas gifts without sufficient funds in her account. Like a character in a Victor Hugo novel, she tearfully explained her heartbreaking tale to me. I couldn't accept the truth of what she was saying until I checked her file and discovered that she had, in fact, been convicted and sentenced to over ten years in prison for writing five checks, including three to Toys "R" Us. None of the checks was for more than $150. She was not unique. Thousands of women have been sentenced to lengthy terms in prison for writing bad checks or for minor property crimes that trigger mandatory minimum sentences.[44]

This tragic reality was exacerbated by congressional welfare reform passed in 1996. This legislation, Stevenson explains,

> gratuitously included a provision that authorized states to ban people with drug convictions from public benefits and welfare. The population most affected by this misguided law is formerly incarcerated women with children, most of whom were imprisoned for drug crimes. These women and their children can no longer live in public housing, receive food stamps, or access basic services. In the last twenty years, we've created a new class of "untouchables" in American society, made up of our most vulnerable mothers and their children.[45]

Scripture calls the church to seek the peace and prosperity of our cities, to defend the dignity of the least of these, and to protect society's most vulnerable. Our criminal system preys upon these vulnerable groups and is perpetuating intergenerational poverty and trauma.

THE TULIA RAIDS

Due to the policies set in place by the War on Drugs, Kathryn Johnston's case is not an anomaly. Before dawn on July 23, 1999, SWAT officers, armed in combat gear, conducted synchronized dynamic entry raids on the homes of forty-seven citizens of Tulia, Texas, a rural town of about five thousand. These residents were arrested and paraded (half-dressed, hair unkempt) before news cameras, charged with dealing drugs.[46] Amid the chaos, a neighbor shouted, "They're arresting all the black folks!"[47] This seemingly hyperbolic assessment was not completely erroneous.

Of the forty-seven people arrested, forty were black.[48] This number constituted nearly 30 percent of the town's black males and 20 percent of its black adults.[49] Every arrest was based exclusively on the sole testimony of an undercover Caucasian officer. The raid's convictions resulted in draconian sentences ranging from twenty to forty-five and even ninety-nine year charges. These outlandish verdicts were even issued to defendants without criminal records. These punitive sentences coerced defendants awaiting trial to consent to plea bargains despite vowing their innocence.

The defendants were mired in poverty. They could not afford a lawyer, much less the experienced legal representation that these severe charges warranted. In fact, most defendants could not even muster funds to post bail. With their lives hanging in the balance, most defendants elected not to take the risk of hoping for a fair trial in a Tulia court legislated by a Caucasian judge and jury. Attorney Erick Willard said that he advised clients to accept pleas "because they did not believe and I did not believe they could get a fair hearing."[50]

LaWanda Smith, who agreed to a plea, only agreed because she feared a biased trial. Smith said that not only had she never sold drugs to the undercover agent, Tom Coleman, she had "never met the guy . . . not ever."[51] While many defendants agreed to pleas, they did so out of self-preservation, not guilt. Repeatedly, poor, vulnerable minorities were intimidated into acquiescing to guilty pleas—knowing that they did not commit the alleged crimes—because of the fear the inflated sentences confronting them induced.

THE TRIALS AND AFTERMATH

In a financially incentivized climate created by the War on Drugs, Tom Coleman was named Texas's Outstanding Narcotics Officer and the Outstanding Lawman of the Year. Randy Credico of the Fund for Racial Justice explains the drug sting: "The Panhandle task force was the beneficiary of Coleman's lies. The more busts he made and the more convictions he helped win, the more federal grant money the task force received."[52] The drug war's economic incentives have repeatedly led to innocent people being railroaded by a corrupt system.

While the vast majority of defendants in the Tulia drug bust agreed to plea bargains, the few who went to trial saw their court proceedings last for up to three years. Nearly four years after the raid, a judge threw out all thirty-eight convictions, and the governor released the twelve remaining incarcerated defendants. In trial, it became clear that Coleman repeatedly lied, practiced with racial bias, and had no corroborating evidence. The court determined that Coleman had falsified reports, distorted his evidence, and misidentified defendants. Cumulatively, defendants spent over seventy years wrongly incarcerated because of Coleman's immorality.

They cannot get those years back. They cannot undo the relational harm their incarceration caused. Estranged from family—particularly their children—defendants missed developmental milestones, graduations, birthdays, and holidays. While a five-million-dollar settlement was eventually reached and divided among forty-five defendants, Kizzie White, who spent four years behind bars, summarizes things well: "The money is good . . . but that can't bring back the time I missed with my kids."[53]

While it is tempting to dismiss Johnston's case and Tulia as aberrations, the ACLU filed a lawsuit in 2000—a year after Tulia—in a case mirroring Tulia. In Hearne, Texas, another rural community of about five thousand residents, another undercover officer's drug bust led to 15 percent of the town's black men aged eighteen to thirty-four being falsely arrested.[54] While overt racial corruption of this nature is not necessarily commonplace, the policies and practices that made these flawed raids possible are.

THE BROADER CONNECTION

A 1995 survey asked, "Would you close your eyes for a second, envision a drug user, and describe that person to me?" The *Journal of Alcohol and Drug Education* published the results. While in reality a strong majority of drug users are white, most respondents—95 percent—pictured African Americans.[55]

Only 15 percent of drug users at that time were black (and the same is roughly true today). Studies have shown that whites are more likely to use and deal drugs. White youth in particular are seven times more likely to use cocaine and heroin than black youth, and three times more likely to sell drugs.[56] Despite these facts, African Americans represent the vast majority of drug offenders sent to prison (see fig. 1.1).

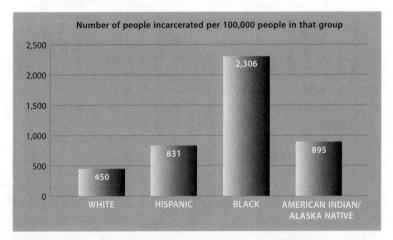

Figure 1.1. United States incarceration rates by race/ethnicity 2010
Note: Incarcerated populations are all types of correctional facilities in a state, including federal and state prisons, local jails, and halfway houses. Statistics for whites are for non-Hispanic whites.
Source: Calculated by the Prison Policy Initiative from US Census 2010 Summary File.

Our justice system is fundamentally broken, but so is our vision. We are socialized to see entire ethnic groups as being more prone to criminal activity than others. We are trained by this society to believe that members of certain communities of color will inevitably end up behind bars. After all, many believe that the statistics validate this belief.

Today, it is predicted that nationwide one in three black males and one in six Hispanic males will be incarcerated in their lifetime.[57] We have come to accept this as natural. But why doesn't our discipleship inspire us to interrogate this belief?

SILENCE IS NOT AN OPTION

This view of black and Hispanic men is ungodly, and we must repent. Stigmatizing entire communities is nothing new. In fact, Jesus came from Nazareth, and it was believed that nothing good could come from there. When black and brown people are universally criminalized, we all suffer. And when the church fails to name, renounce, and reshape this through biblically based discipleship, we too have blood on our hands. As Bryan Stevenson writes, "We are all implicated when we allow other people to be mistreated. An absence of compassion can corrupt the decency of a community, a state, a nation."[58]

When we dehumanize others, we become less human ourselves. In his seminal text *The Hidden Wound*, Wendell Berry says, "No man will ever be whole and dignified and free except in the knowledge that the men around him are whole and dignified and free." Taking this even further, Berry continues, "If the white man has inflicted the wound of racism upon black men, the cost has been that he would receive the mirror image of that wound into himself. As the master, or as a member of the dominant race, he has felt little compulsion to acknowledge or speak of it; the more painful it has grown the more deeply he has hidden it within himself. But the wound is there, and is a profound disorder, as great a damage in his mind as it is in his society."[59] With this knowledge, the church must not shy away from political activism. We helped pass the laws that incited the War on Drugs, and now we must mobilize to change them.

We have a responsibility to defend the dignity of society's most vulnerable, and policies such as mandatory minimums and no-knock warrants put both police and citizens at risk. These policies do not enhance our society, make our communities safer, or reflect God's love and justice. They are legislative issues that the church can, and must, work to change. We have an ethical and theological responsibility to advocate for a justice system that brings restoration to individuals and communities.

A CRITICAL MOMENT

While the United States constitutes only 5 percent of the world's population, we have 25 percent of its incarcerated populace. Statistically, our nation currently has more people locked up—in jails, prisons, and detention centers—than any other country in the history of the world. We currently have more jails and prisons than degree-granting colleges and universities. In some areas of the country, there are more people living behind bars than on college campuses.[60]

One out of every twenty-five people sentenced to the death penalty are falsely convicted.[61] In many states, pregnant women are shackled to gurneys during their delivery.[62] Thirteen states have no minimum age for prosecuting children as adults, such that children as young as eight have been tried and sentenced as adults, left vulnerable to trauma and abuse while living among adults in jails and prisons.[63]

Eighty thousand inmates per day are locked in solitary confinement, where they are quarantined in a twelve-by-seven-foot concrete cell (smaller than a standard horse stall), frequently for twenty-three hours a day, and are only allowed outdoor access and human interaction for one hour. This dehumanizing form of "incarceration" is more accurately defined as torture—a slow assault on the dignity of individuals and a strategic disintegration of their body and psyche. The Geneva Convention defines torture as

> any act by which severe pain or suffering, whether physical or mental, is intentionally inflicted on a person for such purposes

as obtaining a confession, punishment for an act that a person is suspected of having committed, or intimidating or coercing a person for any reason based on discrimination of any kind, when such pain or suffering is inflicted by or at the instigation of or with the consent or acquiescence of a public official or other person acting in an official capacity.[64]

How did this become our reality, and who are the people serving time behind bars? Lawyer and criminology expert Elliott Currie writes, "Short of major wars, mass incarceration has been the most thoroughly implemented government social program of our time."[65] While most theorists trace our criminal justice system's exponential growth back to Richard Nixon's commissioning of the drug war, this—in isolation—is an inadequate analysis. The history that bred our carceral quagmire predates Nixon's presidency, and it is much more expansive than the War on Drugs. While the drug war is undoubtedly a primary driver of our nation's incarceration explosion, it is inaccurate to depict it as the independent impetus of mass incarceration. The War on Drugs is only one of five pipelines currently funneling people into prison, jails, and detention centers nationwide. The other four carceral conduits are the crackdown on immigration offenses, decreased funding for mental health, private prisons and detention centers, and the school-to-prison pipeline.

Each of these pipelines is built on a legacy of racist and classist legislation that has paved the way for our present carceral epidemic. To comprehensively understand the evolution of mass incarceration, we must do something that will surprise most: begin our exploration at the time before slavery ends.

HOW DID WE GET HERE?

From Black Codes to Neoslavery

MASS INCARCERATION IS AND ALWAYS HAS BEEN inextricably connected to race and class. Poor people, people of color, and particularly poor people of color have served as cannon fodder for an exploitative system since before the abolition of slavery. In the late 1700s the incarceration of black people began to rise in the North while black people were still shackled, *owned*, and legally constituted as property in the South.

THE UNTOLD STORY OF BLACK WOMEN

Seminal texts on mass incarceration have a glaring blind spot. While the most acclaimed books have masterfully documented the experience, systemic plight, and oppression of black men, they have simultaneously—even if inadvertently—erased black women's tumultuous history of being racially profiled and incarcerated in mass. In 2003, Angela Davis named this oversight in her book *Are Prisons Obsolete?*, claiming that public discussions about the American prison system have historically left women out.[1] The history of the criminalization of black women must be lifted up in any legitimate effort to understand the roots of mass incarceration.

Free black women in the North—during the era of slavery—worked primarily as domestics in white homes, which made them extremely vulnerable to sexual assault and accusations of theft. Consequently, the history of African American women's incarceration begins with larceny, and this history starts before the abolition of slavery. When black women were charged with stealing from white families, they were issued some of the harshest sentences handed down by the criminal system. According to historian Kali Nicole Gross, at that time, black women in Philadelphia constituted approximately 50 percent of the female prisoners, while black men constituted approximately 30 percent of male prisoners. This is at a time when blacks made up less than a quarter of the city's total population.[2]

Immediately following the Emancipation Proclamation, this targeting proved to be true in other parts of the nation as well, in both the North and South. According to Gross, there was a great disparity between the incarceration rates of black women and black men through the early twentieth century. Illinois, a state notorious for its disproportionate incarceration rates, serves as a prime illustration, particularly with regard to felony offenses. During the decade slavery was abolished—the 1860s—the population of Illinois was 2 percent black, but 15 percent of female felons and 7 percent of male felons were black. Those numbers rose throughout the twentieth century to extreme levels—by the 1960s, when blacks made up 11 percent of the population, black women made up 70 percent of female felons, and black men made up 46 percent of male felons. While Illinois is distinguished by its elongated history of disproportionate incarceration rates, it is not an aberration. In fact, the state's statistics do not sharply diverge from national trends. The overrepresentation of black people within our criminal justice system is not a new reality that emerged because of the drug war (although these disparities worsened during this era)—this trend predates the abolition of slavery.

Another harsh reality is that black women have been consistently incarcerated for defending themselves from assault, both sexual and physical. These arrests began right after the Emancipation Proclamation, as recently liberated black women sought to enforce their newfound freedom by thwarting the sexual violence of white men who previously "owned" them and were therefore legally entitled to prey on their bodies whenever they wished. Whether it be the woman arrested and tried for murder after fatally stabbing an intoxicated man who was attempting to sexually assault her on a streetcar in Philadelphia in 1919, or Marissa Alexander, the woman who was sentenced to twenty years in prison for firing a warning shot into the air when confronted and threatened by her abusive former husband (whom she had a restraining order against), there is a long, troublesome history of incarcerating black women for simply practicing their legal right of self-defense.

RECONSTRUCTION AND THE RESURGENCE OF RACIAL CONTROL

In 1865, Congress passed the Thirteenth Amendment to the US Constitution. Section 1 of this Amendment reads, "Neither slavery nor involuntary servitude, *except as a punishment for crime* whereof the party shall have been duly convicted, shall exist within the United States, or any place subject to their jurisdiction."[3] The amendment that abolished slavery did so with one caveat. Shortly after this amendment went into effect, the exception was exploited by a disgruntled white gentry, and this exception continues to be abused today.

Immediately after slavery was abolished, Reconstruction began, leaving Confederate leadership lamenting in sackcloth and ashes. Their economy was reeling, the free labor—which made them wealthy—dissipated, and the humans they *owned* just days before were now legislatively becoming their equals. These unwelcome changes compelled Confederate leaders to feverishly seek new ways of reestablishing racial control. Their zealous search produced an unholy trinity that resuscitated white supremacy: sharecropping, lynching, and a series of restrictive laws known as "black codes."

Sharecropping emerged as an oppressive economic system predicated on weighted scales. It was designed to keep black labor consistent, exploitable, and indebted to the Confederate aristocracy. Sharecropping was peonage slavery where blacks who rented a plot of land from white plantation owners were forced to labor as indebted slaves.

The law emboldened this form of entrapment, which meant that blacks who were caught within this immoral arrangement were now shackled to the same white elites who previously owned them—only this time their enslavement was legally justified because of their debt.

Lynching was domestic terrorism. It was a barbaric expression of white supremacist anarchy enacted to keep blacks subjugated and disenfranchised. Lynching was also deployed as a sociopolitical tool of coercion, whereby white thugs were sanctioned to function as judge, jury, and executioners of "black criminality." Consequently, between 1890 and 1940 over five thousand black people were lynched nationwide.[4] The lynching of African Americans was so acceptable that James Cone notes in *The Cross and the Lynching Tree* that "Cole Blease, the two-time governor and U.S. senator from South Carolina, proclaimed that lynching is a 'divine right of the Caucasian race to dispose of the offending blackamoor without the benefit of jury.'"[5] From 1889 to 1929, someone was lynched every four days.[6] The Tuskegee Institute, which documented lynching nationwide, could not report a year without a lynching for seventy-one consecutive years—until 1952.[7]

Black codes were the most insidious of the three innovative tactics white southerners used to reestablish control—they were adapted from slave codes. This legislation aimed to criminalize blackness and arrest African Americans' newfound freedom.

Douglas Blackmon, author of the seminal text *Slavery by Another Name*, explains black codes:

> Across the South, the state legislatures of every state passed laws which began to effectively criminalize Black life and to create a situation in which African American men found it almost impossible not to be in violation of some misdemeanor statute at almost all times. And the most broadly applied of those was that it was against the law if you were unable to prove at any given moment that you were employed.[8]

For example, South Carolina passed an apprenticeship law for black children. This law meant that even against their will black children who were deemed orphans or whose parents were deemed unfit were legally endowed to their former masters until males were twenty-one years old and females were eighteen years old. These black children were yet again forced to labor for the white families who previously owned them, and their masters had the right to physically punish and recapture runaways.[9]

Other examples of black codes include:

No negro shall be permitted to preach, exhort, or otherwise de-claim to congregations of colored people, without a special per-mission in writing from the president of the police jury.[10]

It shall be the duty of every citizen to act as a police officer for the detection of offences and the apprehension of offenders, who shall be immediately handed over to the proper captain or chief of patrol.[11]

No person of color shall migrate into and reside in this state, unless, within twenty days after his arrival within the same, he shall enter into a bond with two freeholders as sureties.[12]

While black codes varied from state to state, historian Mary Ellen Curtin has argued that they had a unified purpose. They were de-signed "to subject free [black] people to their own particular kinds of control."[13] Blackmon explains the long-term socioeconomic impact of the black codes:

This whole regime of the Black Codes, the way that they were enforced, the physical intimidation and racial violence that went on, all of these were facets of the same coin that made it in-credibly less likely that African-Americans would emerge out of poverty in the way that millions of white Americans did at the same time.[14]

Vagrancy statues in southern states made it illegal to be black and unemployed. Jobless blacks were arrested, imprisoned, and rented out to private entities as cheap laborers because of the loophole in the

Thirteenth Amendment. Michelle Alexander writes, "Nine Southern states adopted vagrancy laws—which essentially made it a criminal offense not to work and were applied selectively to blacks—and eight of those states enacted convict laws allowing for the hiring-out of county prisoners to plantation owners and private companies."[15] Black codes increased the severity of punishable offenses against black people and legislatively coerced them into low wage, exploitative labor. In many states, blacks were required to sign labor contracts each year. Without a contract, they could be arrested and forced to work without pay.[16]

These exploitative laws resulted in a significant growth in black imprisonment throughout the South. This period was the first of many racialized explosions in our criminal justice system. Mary Ellen Curtin illuminates how black codes functioned as the roots of what has evolved into mass incarceration: "You have people being arrested from the black codes and being put to work on the streets. And, this is before the big convict leasing system emerges."[17] As a consequence of the black codes, thousands of black people were arrested for trumped up charges, jailed, and sold to coal mines, railroad companies, lumber camps, mills, and tobacco factories in accordance with the Thirteenth Amendment.[18]

CONVICT LEASING

Black codes gave rise to the convict leasing system. Convict leasing was a penal labor system practiced predominately throughout the South, where "convicts" were leased out to private businesses—mostly plantation owners and major industrial corporations like the Tennessee Coal and Iron Company—as cheap laborers. Mirroring slavery, the lessee—with no oversight or accountability—was responsible for feeding, clothing, housing, and supervising leased "laborers." While convict leasing began as early as 1844 in Louisiana, the comprehensive system truly expanded after the Civil War.

Matthew Mancini, author of *One Dies, Get Another*, explains there was a fundamental distinction between the treatment of slaves and convicts. Since convicts were not owned by those they labored for, they were driven harder and often literally worked to death. Convicts, unlike slaves, were merely rentals, which meant that because no one owned them, no one truly had a vested financial interest in their livelihood. Therefore, unlike slave owners, most lessees did not care if convicts were malnourished or died while laboring because leased convicts were not their property, and they simply could be replaced without any financial penalty to the lessees. Consequently, every ounce of labor was extracted from leased convicts, and then they were disregarded like trash. This dehumanizing mindset caused most leased convicts to die prematurely. Mancini concludes that the institutional corruption, lack of accountability, and love of money that the convict leasing system was predicated on culminated in "one of the harshest and most exploitative labor systems known in American history."[19]

Douglas Blackmon goes even further than Mancini, defining this seventy-six-year period—1865 to 1941—as *neoslavery*. Blackmon says neoslavery "describes a whole range of ways in which across the South in the late 19th century and deep into the 20th century millions of African-Americans found themselves in a form of de facto slavery and involuntary servitude."[20] Blackmon further parallels slavery and the systems of convict leasing:

> It was a form of bondage distinctly different from that of the antebellum South in that for most men, and the relatively few women drawn in, this slavery did not last a lifetime and did not automatically extend from one generation to the next. But it was nonetheless slavery—a system in which armies of free men, guilty of no crimes and entitled by law to freedom, were compelled to labor without compensation, were repeatedly bought and sold, and were forced to do the bidding of white masters through the regular application of extraordinary physical coercion.[21]

Historian Mary Ellen Curtin also affirms this comparison, adding that under the convict leasing system, "whipping, keeping people chained up, brutal kinds of physical torture and mental abuse are the norm. A lot of the things that kept people in control under slavery are amplified under this convict system."[22]

Explaining the socioeconomic significance of the convict leasing system in an interview with Bill Moyers, Blackmon says,

> I began to realize the degree to which this form of enslavement had metastasized across the South, and that Atlanta was one of many places where the economy that created the modern city, was one that relied very significantly on this form of coerced labor. And some of the most prominent families and individuals in the creation of the modern Atlanta, their fortunes originated from the use of this practice. And the most dramatic example of that was a brick factory on the outskirts of town that, at the turn of the century, was producing hundreds of thousands of bricks every day. The city of Atlanta bought millions and millions of those bricks. The factory was operated entirely with forced workers. And almost 100 percent black forced workers. There were even times that on Sunday afternoons, a kind of old-fashioned slave auction would happen, where a white man who controlled black workers would go out to Chattahoochee Brick and horse trade with the guards at Chattahoochee Brick, trading one man for another, or two men.[23]

Moyers responded, "And yet, slavery was illegal?" Blackmon replied, "It had been illegal for 40 years. And this is a really important thing to me. I was stunned when I realized that because the city of Atlanta bought these millions and millions of bricks, well, those are the bricks that paved the downtown streets of Atlanta. And those bricks are still there. And so, these are the bricks that we stand on."[24] It is vital to note that while Blackmon details the history of Atlanta here, my hometown is not unique in this regard. Many other cities still depend on infrastructure that was created, enhanced, and constructed by leased convicts. Thus, convict leasing not only financed Atlanta's modernization, it kept the southern economy afloat after the Emancipation Proclamation and buttressed the industrial revolution that was evolving in the North.

Due to a lack of data collected, it is impossible to accurately deduce the precise number of African Americans that were entrapped within this oppressive system. However, we know that in Alabama alone at least two hundred thousand African American men were leased convicts. Blackmon, addressing the arrest of black men during neoslavery, writes,

> Instead of thousands of true thieves and thugs drawn into the system over decades, the records demonstrate the capture and imprisonment of thousands of random indigent citizens, almost always under the thinnest chimera of probable cause or judicial process. The total number of workers caught in this net had to have totaled more than a hundred thousand and perhaps more than twice that figure. Instead of evidence showing black crime waves, the original records of county jails indicated thousands of arrests for inconsequential charges or for violations of laws specifically written to intimidate blacks.[25]

One of the African American men entrapped within this exploitative system was Green Cottenham.

GREEN COTTENHAM

Slavery by Another Name highlights the narrative of Green Cottenham as a way of narrating the broader realities of black life throughout the South during this era. Cottenham was born in 1886 to two former slaves. He grew up in extreme poverty and was arrested on vagrancy charges in Shelby County, Alabama, when he was twenty-two. Cottenham was convicted by a white judge and an all-white jury. He was initially sentenced to thirty days of hard labor, but, like most blacks charged with vagrancy, he could not pay the legal fees connected to his imprisonment.[26] Consequently, Cottenham's sentence was extended to a year. The day after his conviction, Cottenham was sold by the state of Alabama as a convict to labor for the US Steel Corporation.

Cottenham began toiling in the Pratt Coal Mines the same day he was sold. In these mines, according to Blackmon, Cottenham "was chained inside a long wooden barrack at night and required to spend nearly every waking hour digging and loading coal. His required daily 'task' was to remove eight tons of coal from the mine. Cottenham was subject to the whip for failure to dig the requisite amount." The inhuman working and living conditions of the mines bred a plethora of diseases, particularly pneumonia and tuberculosis. Many convicts died because of these diseases and malnutrition. When convicts died in the mines, they were either buried in shallow graves inside the mine or incinerated in company ovens, further exacerbating the toxic work environment. Like so many other convicts, months after laboring in this cesspool, Cottenham—at the ripe age of twenty-two—died in the mines.

Forty-five years after Lincoln's Emancipation Proclamation, Green Cottenham embodied the reality of over a thousand imprisoned black men in the antebellum South. He was racially profiled, unjustly arrested, convicted by a biased court, sold, forced to work without pay, guarded by overseers with whips, and physically assaulted when imposed deadlines were not met. Blackmon concludes that Cottenham and other convicts were "slaves in all but name."

What convicts endured in coal mines, steel mills, tobacco factories, and lumber mills would have been intolerable within the system of slavery. It would have been economically irresponsible for slave owners to work slaves to death, forsaking their property, forfeiting a lifetime of labor, and surrendering an immense amount of profit. Many scholars believe labor under the confines of convict leasing was worse than slavery. Without financial liability, leasers abused the system; convicts became disposable bodies that were rented, worked to death, and swapped out like insignificant commodities.

PROFITING FROM CONVICTS

Convict leasing was prevalent because it was lucrative. In 1898, convict leasing supplied 73 percent of Alabama's entire annual state revenue.[27] Neoslavery produced revenue for the treasuries of eight southern states that would equate to tens of millions of dollars today.[28] Blackmon explains that this quasi-slavery of the twentieth century was rooted in the nascent industrial slavery that had begun to flourish in the last years before the Civil War. The same men who built railroads with thousands of slaves and proselytized for the use of slaves in southern factories and mines in the 1850s were also the first to employ forced African American labor in the 1870s.[29]

Convict leasing—reconstituted slavery—resurrected the deflating southern economy. This neoslavery is the bedrock of what became the "New South." While northern states also leased convicts, historian Alex Lichtenstein argues in *Twice the Work of Free Labor* that only in the South was the punishment for conviction invariably equivalent to being bought and sold for labor.[30] By the beginning of the twentieth century, a primary purpose of the judicial system had become the South's insidious method of forcing blacks to fulfill the labor requirements of whites and diminishing the newfound freedom of African Americans.[31] In this system, as was the case in slavery before it, convicts were priced relative to their age, health, and capacity to work under brutal conditions, and failing to meet a quota resulted in brutal beatings.[32]

Thus, the same racialization that appraised blacks as subhuman during slavery now criminalized blackness after the Thirteenth Amendment and led to blacks being legally reenslaved. Yet again, the law made it permissible for elite whites vested in a depraved system to get filthy rich off the blood, sweat, and dehumanization of subjugated blacks. The convict leasing system was not formally outlawed until 1921, but it managed to exist as "peonage" until 1941.[33]

Leon Litwack writes that the disproportionate number of black people incarcerated during the convict leasing era was undoubtedly due to the "vigorous and selective enforcement of laws and discriminatory sentencing."[34] While polices have changed in the current era, the system and its disproportionate results remain the same. Racially biased legislation continues to be enforced by overzealous law enforcement within impoverished black communities. This stark reality has amplified the overrepresentation of black bodies caged behind bars and has preserved a national ritual: financially exploiting black bodies for their labor. Despite the passing of the Thirteenth Amendment and the law banning convict leasing, both individuals and corporations continue to profit from legislatively sanctioned racism and mass incarceration today.

ANGOLA PRISON

While the United States has worked hard to obscure this reality, slavery was never fully abolished—it persists today in modified forms. The operation of Angola prison (also known as the Louisiana State Penitentiary) is a prime example of what we could call modern slavery.[35]

At Angola, once prisoners are deemed fit to work, they are subjected to mandatory labor in environments from fields to manufacturing—sometimes uncompensated, sometimes paid as little as two cents per hour.[36] Angola was originally an eight-thousand-acre slave plantation. Confederate major Samuel James, who was entrusted with directing the state of Louisiana corrections system in 1869, bought the Angola plantation in 1880. In the year of purchase, James began incarcerating prisoners in what were old slave quarters. James leased the prisoners to private individuals. In 1894, James died, and his son took over Angola. But amid this transference the public caught wind of the way prisoners were being exploited and brutalized at Angola. A newspaper account published the gory details and prompted concerned citizens to mobilize and advocate for reform.[37]

In 1901, after fifty-five years of convict leasing at Angola, the state of Louisiana took control. At that time, the brutal treatment of prisoners was curbed, and the death rate was significantly reduced. In 1922 the state of Louisiana expanded Angola, buying property surrounding the original plantation and bringing the penitentiary to its present size of eighteen thousand acres. As public concern dissipated around the humane treatment of prisoners incarcerated in Angola, the brutality increased again. So much so that in 1952 Robert Kennon—a Minden, Louisiana, judge—found the need to clean up Angola a reasonable platform for his campaign for governor. This occurred after thirty-one inmates intentionally cut their Achilles' tendons in protest of the conditions at Angola. By the late 1960s, Angola had become known as "the Bloodiest Prison in the South" due to the violence against the prisoners there.[38]

PRISON LABOR TODAY

In the decades since, prison labor has only expanded. Prisoners toil both in-house and in corporations—even though convict leasing was technically abolished. The present convict-leasing partnerships endure as a modernized form of the exploitative system of yesteryear.

In 1979, Congress created a loophole that is now being exploited by many companies that are household names. This congressional loophole is called the Prison Industry Enhancement Certification Program (PIECP), and for the last thirty-eight years it has stealthily enabled prisoners to be exploited by for-profit businesses, for slave-like wages. The Department of Justice (DOJ) says,

> The Prison Industry Enhancement Certification Program (PIECP) exempts certified state and local departments of corrections from normal restrictions on the sale of inmate-made goods in interstate commerce. In addition, the program lifts restrictions on these certified corrections departments, permitting them to sell inmate-made goods to the federal government in amounts exceeding the $10,000 maximum normally imposed on such transactions. PIECP was created by Congress in 1979 to encourage states and units of local government to establish employment opportunities for inmates that approximate private-sector work opportunities. The program is designed to place inmates in a realistic work environment, pay them the prevailing local wage for similar work, and enable them to acquire marketable skills to increase their potential for successful rehabilitation and meaningful employment upon release. A total of 50 jurisdictions may be certified under PIECP. To become certified, each program must demonstrate to the Director of the Bureau

of Justice Assistance (BJA), U.S. Department of Justice, that it meets statutory and guideline requirements as listed under Mandatory Criteria for Program Participation.[39]

Although the PIECP declares that inmates should be paid "the prevailing local wage for similar work," this is not enforced. Slave-like wages endure in our nation.

The DOJ says that the PIECP has two primary objectives:

- Generate products and services that enable inmates to make a contribution to society, help offset the cost of their incarceration, compensate crime victims, and support their families.

- Reduce prison idleness, increase inmate job skills, and improve the prospects for successful inmate transition to the community upon release.[40]

Despite this mission statement, this congressional program has led to incarcerated laborers being exploited for their labor in vocations ranging from mining to agriculture and manufacturing work, and doing work such as farming, putting out wildfires, building airplane parts, constructing military weaponry, and sewing lingerie garments.[41] These corporate prison programs also extend into the service sector, with incarcerated laborers serving in telemarketing and corporate call-center operations.

In 1963, Texas created Texas Correctional Industries (TCI) with the passage of Senate bill 338, the Prison Made Goods Act. TCI "manufactures goods and provides services to state and local government agencies, public educational systems and other tax-supported entities."[42] This includes making "garments and cloth products, janitorial supplies, laundry supplies, name plates and easels, park equipment, stainless steel security fixtures and food service equipment, school bus renovation services, tire repairs and retreading."[43] *Prison Legal News* reports that TCI also

manufactures a wide selection of goods that range from furniture and garments to refurbished computers. TCI also operates soap and detergent factories, metal fabrication facilities, sign shops, and boot and shoe manufacturing plants, and produces bedding, janitorial supplies, Texas state flags and, of course, license plates. Industry programs also include tire repair and retreading, printing services, renovating school buses and Braille transcription.[44]

TCI employs more than five thousand prisoners at thirty-seven factories, and its sales garnered almost ninety million dollars in 2014. Most of TCI's laborers are not paid.[45] A small number of laborers— some of those part of TCI's Prison Industry Enhancement (PIE) Certification Program—receive wages for their toil. PIE partners the Texas Department of Criminal Justice with private employers. According to *Prison Legal News*, prisoners in this program "manufacture goods that are sold on the open market," and their wages are garnished for "room and board, dependent support, restitution, and a contribution to a crime victims' fund." Just two PIE programs are paid—and still well below the market rate. Since the PIE program was implemented in Texas (1993), "nearly $20 million has been returned to the state through deductions from prisoners' wages."[46]

One of the worst things about programs like PIE is they integrate prisoners in a wide variety of trades, but prisoners' experience and mastery is usually meaningless on release. The same individuals corporations and employers depended on during their stints of incarceration will frequently be rejected when they are released from prison and return to these companies to apply for jobs. Their work, it seems, is only desired when it is exploitable. All told, at least thirty-seven states have legalized the contracting of prison labor to private companies in some form.[47]

Do incarcerated laborers benefit from the protections other laborers maintain? As Whitney Benns explains in her *Atlantic* article, "Employment law makes the status of the worker as an 'employee' a critical distinction. If you are an employee, you get protections; if not, you don't."[48] Incarcerated laborers can be defined as employees in workers' protection statutes.[49] But in lawsuits against their employers for the application of minimum wage laws, the courts have ruled that these laborers are not protected because the relationship of the prison to the inmate is not economic.[50]

TIME FOR CHANGE

The church must reckon with the reality that ever since black people were stolen from Africa and trafficked to this land, they have been dehumanized, abused, criminalized, incarcerated, exploited for profit, and governed in distinctively sinister ways. This oppression has been personal, institutional, systemic, and legislative. It has been authorized and sanctioned by our local, state, and federal government. As the church, do we have the wherewithal to confront the austere reality that our national economy has been subsidized by a criminal justice system that is, and has been, predicated on the exploitation of cheap labor extracted from poor, racially profiled people of color?

In 1903, W. E. B. Du Bois crystallized our present crisis in his classic text *The Souls of Black Folks*. Du Bois wrote, "The black folks say that only colored boys are sent to jail, and not because they are guilty, but because the State needs criminals to eke out its income by their forced labor."[51] In many ways, Du Bois had eyes to see and ears to hear what many of us have not yet fully come to grips with. When we muster the strength to have difficult conversations about history, race, and governmentally sanctioned institutional injustice, we will realize that it is counterproductive to characterize our current situation as merely a byproduct of the War on Drugs. This inadequate assessment inhibits us from developing the comprehensive analysis needed to reimagine our criminal justice system.

Therefore, given the racism, dehumanization, and economic exploitation of our criminal justice system, the church must refuse to remain silent. We must advocate for another way—our credibility depends on it. Christians must join the freedom caravan and take part in the ongoing work of reimagining true justice. We can no longer wait until it is socially expedient. We are called to be a prophetic presence in the world, not merely an echo chamber that resounds once there is no longer any social risk involved in speaking up.

While the church must awaken to the need for a systemic shift within our criminal justice system, we also need to realize that a shift in posture is required within the body of Christ. The work will draw many of us outside of our comfort zones, forcing us to depend on the Spirit's guidance. It will entail facing difficult truths and developing the integrity and fortitude to look within, honestly confronting Christianity's role in our nation's history of injustice. And we must ultimately reassess our presuppositions about God's justice and our role in pursuing it as colaborers within the inaugurated kingdom of God.

BEYOND LAW AND ORDER

THROUGHOUT SCRIPTURE, GOD'S PEOPLE are called to pursue righteous relationships and just standards as a community. For example, Deuteronomy 1:16-17 states that whether someone is a citizen or resident alien, regardless of their place and caste in society, "you must not be partial in judging: hear out the small and the great alike; you shall not be intimidated by anyone, for the judgment is God's." But while our criminal justice system has repeatedly manifested unbalanced scales and partial judgments—particularly for poor minorities—many Christians remain the staunchest defenders of our justice system.

The church must confess that its support of a broken criminal justice system has emboldened systemic injustice. One of the ways the church has been complicit in our criminal injustice system is our uncompromising support of law-and-order legislation. We must repent of our complicity. Repentance requires naming sin, renouncing it, and turning away from it in order to return to God.

Since the drug war began—during an era when most citizens believed that drugs were not a significant societal threat—the media has been used to alter the public's perception. News, advertisements, and political speeches have been strategically curated to induce fear. The media sensationalized crack, depicting it as a new, more potent drug that would destroy our nation. Politicians capitalized on this fearmongering by deploying "get tough on crime" rhetoric and passing punitive legislation. Law and order has always functioned as dog-whistle politics—racial legislation ensconced within coded rhetoric about the common good.

We cannot talk authentically about mass incarceration without exposing dog-whistle politics and political double talk used to incite racialized fear. According to Michelle Clifton-Soderstrom, the 1988 election epitomized this.

> In the 1988 Presidential campaign, the National Security Political Action Committee ran an attack ad against Michael Dukakis. The ad featured Willie Horton—a convicted murderer in Dukakis' state who allegedly raped, stabbed, kidnapped a young white couple while on a weekend furlough from prison. The issue with the ad was not George Bush's "tough on crime" vs Dukakis' "soft on crime" record. Or bringing up the question of the risks of weekend furloughs for convicted murderers. The problem was the visual that definitively associated violent crime with a menacing picture of a black man—Willie Horton—whose face hovered over three words: kidnapping, stabbing, raping.

Clifton-Soderstrom goes on to describe how Horton's image was etched into the American psyche, also noting its reverberating effect today. She writes, "It has remained infamous for its effect (especially on white women), and reinforced our views of 'the threatening black man.'" Throughout the entire election cycle, not a single political representation of Horton identified him by his name, William. *Time* magazine even dared to name Horton "Bush's most valuable player."[1]

Clifton-Soderstrom explains that in an attempt to show that Bush was actually soft on crime, Dukakis ran a counter campaign. His ad featured Angel Medrano—a felon convicted for rape and heroin dealing—as his "poster criminal." Medrano also committed his violent crime while out on furlough. Instead of highlighting a black face, Dukakis elected to use a Hispanic one. Nevertheless, the victim was again a white woman.

Clifton-Soderstrom concludes,

> These alarming examples of powerful white politicians dehumanizing black and brown bodies to bolster their political

agenda not only exposes the pathology of equating black and brown bodies with criminality, it exposes white supremacy as it seeks to maintain power, dictate the narrative, and preserve social and political space by defining non-whites by "the worst thing they've ever done."[2]

While criminal activity must be addressed, we cannot be blinded to the ways law-and-order rhetoric is deployed to camouflage racism. Christians must resist propaganda and overcome fear in scriptural ways.

THE ROOTS, RISE, AND EVOLUTION OF LAW AND ORDER

Law and order rhetoric and legislation is rooted in racial control. The politicians who rigorously fought to maintain slavery, seceded from the union, and endorsed Jim Crow became ardent advocates of law and order. George Wallace, an infamous segregationist, was one of the initial politicians to champion law and order. Michelle Alexander explains,

> The rhetoric of "law and order" was first mobilized in the late 1950s as Southern governors and law enforcement officials attempted to generate and mobilize white opposition to the Civil Rights Movement. In the years following Brown v. Board of Education, civil rights activists used direct-action tactics to force reluctant Southern States to desegregate public facilities. Southern governors and law enforcement officials often characterized these tactics as criminal and argued that the rise of the Civil Rights Movement was indicative of a breakdown of law and order. Support of civil rights legislation was derided by Southern conservatives as merely "rewarding lawbreakers." For more than a decade—from the mid-1950s until the late 1960s—conservatives systematically and strategically linked opposition to civil rights legislation to calls for law and order, arguing that Martin Luther King Jr.'s philosophy of civil disobedience was a leading cause of crime.[3]

As Fannie Lou Hamer said, "Black people know what white people mean when they say 'law and order.'"[4]

Barry Goldwater took the rhetoric of law and order to the next level in his 1964 presidential campaign. Goldwater strategically exploited the fear of blackness and black crime, commencing what would evolve into the racially charged "get tough on crime" movement plaguing our nation today. At that time Goldwater warned voters, "Choose the way of [the Johnson] Administration and you have the way of mobs in the street."[5] Conservatives dismissed civil rights activists who connected uprisings in the black community to the scourge of widespread police brutality. Conservatives were empowered to negate the claims of civil rights activists because of politicians such as Robert Byrd, who argued that police brutality would cease to be a problem if blacks would only get themselves in order and under control.[6]

NOT SO BLACK AND WHITE

Nevertheless, support for law and order was not black and white. Michael Javen Fortner, author of *The Black Silent Majority*, illustrates that law and order was not exclusively championed by white politicians. This rhetoric was also espoused by black politicians and activists. Fortner explains that many tough-on-crime policies since the late 1960s were supported by a sizable number of black upper- and middle-class families like his own. Black leaders who supported law and order, he argues, saw it as an imperfect but necessary measure to thwart violence in poor, black, urban neighborhoods. Fortner contends that black people had political agency: "Their voices had a huge impact in changing the narrative around urban crime and drug addiction and pushing it in a way that validated very punitive crime policies."[7] Fortner points to, among other things, Ronald Reagan's crack cocaine bill of 1986, which was cosponsored by thirteen members of the Congressional Black Caucus.

Additionally, Fortner says that the support of black leaders was indispensable to Bill Clinton's 1994 crime bill. He writes that "there was grassroots mobilization of the community, particularly by black pastors. There was a group of influential black pastors who signed a letter encouraging the Congressional Black Caucus to support the bill. And then later, on top of that, black elected officials, who portrayed themselves at various points as uncomfortable with some of these laws, went along anyway because of pressure coming from their communities, and because they also realized the problem was so bad."[8]

Fortner writes that the black middle and upper class

> did not blame their problems on white racism or capitalism. . . . They no longer understood their community in strictly racial terms; crime threats prompted them to view themselves as members of a broader class-based community of "decent citizen," "hard-working people," and Bible-believing churchgoers. When they thought about the black underclass, they did not see brothers. They saw hoods. They saw monsters.[9]

Likewise, James Forman Jr., a professor at Yale Law School, asserts that between the 1960s and the 1970s, African American law-and-order advocates emerged on the national stage, shaping drug and punishment policy and helping give rise to mass incarceration. In *Locking Up Our Own*, Forman focuses on the nation's capital, trying to explain how a generation of black elected officials sought to deal with a crisis of violence and drugs. Forman argues that drug addiction to heroin, and later crack, during this period incentivized black support for law and order. "Forty-five percent of male jail detainees tested positive for heroin in 1969, up from 3 percent in the early '60s. During roughly the same period the city's murder rate tripled. By 1987, officials found that 60 percent of Washington arrestees tested positive for crack cocaine."[10]

Forman also explains that the black community was divided on what to do. There was agreement by the late 1970s that drug rates were rising, and violence was increasing in the city. Some of the initial options for responding ranged from decriminalizing marijuana to increasing the severity of sentences. Far too many ultimately chose to embrace punitive solutions driven by law-and-order policies. Citing a 1966 study conducted by the University of Michigan, Forman writes that "a surprising number" of working-class black cops "didn't like other black people—at least not the poor blacks they tended to police."[11] This silent black majority was used to buttress Nixon's law-and-order agenda and the southern strategy.

Daniel Patrick Moynihan, former assistant secretary of labor, composed a 1970 memo to President Richard Nixon in which he claimed that dangerous young black men were among the greatest challenges facing black America. Moynihan coined the term "silent black majority" and used it to convince Nixon that he should intentionally court middle- and upper-class blacks who were "politically moderate" and fed up with "antisocial behavior."

EVANGELICAL SUPPORT OF LAW AND ORDER

Evangelicals have staunchly supported law and order. While this is undoubtedly truer within conservative strains, as a voting bloc, particularly since the 1970s, evangelicals have aligned with get-tough-on-crime rhetoric and legislation. Tony Campolo underlined the significance of this, saying, "Evangelical Christians, who once were a ridiculed irrelevant sectarian movement, have, over just three decades, become a powerful voting bloc that can no longer be ignored."[12] In affirmation of Campolo's point about evangelicals' rise to political significance, Billy Graham said in 2005, "If you'd have said Evangelical in 1957, most people wouldn't know what you were talking about."[13]

Given this newfound political significance, it is noteworthy that evangelicals like the late Jerry Falwell and Billy Graham and their influential children Jerry Falwell Jr. and Franklin Graham have used their platforms to tout law and order, endorsing it as inherently biblical. These key evangelical leaders have mobilized movements such as the Moral Majority, which called for harsher penalties and a heavier use of the death penalty. As a result some representatives withdrew from initiatives that would have made criminal law more moderate. Jerry Falwell even went as far as to compose editorials bemoaning that "crime is epidemic" and declaring that "criminals are better protected by the law than the people on whom they prey."[14] Jerry Falwell supported political candidates whose platform touted law and order by hosting rallies and contributing to their campaigns. Evangelical leaders have zealously aided the Christian right in its effort to reclaim law and order amid the broader culture wars that have been waged over the last forty years.

Today, Franklin Graham commonly espouses law and order in oversimplified ways that trivialize the pain, suffering, trauma, incarceration, and deaths of those targeted by law and order. Graham frequently makes simplistic statements that seem more political than pastoral. Following the presidential election, Graham said, "Political pundits are stunned. Many thought the Trump-Pence ticket didn't have a chance. None of them understand the God factor. . . . While the media scratches their heads and tries to understand how this happened, I believe that God's hand intervened."[15]

About six months later, in an interview with *The Atlantic*, Graham said, "He did everything wrong, politically. . . . He offended gays. He offended women. He offended the military. He offended black people. He offended the Hispanic people. He offended everybody! And he became president of the United States. Only God could do that." The interview continued, "Now, there's 'no question' that God is supporting Trump," Graham said. "No president in my lifetime—I'm 64 years old—can I remember . . . speaking about God as much as Donald Trump does."[16]

Graham also provided an oversimplified response to police brutality, as the number of unarmed black and brown citizens losing their lives to police brutality climaxed in March of 2015. In a political statement that mirrored Senator Robert Byrd's inadequate commentary on police brutality decades before, Graham wrote, "Listen up—Blacks, Whites, Latinos, and everybody else. Most police shootings can be avoided. It comes down to respect for authority and obedience. If a police officer tells you to stop, you stop. If a police officer tells you to put your hands in the air, you put your hands in the air. If a police officer tells you to lay down face first with your hands behind your back, you lay down face first with your hands behind your back. It's as simple as that."[17] This comment lacks pastoral care and presence. It was insensitive, alienating, and paternalistic. Graham's instructions oversimplified a profoundly complex issue, and belittled the pain, oppression, and deaths that black and brown communities were enduring.

Likewise, Falwell Jr. declared, "I think evangelicals have found their dream president," referring to President Trump. Falwell Jr., who is the president of Liberty University, also said, "I've never seen a White House have such a close relationship with faith leaders than this one."[18] These sentiments and ringing endorsements from noted conservative evangelical leaders go a long way toward explaining why white evangelicals showed up in record numbers to support Trump—who ran a campaign rooted in law-and-order rhetoric.

LAW AND DISORDER

From an early age most Christians are taught that laws provide structure for healthy communities, ordering society by providing ethical standards and social accountability. We grow up resolute in our belief that laws are solely intended to protect, govern, and provide social stability. We are trained to see them as inherently linked. Therefore, it is only natural for us to wed law and order.

However, what happens when the law does not provide the structure necessary for communities to thrive? How do we make sense of the law when it does the inverse—when laws disproportionately create and sustain injustice, oppression, and immorality in certain communities? While most of the church has been taught to view the law in exclusively positive ways, history illustrates that laws are not always just, nor are they implemented only to aid societal flourishing. The reality is that we live in a nation of legislative fluidity where the law has functioned in both positive and negative ways. It has both guarded and violated the sanctity of human life. When the church is unable to acknowledge these contradictions, it loses social credibility, particularly within communities that have borne the weight of legislative injustice.

Given the fallen nature of humanity and the fact that fallible people govern institutions, organizations, and structures, systems are susceptible—if not prone—to distortion and corruption. Therefore, how are Christians to view the law? Is it faithful for us to assume that law creates order categorically? These questions are complicated because much of Western theology endorses a blind allegiance to law and order, citing Romans 13:1-7. But other Christians subscribe to an Augustinian logic, which professes that "an unjust law is no law at all."

Augustine profoundly shaped Dr. King's thinking. King said that we must "never forget that everything Hitler did in Germany was legal."[19] This helped him determine that "one has not only a legal, but a moral responsibility to obey just laws. Conversely, one has a moral responsibility to disobey unjust laws."[20] Moreover, King said that "an individual who breaks a law that conscience tells him is unjust, and who willingly accepts the penalty of imprisonment to arouse the conscience of the community over its injustice, is in reality expressing the highest respect for the law."[21]

King's nonviolent agitation and protest of the law frequently gets shrouded within the church. King's theology of militant civil disobedience entailed resistance and disruption when laws legitimated oppression, injustice, and death. After being arrested for the Montgomery bus boycott King wrote,

> I knew that I was a convicted criminal, but I was proud of my crime. It was the crime of joining my people in a nonviolent protest against injustice. It was the crime of seeking to instill within my people a sense of dignity and self-respect. It was the crime of desiring for my people the unalienable rights of life, liberty, and the pursuit of happiness. It was above all the crime of seeking to convince my people that noncooperation with evil is just as much a moral duty as is cooperation with good.[22]

So how are Christians supposed to view and respond to the law when it conflicts with God's will and desire for shalom?

SYSTEMIC CORRUPTION

Acts 16:16-40 tells the story of Paul and Silas, who were imprisoned for bearing witness to the gospel. Verses 16-21 provide the context for what transpires.

Once when we were going to the place of prayer, we were met by a female slave who had a spirit by which she predicted the future. She earned a great deal of money for her owners by fortune-telling. She followed Paul and the rest of us, shouting, "These men are servants of the Most High God, who are telling you the way to be saved." She kept this up for many days. Finally Paul became so annoyed that he turned around and said to the spirit, "In the name of Jesus Christ I command you to come out of her!" At that moment the spirit left her.

When her owners realized that their hope of making money was gone, they seized Paul and Silas and dragged them into the marketplace to face the authorities. They brought them before the magistrates and said, "These men are Jews, and are throwing our city into an uproar by advocating customs unlawful for us Romans to accept or practice."

Willie Jennings says that the oppressed, enslaved body of this nameless woman was "where the demonic and the economic were bound together."[23] Paul, Jennings writes,

> speaks to her and to the spirit at work in her that binds her to her owners. . . . The point was not to silence her voice but to release it from its networked captivity. Ministry in the name of Jesus Christ releases people to speak, especially poor women, by challenging the voices of their oppression that constantly wish to speak through them.[24]

However, Jennings notes that "to free someone is never without cost."[25]

In exorcising this spirit, Paul and Silas usurped the ill-gotten gains of powerful men, and they were charged with throwing the city into an uproar. Infuriated by Paul and Silas's liberating action, the slave owners were determined to make them pay. Because their "hope of making money was gone," they dragged Paul and Silas into the marketplace where the worship of mammon (the idolatry of worshiping money or material things) was institutionalized. These slave owners knew where the loyalties of the authorities and magistrates of the marketplace lay.

When the slave owners stated their claim against Paul and Silas, they did more than name the economic disruption they caused—they also named them as the other. Willie Jennings notes that in doing this, "the owners perform through their words the great demonic juxtaposition—the stability of a city, a social world, and a people on one side and the 'problem' of the Jew on the other side."[26] These men unleash the crowd's repressed xenophobia. They play on the crowd's fears to trigger bigotry and violence. They use law and order to appease their ethnocentric aggression. Exploiting their punitive criminal justice system, they satisfied their craving for ethnic violence.

Scripture says the crowd joined in the attack on Paul and Silas, which suggests that the citizens were primed to participate in Jewish persecution. Corrupt judges convict Paul and Silas, sentencing them to be bludgeoned before being thrown into prison. Paul and Silas were publicly humiliated: stripped naked, beaten with rods, and severely flogged in front of a jeering crowd. The marketplace and its authorities collaborate to send a public service announcement: *Anyone who disrupts the city's status quo of economic exploitation will endure this fate.*

Paul and Silas endure what would be analogous to police brutality before being imprisoned. Undeterred by this persecution, Paul and Silas continue to persist, bearing witness to the gospel. They refused to be silenced, repudiating the authorities seeking to silence them. Bound in jail, they continued praising God, praying aloud, and singing hymns of resistance (as in the civil rights movement). They prophetically proclaimed the good news until the very foundations of the prison shook and the prison gates flung open. Evil could not imprison the gospel, shackles could not constrain the good news, and the captive's liberation could not be arrested by law and order! With this zeal, authority, and conviction the church must relentlessly confront mass incarceration if we are going to deconstruct this exploitative system.

Ending mass incarceration will require some Christians to be arrested. Protesting evil and counteracting injustice will require nonviolent protests that expose the system and the collaborating structures supporting it. We will endure persecution when we illuminate the way individuals, institutions, and our government are reaping unholy dividends.

Willie Jennings declares that Luke, particularly in Acts, never allows Christians to wander too far from prisons. He writes,

> Torture and violence are signs of the prison. Lies, deceptions, and falsehoods that lead people to be incarcerated are signs of the prison. Exploitation, racism, and bigotry also encircle the prison and its judicial system. . . . We must see the operations of incarceration in their intimate relation to the forces of death. The disciples of Jesus cannot escape our necessary confrontation with prisons. Arrest, incarceration, and imprisonment have never been and never are neutral processes, functioning according to basic rules of justice and human utility. Incarceration is a process at the disposal of the rich and powerful, and here we see it unleashed against the servants of Jesus.[27]

GRACE TRUMPS THE LAW

John 8:1-11 provides insight from an alternative vantage point concerning how Christians are supposed to view and respond to the law, especially when the law conflicts with God's will and desire for *shalom*. In this passage religious leaders approach Jesus with a woman who had broken the law. They bring her before Jesus, explaining to him that according to the law, her transgression warrants capital punishment. They ask Jesus for his thoughts on the matter. Rather than affirming the law and its punitive response to crime, Jesus demonstrates unmerited grace towards this "criminal."

Figure 3.1 illustrates that evangelicals—particularly white evangelicals—are more prone to respond like the religious leaders who brought this woman before Jesus, seeking the death penalty. As followers of Jesus—himself a victim of the death penalty—one would think Christians would rebuke capital punishment as an antiquated, inhumane method of torture disguised as justice.[28] In John 8 we see Jesus extend grace to this woman in a way that causes all her accusers—those who considered themselves righteous and in a position to judge—to see themselves as fallible before indicting this woman. This leads me to wonder what would happen if the church took this humble approach today. If this were our posture, how would our response to both "criminals" and the punitive nature of the law shift? If the church prophetically responded out of these convictions, the death penalty would cease to exist!

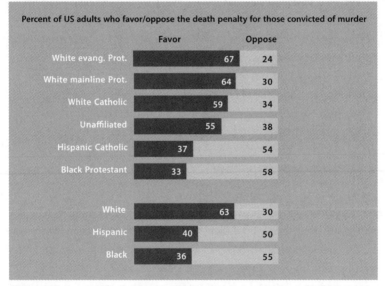

Figure 3.1. Support for death penalty across religious and racial/ethnic groups
Note: Whites and blacks are non-Hispanic only; Hispanics are of any race. Those saying "don't know" are not shown.
Source: Pew Research Center survey conducted March 21–April 8, 2013.

Rather than affirming the law and its "tough on crime" approach, Jesus counteracts it and responds to the violator of the law restoratively. Where the law demanded punishment, Jesus offers grace. Where the law required bloodshed, Jesus calls for restoration, repentance, and forgiveness. Where the law suggested that order comes through purging out the criminal, Jesus shows us that order is restored when our communities are reconciled. Jesus calls us in the face of crime to move forward together—both the violated and the violators—under the confines of covenant relationship.

Jesus not only saved this woman from capital punishment—what the law demanded—he also urged her to reenter society, be restored to community, and turn away from her sinfulness. What might Jesus' response say to the church today with regard to the belief that the law is exclusively what brings order to our society? While Jesus undoubtedly affirms ethically grounded laws as well as the individuals who morally enforce them, he chooses to counteract laws that contrast kingdom values. As Shane Claiborne writes in *Executing Grace*, "It's not that the law has no meaning; it's just that grace has the last word."[29] What does this suggest about how we should teach and disciple followers of Christ to observe the law? Is it faithful to train people to blindly support and adhere to any and every law—even those that breed death and destruction?

Historically, as unjust laws have brought death, oppression, and injustice, far too many Christians have acquiesced to a patriotic doctrine of unquestioning allegiance to law and order. I raise this point in part because it is so easy to forget that if Mary and Joseph had blindly followed the law, Jesus would have been executed at birth—as would have Moses. Jesus embodied God's heart for restoration. Jesus came to save, redeem, and restore those who are separated from God and their community because of their sin. But Jesus also came to remove the stones of judgment from the hands of religious people who impede the path of restoration for those who have stumbled along the way.

THREE OVERLOOKED PIPELINES

Mental Health, Private Prisons, and Immigration

WHILE A FEW SCHOLARS HAVE NAMED convict leasing as an exploitative antecedent of mass incarceration, most have failed to properly name Japanese internment as such. Shortly after the bombing of Pearl Harbor, President Franklin Roosevelt ordered that all Japanese persons residing in the Unites States, including US citizens, would be banned from portions of four western states. This was claimed to be "military necessity," but it was rooted in the fear that Japanese Americans were a national security risk in the conflict with Japan. Consequently, around 120,000 persons—men, women, and children—were placed in internment camps, which were located in isolated parts of rural America.[1] According to the 1940 census, only 127,000 persons of Japanese ancestry lived in the United States at that time.[2]

Executive Order 9066, which came on the heels of the Chinese Exclusion Act, unconstitutionally profiled, targeted, and incarcerated Japanese communities. Over 60 percent of the Japanese who were incarcerated were citizens of the United States, and many others had lived in the United States for several decades. Japanese Americans, especially those of the second generation, were very loyal to the United States. No Japanese person was found guilty of sabotage or espionage.[3]

Internment camps, therefore, are a disingenuous nomenclature used to describe Japanese persecution. The Japanese were ethnically profiled, imprisoned without due process, caged within barbed wire fences, and patrolled by armed soldiers. They were a siloed ethnic group made vulnerable by racist legislation and ultimately victimized by mass incarceration. Our federal government initiated xenophobic legislation that stripped the Japanese of their dignity, civil liberties, and community wealth. Fear of the perpetual foreigner provoked institutionalized injustice. Consequently, the Japanese were warehoused in incarceration camps for four years and forced to live in barracks without running water, insulation from the frigid winter cold, and furnishings other than used, tattered, and torn army cots.

In some ways, mass incarceration even inadequately names what the Japanese were subjected to. The Children of the Camps Project says that "President Roosevelt himself called the 10 facilities 'concentration camps.'"[4] The same group also explains that "several [Japanese] were killed by military guards posted for allegedly resisting orders."[5]

THE EVOLUTION OF PRIVATE PRISONS

Private prisons are the offspring of convict leasing and Japanese incarceration camps. Private prisons model their economic enterprise of profiteering off of prison labor, based on the model set forth by the convict leasing system. Private prisons have found innovative ways to emulate their predecessors. Similarly, private prisons frame the strategic placement of their facilities off the geographic blueprint prescribed by Japanese incarceration camps (and Native American reservations). Private prisons, like incarceration camps before them, abide by the mantra "out of sight, out of mind." Private prisons, echoing incarceration camps, strategically place facilities in sparsely populated rural communities, where the injustice that transpires within is out of the public's purview.

In 1984 there was a revolutionary change in the trajectory of incarceration. The Corrections Corporation of America (CCA), a private entity, took control of a prison in Hamilton County, Tennessee.[6] The number of privately operated prisons skyrocketed in the decades that followed. By 2013, 10 percent of prisons nationwide were privately operated, and the growth of private prisons now outpaces the growth of public prisons.[7]

Private prisons are operated by a third party contracted by the government. Private prison companies sign government contracts—federal, state, and local—which usually include bed occupancy requirements. Private prisons are paid a per diem or monthly rate, either per inmate or for each available facility bed, whether occupied or not. These quotas dictate the number of prisoners who must occupy beds in these facilities nightly, and the quotas range from requiring a minimum of 70 percent to 100 percent occupancy. Most contracts mandate that at least 90 percent of beds are filled nightly, and when beds go unfilled, the government must pay for the unfilled beds. Private prisons profit immensely from bed quotas. Arizona has three prisons with one-hundred percent occupancy requirements.[8]

In 2015, Joe Watson wrote an article exposing the dangers of quota-based prisons. Watson exposed the contractual relationship between the Arizona Department of Corrections (ADC) and Management and Training Corporation (MTC) in running a prison complex in Kingman, Arizona. After several prisoners escaped the complex in 2010, the ADC found numerous breaches of security, including malfunctioning alarms. The ADC removed over two hundred high-risk prisoners from the complex and refrained from sending new prisoners while the breaches were addressed. Since the contract called for a 97 percent bed occupancy guarantee, MTC filed a claim against the ADC, requesting ten million dollars to cover their losses during the year of action. Ultimately, the ADC paid the MTC three million dollars and agreed to resume honoring the 97 percent quota.[9]

As this story illustrates, beds help make private prisons a multimillion-dollar enterprise. They prioritize profit over people, making a mockery of justice. We must ask, How can communities dependent on the jobs these facilities bring, officers who know that they will be overlooked for promotions if they fail to tally arrest statistics paralleling or exceeding their peers, and judges who are implicated in an entire community's economic livelihood—by their sentencing—act ethically? Bed quota contracts induce institutional injustice and empower private prisons to function as the latest iteration of governmentally sanctioned racketeering.

In *Race to Incarcerate*, Marc Mauer highlights a 1997 *New York Times* interview with former president Jimmy Carter. In the interview Carter "cited inequities in the criminal justice system that often penalize blacks and other minority groups more than whites. He said that as a young governor of Georgia, he and contemporaries like Reuben Agnew in Florida and Dale Bumpers in Arkansas had 'an intense competition' over who had the smallest prison populations. Now it's totally opposite." Carter said, "Now the governors brag on how many prisons they've built and how many people they can keep in jail and for how long."[10] Carter's commentary occurred during private prisons' zenith. His statement reveals how discriminatory legislation, which masquerades under the guise of "law and order," is inherently connected to populating prisons.

The GEO Group and CCA are the two largest prison corporations in the United States. Neither CCA nor the GEO Group is classified as a correctional facilitator; they are incorporated as real estate investment trusts. This status limits corporate tax liability and makes them exempt from federal taxation. Forty percent of their income comes from the federal government.[11] Collectively, they made $3.3 billion in 2011.[12]

INVESTING IN INCARCERATION

Companies and individuals also profit from private prisons through the stock market. Citizens aggressively buy and trade stock in private prisons, illuminating how money is wed to elevated incarceration rates.[13] In a 2010 annual report filed with the Securities and Exchange Commission, CCA stated, "The demand for our facilities and services could be adversely affected by . . . leniency in conviction or parole standards and sentencing practices."[14]

The profiteering of private prisons was most evident on August 18, 2016, when the Department of Justice announced it would no longer use private prisons, due in large part to concerned citizens who opposed this exploitative system. When the Justice Department made this announcement, shares in CCA plummeted about 40 percent, and GEO shares dropped nearly 35 percent.[15] While the drop was temporary, primarily because the announcement only affected federal facilities, it revealed how many people are investing in and fiscally monitoring our incarceration epidemic.

Our broader criminal justice system—private prisons included—recapitulates the convict leasing system by profiting immensely from contracting out prison labor to private companies. Inmates are cheap, if not free, labor. They usually cost between 93 cents and $4 a day, and they cannot collect benefits or join labor unions.[16]

Scripture is explicitly clear: the love of money is the root of all kinds of evil. The worship of money is idolatrous, and mammon perverts the human soul. Placing profit over people has corroded our criminal justice system. Greed has bred a system of mass incarceration predicated on the financial exploitation of inmates rather than a system dedicated to reformation, transformation, and restoration.

IMMIGRATION

Immigration is the third conduit of mass incarceration. According to the ACLU, "The federal government is in the midst of a private prison expansion spree, driven primarily by Immigration and Customs Enforcement (ICE), an agency that locks up roughly 400,000 immigrants each year and spends over $1.9 billion annually on custody operations."[17] This claim is statistically substantiated, as arrests for immigration offenses increased 610 percent between 1990 and 2000.[18] This astronomic rise mirrors the previously unprecedented upsurge in incarceration arrests upon the federal government's launch of the War on Drugs (see fig. 4.1). This and other evidence suggest that our government has also—stealthily—launched a second war, this time on immigration, and particularly on Latino immigrants crossing our southern border.

In the year 2000, while Hispanics represented only 13 percent of the population, they accounted for 31 percent of those incarcerated in federal prisons.[19] Additionally, in 2011, Hispanics represented 16.3 percent of the population yet accounted for 50.2 percent of those incarcerated for felonies within the first nine months of the year.[20]

Furthermore, half of the 165,265 arrests made by the federal government in the 2014 fiscal year were for immigration-related offenses. This rise in arrest by Customs and Border Protection coincides with a substantial staffing expansion within this agency during the mid- to late 2000s. The number of Border Patrol officers almost doubled between 2004 and 2010, rising from 10,819 to 20,558. The increase of Border Patrol officers has centralized where this war is being waged; in 2014, 61 percent of all federal arrests—over 100,000—occurred in just five federal judicial districts along the US-Mexico border.[21]

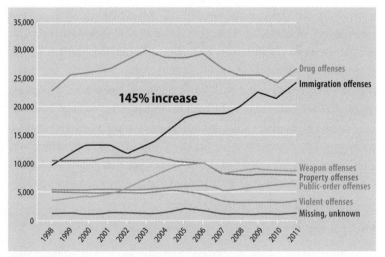

Figure 4.1. Prisoners entering federal prison, 1998–2001

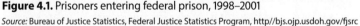

Source: Bureau of Justice Statistics, Federal Justice Statistics Program, http//bjs.ojp.usdoh.gov/fjsrc

According to NBC News, "Over the past 24 years, the amount of money spent on border security has increased 14 times; the number of border patrol agents have increased 500 percent; the amount of border wall has grown from 77 miles to 700 miles since 2000; and the number of people being apprehended trying to cross the border have decreased by four-fifths."[22] The increase in Border Patrol staffing, funding, and legislative authority parallels the War on Drugs. In addition to the increases that have already transpired, in early 2017

President Trump expressed his desire to add five thousand more Border Patrol agents and ten thousand more ICE officers in the interest of enforcing his initial executive orders on immigration.[23]

Private prisons and county jails hold 90 percent of immigration detainees.[24] Private prison companies' financial success is intertwined with immigration legislation. For example, in 2010, an immigration "bed mandate" was introduced by democrat Robert Byrd.[25] This congressional directive mandates ICE to keep an average of 34,000 detainees in its custody daily.[26]

This legislative dependency was also corroborated by a Geo Group fourth-quarter earnings conference call, where George C. Zoley, the chief executive of the Geo Group, bragged to Wall Street analysts that his company was "the largest provider of detention services to the three federal agencies" involved in the protection of the southern border of the United States.[27] This statement was made to reassure investors that GEO is a prime player in the protection of the southern border. Brian W. Ruttenbur, a managing director at CRT's (an LLC providing security brokerage) Capital Group research division, said "the big growth in recent years has been with [US Immigration and Customs Enforcement, or ICE] and both of these companies have historically made heavy investments there."[28]

TRYING TO STAY AHEAD OF THE CURVE

As private prisons were economically flourishing, they noticed that public sentiment on incarceration was shifting in 2010. Private prisons saw a dip in their popularity as activists began shining a light on their unscrupulous tactics. These companies saw the writing on the wall; realizing they could no longer house all their lucrative eggs in one basket, they began diversifying.

In the article "What Private Prisons Companies Have Done to Diversify in the Face of Sentencing Reform," Matt Stroud explains that both CCA and the GEO Group began expanding their portfolio by investing in offender rehabilitation services. Stroud writes, "Both GEO Group and CCA—which last year pulled in a combined $3.3 billion in annual revenue—have taken moves in recent years to diversify into services that don't involve keeping people behind bars."[29]

These expansions proved to be important strategic moves, because on August 18, 2016, the federal government announced its plan to phase out the use of private prisons. A few months later, after the September 2016 presidential debate, stock in these companies took another hit, with CCA stock plunging nearly 8 percent and stock in the GEO falling 4 percent. During the debate Hillary Clinton (who has her own troublesome history with mass incarceration) said, "I'm glad that we're ending private prisons in the federal system." And, "I want to see them ended in the state system. You shouldn't have a profit motivation to fill prison cells."[30] This market activity illuminates the profound impact legislation has on private prison profits.

To curtail this market freefall, CCA surreptitiously employed a tactic that organizations revert to when their names become unredeemable, tarnished by bad publicity and unethical behavior. They rebranded themselves. The organization that used to be CCA now functions as CoreCivic and claims to have "a growing network of residential reentry centers to help tackle America's recidivism crisis."[31] Christians must ask, Can we trust companies who directly profit from incarceration to ethically steward the reentry process?

The fortunes of private prisons turned with the November 2016 election results. Days after the presidential inauguration, CBS Money-Watch declared, "When it comes to companies that are set to profit from President Donald Trump's policies, here's a clear winner: private prison operator CoreCivic (CXW)." CBS explained that CoreCivic "experienced almost a complete turnabout since Mr. Trump emerged victorious in the November election. Before voters cast their ballots, CoreCivic was having a rough year. Its stock had plunged by almost 50 percent from January 1, 2016 through Election Day." Since the election, CoreCivic's shares have more than doubled, and SunTrust analyst Tobey Sommer described it as one of his best financial investment picks for the year.[32]

Additionally, on February 24, 2017, it was reported that "the stocks of the two biggest private prison operators—CoreCivic and

Geo Group—have doubled since election day. CoreCivic (CXW) is up 140% since Trump won in November; Geo Group (GEO) has risen 98%."[33] Jeff Sommer of the New York Times wrote, "When a member of the Trump administration issues a memo or executive order, gives a speech or tweets about the crackdown on immigrants, shares of the two companies rise: Since the election, CoreCivic's stock price has climbed 120 percent, and Geo's has gained 80 percent." In 2017 alone, CoreCivic's shares are up about 30 percent; Geo has gained about 20 percent.[34]

Carl Takei, a staff attorney for the ACLU, explained that while investors will profit from private prisons, they cannot lose sight of the immorality of this industry. Takei said, "No matter what they say about being a government services company or providing valuable services to government agencies, this is a business model that doesn't need to exist." Takei concluded, "It represents the outsourcing of an essential government function to for-profit companies that have a fiduciary responsibility to shareholders, but not to the public."[35]

Private prisons also profit by unethically cutting corners. An example of this was exposed in Colorado, where Grisel Xahuentitla was detained. Shortly after her release, she, along with eight others, took legal action against the GEO Group. Their lawsuit alleges that GEO profited by exploiting inmate labor. Xahuentitla spent "six hours a day passing out trays before meals, scrubbing toilets and scouring showers." She said she was coerced into doing the janitorial and maintenance work for the facility as part of a work program that helps with the upkeep of the facility. These kinds of "voluntary" work programs are legitimated because most people believe that lawbreakers should be put to work, and this logic emboldens private prisons to claim coerced labor is "rehabilitative work" that just happens to keep operations costs down. Xahuentitla represents thousands of people exploited daily for their labor. Prisoners who labor in private facilities usually earn $1 a day.[36]

In Isaiah 58, Israel comes before God inquiring about their fast. They ask God why their fast has not been seen. God responds that Israel's systemic injustice has distorted their fast, making it illegitimate. Scripture says Israel chose to do as it pleased: exploiting all its workers and striking each other with wicked fists. In this text, God says those who prey on the vulnerable, exploit laborers, and profit from systemic injustice will not be honored. Our criminal justice system enacts each of these sins. If the church does not stand up, speak out, and advocate for change, we too will have to answer for the injustice that has occurred on our watch.

MENTAL HEALTH

Mental health is the fourth and most overlooked pipeline feeding mass incarceration. While mental health has always been connected to incarceration, this relationship has intensified as funding for mental community health has dissipated. Sociologist Bernard Harcourt writes that "state hospital populations have declined substantially since the mid-1950s, falling by more than 75% from 1955 to 1980." Moreover, the deinstitutionalization of mental health facilities resulted in additional state prisoners accounting for up to 14 percent of the total prison population.[37]

As the twentieth century ended, the number of mentally impaired prisoners skyrocketed to 283,800 (in 1998), representing 16 percent of prisoners.[38] Conversely, by 1999, the number of individuals in mental hospitals plummeted to the point that professionals deemed the rate of mental hospitalization insignificant.[39] Fifteen years later, a 2014 report by the Treatment Advocacy Center bluntly declared, "Prisons and jails have become America's new asylums." In 2016, almost 400,000 people behind bars had a mental health condition.[40]

Mental health is a challenging subject, and most people feel unqualified to address it, due to either a lack of education or lived experience. While this is understandable and responsible to an extent, the church cannot wade into the water only when the waves are calm and familiar. We must learn to entrust ourselves to God, following the Spirit into the unknown and believing that God will lead, direct, and make straight the path before us. Nevertheless, I contend there are less noble reasons why we avoid the topic of mental health.

Michel Foucault names these reasons in *Madness and Civilization*. He traces the communal experience of socially stigmatized people (criminals, and those with diseases and mental impairments), illustrating how society has moved from exiling to confining and then institutionalizing these populations. Foucault begins his examination by exploring the experience of lepers within Christian communities.

Foucault explains that leprosy had faded from the Western world by the end of the Middle Ages. He writes,

> In the margins of the community, at the gates of cities, there stretched wastelands which sickness had ceased to haunt but had left sterile and long uninhabitable. For centuries, these reaches would belong to the non-human. From the fourteenth to the seventeenth century, they would wait, soliciting with strange incantations a new incarnation of disease, another grimace of terror, renewed rites of purification and exclusion.[41]

Foucault details the history of leprosy in the West, giving special attention to the distorted theology that led the church to exclude lepers while still charging them to live for God. He writes, "If the leper was removed from the world, and from the church visible, his existence was yet a constant manifestation of God, since it was a sign both of His anger and of His grace."[42] Foucault then tells a horrific story of a leper being kicked out of a church, and as he is literally dragged out of the sanctuary—by believers—a priest blesses him, thereby simultaneously claiming him as God's child as the church excludes him.

Foucault declares,

> Leprosy withdrew, leaving derelict these low places and these rites which were intended, not to suppress it, but to keep it at a sacred distance, to fix it in an inverse exaltation . . . what doubtless remained longer than leprosy . . . where the values and images attached to the figure of the leper as well as the meaning of his exclusion, the social importance of the insistent and fearful figure which was not driven off without first being inscribed within a sacred circle.[43]

He then observes,

Leprosy disappeared, the leper vanished, or almost, from memory; these structures remained. Often, in these same places, the formulas of exclusion would be repeated, strangely similar two or three centuries later. Poor vagabonds, criminals, and "deranged minds" would take the part played by the leper, and we shall see what salvation was expected from this exclusion, for them and those whom excluded them as well.[44]

This analysis frames how mental health became a conduit of mass incarceration.

Asylums have historically functioned as warehouses for undesirables, deviants, and individuals with mental health challenges. Research indicates that from 1770 to 1820, people with mental illness were routinely rounded up and left in prisons and jails. Because this practice was deemed cruel, the mentally impaired were instead confined in hospitals until 1970. Since then we have reverted to imprisoning them.[45]

Foucault concludes that although our exclusion of stigmatized people evolves overtime, our rationale for exclusion remains consistent. He states that exclusion is practiced with salvific hope for both the excluded and the excluder. He writes, "With an altogether new meaning and in a very different culture, the forms [of confinement] would remain—essentially that major form of a rigorous division which is social exclusion but spiritual reintegration."[46]

Foucault names a lamentable component of the church's legacy: Christianity has consistently been misused to legitimate exclusion. Misappropriated faith has been used to create a buffer between us and them, be it between "moral citizens" and "criminals," the cognitively impaired and those without, or the haves and the have nots. The fact that many people link exclusion to the church and our definition of salvation is heartbreaking! It illuminates our flawed nature as fallible humans and our inability to fully comprehend God's reconciling work in the world and our role in it.

PEOPLE AT THE MARGIN OF SOCIETY:
INSANITY AND CRIMINALITY

Building on Foucault, Bernard Harcourt notes, "The question is not, how many people with mental illness are in the criminal justice system? Rather, the question should be, has the criminal justice system caught in its wider net the type of people at the margin of society—the class of deviants from predominant social norms—who used to be caught up in the asylum and mental hospital?"[47] These sociologists' analysis beckons us to reassess the function and purpose of confinement. They compel us to reckon with how we have historically seen, treated, and responded to those labeled "insane" and "criminals."

Harcourt crystalizes the need for this by linking the experience of these two defamed groups:

> The category of the "insane" was created in modern times to capture the deviant and marginal. But to make sense of the larger trend in institutionalization, we need to view the "criminal" through the same prism. Is it possible that the category of the present-day criminal does the same work that used to be done by the category of the insane? Might it capture the same class of norm violators, the same kind of deviants?[48]

Noted sociologist Erving Goffman writes, "Part of the official mandate of the public mental hospital is to protect the community from the danger and nuisance of certain kinds of misconduct."[49] If Harcourt is correct, and I believe he is, then public health's role has been commandeered by prisons. Harcourt's astute observation helps explain the astronomical increase in the number of mentally impaired individuals quarantined behind bars.

Therefore, today incarceration serves the same social function that asylums use to. Incarceration is used to confine and socially exclude people deemed crazy, iniquitous, and contaminated. According to the Treatment Advocacy Center, "Most of the mentally ill individuals in prisons and jails would have been treated in the state psychiatric hospitals in the years before the deinstitutionalization movement led to the closing of the hospitals, a trend that continues even today." Not only is the number of cognitively impaired people in prisons and jails continuously escalating, so is the severity of their illnesses.[50]

PRISONS AS THE NEW ASYLUMS

According to a study by the Treatment and Advocacy Center, in 2012 there were ten times more people with severe mental illness incarcerated than there were treated in psychiatric hospitals. In fact, forty-four states and the District of Columbia had a prison or jail that held more individuals with serious mental illness than the largest remaining state psychiatric hospital. Ohio epitomized this problem with ten state prisons and two county jails each holding more mentally disabled prisoners than the largest remaining state hospital.[51]

In 2016 an estimated 90,000 individuals in jail were found incompetent to stand trial (IST).[52] Individuals given the IST designation have failed to come to trial because they were "too disordered to understand the charges on which they were detained."[53]

The overincarceration of people with mental impairments leads to a plethora of problems. These prisoners are disproportionately abused during their tenure behind bars, have higher rates of deterioration (due to going without treatment), and are grossly overrepresented in solitary confinement. This population is also more prone to die by suicide while incarcerated and is more likely to be reincarcerated.

RACIALIZING MENTAL HEALTH

Given the racialized history of incarceration and the parallels drawn between the "insane" and "criminals," we may wonder if there is crossover regarding the institutionalization of minorities in asylums. Statistically, there is. Mirroring the prison population, there was a significant increase from 1968 to 1978—during the launch of the drug war—in the number of racial minorities admitted to mental hospitals and asylums. Sociologist Bernard Harcourt draws on these and other statistics to devise an important analysis and a question worth pondering.

Throughout the twentieth century, African Americans have represented a consistently increasing proportion of the state and federal prison populations. Since 1926, the year the federal government began collecting data on correctional populations, the proportion of African Americans newly admitted to state prisons has increased steadily from 23% in 1926 to 46% in 1982. It reached 51.8% in 1991 and stood at 47% in 1997. In 1978, African Americans represented 44% of newly admitted inmates in state prisons. That same year, minorities represented 31.7% of newly admitted patients in mental hospitals—up from 18.3% in 1968. Is it possible that, as the population in mental hospitals became increasingly African American and young, our society gravitated toward the prison rather than the mental hospital as the proper way to deal with at-risk populations?[54]

The functional role of prisons in our society—quarantining undesirables—led socialist Loïc Wacquant to deduce that prisons are the last of society's peculiar institutions.[55]

OUR POSTURE TOWARD AND COMMUNION WITH THOSE ON THE MARGINS

When we study the life, teaching, and ministry of Jesus, we see a divergent response to stigmatization and marginalization. In Jesus, we see the living expression of God's love, restoration, and reconciliation; he was literally faith expressing itself in love. Instead of avoiding, confining, and quarantining the sick, Jesus sought, touched, liberated, and reintegrated them into community.

The church must pattern its life after Jesus' example. The Spirit is calling us out of our comfort zones into the margins. Scripture is summoning us to defend the dignity of vulnerable people.

We can, and must, advocate for justice; it is after all what the Lord requires of us.

In this pivotal moment, the church must collectively support the reallocation of medical funding. The clear majority of the people with mental impairments serving time need treatment, not incarceration. We cannot continue to incarcerate people who do not have the mental capacities to understand what they are being sentenced for. This is unethical and immoral!

We also cannot entrust medical and reentry services to for-profit prisons. They will line their pockets as they negotiate exclusive governmental contracts. We have a responsibility as concerned citizens and followers of Jesus Christ to relentlessly advocate for another way, a restorative way!

THE SCHOOL-TO-PRISON PIPELINE

IN 2003 A CATASTROPHIC TREND—which decimated thousands of families—emerged in Luzerne County, Pennsylvania. Juveniles were commonly being arrested for petty crimes, routinely brought before a judge, and convicted at alarming rates. Once sentenced, these juveniles were disciplined in essentially an indistinguishable pattern: they were condemned and shipped off to two private—for profit—juvenile detention facilities.

Mark Ciavarella Jr., the presiding judge, was a well-respected magistrate elected on a tough-on-crime platform in 1995. Lauded for his strictness, Ciavarella became renowned for his judicial style. This approach led to his reelection in 2005. After being reelected, Ciavarella became a circuit speaker for schools on personal responsibility and the ethics of good citizenship.

THE SCANDAL

The number of juveniles who appeared before Ciavarella and ended up behind bars for minor infractions is what initially drew attention to his judicial reign. Many of these cases could, and should, have concluded with youth being diverted into alternative sentencing programs or community service. Another irregularity raising red flags regarding Ciavarella's judiciary tenure was the number of families who waived their right to legal representation. Due in part to renounced legal representation, many juveniles sentenced by Ciavarella got entrapped within the system, spending years behind bars.

A Philadelphia nonprofit—the Juvenile Law Center—was the whistleblower that helped halt and expose Ciavarella in 2009. The Center said,

> In 2007, a frantic call from an alarmed parent prompted Juvenile Law Center to investigate irregularities in Pennsylvania's Luzerne County juvenile court. We discovered that hundreds of children routinely appeared before Judge Mark Ciavarella without counsel, were quickly adjudicated delinquent (found guilty) for minor offenses and immediately transferred to out-of-home placements. We petitioned the Pennsylvania Supreme Court in 2008 to vacate the juveniles' adjudications of delinquency and expunge their records.[1]

While the Pennsylvania Supreme Court initially denied the Juvenile Law Center's petition, when they granted their request it was found that Ciavarella and another judge had accepted over two million dollars in kickbacks from two corporate-run juvenile facilities. Federal criminal charges were filed against both judges, and in 2011 Ciavarella and a host of accomplices stood trial.[2]

The court determined that Ciavarella's commitment to "zero tolerance" was not what drove his overzealous conviction rate. Ciavarella's convictions were primarily driven by an illegal agreement with his friend Robert Powell, the co-owner of the two private juvenile detention centers that Ciavarella's convictions populated. Ciavarella was convicted of racketeering, along with other charges, and sentenced to twenty-eight years in prison. Ciavarella, however, did not act alone. This was yet another example of institutional injustice and systemic corruption.[3]

Robert Powell was sentenced to eighteen months after confessing to paying kickbacks to Ciavarella and Ciavarella's boss, Judge Michael Conahan. Conahan, who was also friends with Powell, pleaded guilty to racketeering and was sentenced to eighteen years in prison. Robert Mericle, the developer of the prisons in question, pleaded guilty and was sentenced to a year in prison.[4]

Ciavarella swept thousands of youth into the juvenile justice system over the course of this scandal. In 2009, "the Pennsylvania Supreme Court vacated the adjudications of all youth who appeared before Ciavarella between 2003–2008, dismissed their cases with prejudice and ordered all of their records expunged."[5] The Juvenile Law Center's relentless advocacy and investigative research was paramount in the overturning these unjust convictions. In the end, four thousand of Ciavarella's convictions were nullified.[6] The greed and corruption of an elected official permanently tainted the lives of thousands of young people and their communities.

Thankfully, the Juvenile Law Center and other partnering organizations granted the victimized youth a new lot in life. Nevertheless, these youth paid a significant price for Ciavarella's transgressions. Because of systemic injustice, youth were severed from their families, psycho-emotionally abused, shackled with onerous debt, removed from school, and socially stigmatized as deviants. While some youth were resilient enough to bounce back from all of this, others, such as Edward Kenzakoski, were never able to recover from this judicial corruption. He killed himself shortly after being released from a six-year stint behind bars.

UNLIKELY ALLIES

A redeeming story that emerged from the ashes of this scandal was the improbable relationship between Hillary Transue and Lauren Ciavarella Stahl. These two epitomize an odd couple. Transue was a juvenile entrapped in the scandal, and Stahl is the daughter of Mark Ciavarella Jr. Despite this, the two have found a way to navigate this juxtaposition and join forces to work together to curb the school-to-prison pipeline.

Transue was arrested and brought before Ciavarella in 2007, when she was fifteen. She was convicted for creating a Myspace page that mocked her assistant high school principal. Fortunately, she was incarcerated toward the end of the scandal and released three weeks after being jailed. Due to this, Transue fared much better than virtually all of Ciavarella's other victims. Subsequently, her abbreviated time behind bars enabled her to finish high school, go to college, and pursue a graduate degree.

Ciavarella's daughter, Lauren, said in an interview, "It was black and white for him. And, obviously, things are not black and white." Stahl, who is a former prosecutor, now aids juvenile advocacy programs, especially those focused on keeping children in their homes. Stahl said later in the interview, "the idea of putting someone like Hillary in front of a judge in the first place is mind-blowing to me."[7] Hillary and Lauren's relationship began via Facebook. They messaged each other back and forth for a few weeks and ultimately became allies. The two now partner to help troubled youth. When asked about their partnership, Hillary said, "We're coming from two completely opposite ends of the spectrum; [yet], we're meeting in the middle. I think that really has the power to move people."[8]

Asked to reflect on the scandal, Lauren said, "Everyone just seemed way too complacent with the status quo."[9] When asked what she would tell her father's victims if given the chance, Lauren said, "I wish I could somehow have them realize that yes, this will shape you, but, my God, don't let this man define you."[10] When Judge Ciavarella was asked what he would want his grandchildren to think about their grandfather, he responded, "to understand that their grandfather screwed up big time and couldn't be in their life because of it."[11]

Proverbs 31:8-9 reads,

Speak up for those who cannot speak for themselves,
    for the rights of all who are destitute.
Speak up and judge fairly;
    defend the rights of the poor and needy.

Most interpreters believe that Lemuel, the author of this poem, is Solomon. Lemuel was a name given to someone who is for God or devoted to God. It was therefore bestowed on men of divine appointment, such as Solomon (Psalm 72), who was appointed king, as a reminder of what he must do with his power, wisdom, and favor: he must administer justice. As a king, Solomon was called to rule with care, courage, and compassion. Kings at this time, and elected officials today, must be advocates of those rendered powerless by systems, structures, and legislation. Proverbs 31:8-9 calls King Solomon to ensure that the judicial system is just. He is to be aware of what his judges and officers do so he can support those who ethically do their duty and remove those who neglect it or rule with partiality. Solomon himself must judge righteously and without fear of popular opinion. Solomon has to pass equitable sentences, especially ensuring that cases involving the least of these are governed justly. God was calling Solomon, as king, to be the patron of the oppressed, because the magistrates were not enacting justice. The judges and courts were routinely failing to ethically plead the cause of the poor and needy. Solomon, therefore, had to interpose and appear as an advocate for the least of these. Solomon was called to defend the rights of the following groups:

- Those who were unjustly charged with capital crimes, as Naboth was (1 Kings 21), and were sentenced to the death penalty to gratify the malice of a person or a group. The king was responsible for ensuring that innocent blood was not shed on his watch.

- Those who had charges unjustly brought against them to defraud them of their rights because they were poor and needy. These vulnerable populations needed an advocate because they were unable to defend themselves and could not afford to hire legal counsel.

- Those who were mentally impaired and literally could not speak for themselves, and for those who were rendered voiceless by systemic injustice or oppressive legislation.[12]

Today, the poor and needy are still in need of judicial defense and advocates. While the president (who would equate to our king) is called by this passage to serve in this capacity, the church is supposed to aid in this process as well. A multitude of people are rendered voiceless by our criminal justice system. In 2016, one in every forty adults, which is more than six million individuals, could not vote because they had a felony on their criminal record. These individuals not having the power to vote shapes judicial outcomes, such as which officials are elected and how long they retain their office. The Bible tells us that leaders are called to a higher standard; when judges act unethically, the church must hold them accountable and speak up for those who cannot speak for themselves, and for the rights of all who are destitute. Speak up and judge fairly; defend the rights of the poor and needy.

THE SCHOOL-TO-PRISON PIPELINE

The school-to-prison pipeline is the fifth conduit feeding mass incarceration. The ACLU defines the school-to-prison pipeline as "the policies and practices that push our nation's schoolchildren, especially our most at-risk children, out of classrooms and into the juvenile and criminal justice systems. This pipeline reflects the prioritization of incarceration over education."[13] The school-to-prison pipeline traces the well-worn path of predominantly impoverished urban youth of color from decrepit, underfunded, antiquated schools to luxurious, earmarked, state-of-the-art prisons.

This school-to-prison pipeline illuminates the detrimental impact of zero-tolerance policies and highlights how these policies are exacerbated by the disproportionate ways they are enforced. This pipeline illustrates how students are often brandished as criminals well before they reach adolescence. It also highlights a philosophical shift in K-12 education regarding how we respond to adolescent misbehavior, outlining our move from in-house administrative discipline to an outsourced, punitive, law-enforcement-based response to juvenile misbehavior.

ZERO-TOLERANCE POLICIES

There has been a dramatic shift in school discipline over the last four decades. School suspensions have grown exponentially, increasing from 1.7 million in 1974 to 3.1 million in 2000.[14] While debates exist about the precise moment when zero-tolerance policies were institutionalized, there is agreement that they became commonplace in the wake of the 1999 mass shooting at Columbine High School. Since 1999, zero-tolerance policies have emboldened the school-to-prison pipeline, adversely affecting millions of students.

Reflecting on the impact of zero-tolerance policies, James Duran, the veteran dean of discipline at Skinner Middle School in Denver, said, "I can tell you that I was suspending upwards of 300 kids a year. And I'll tell you, I'll admit it, that's just what we did in schools. We suspended kids."[15] More than a quarter-million students were charged with misdemeanors after being handed over to police officers.[16]

A US Attorney General–initiated task force found that "many children enter the juvenile justice system because schools rely on that system to enforce discipline. Harsh, exclusionary school discipline policies funnel children into the justice system in large numbers." Additionally, the National Education Policy Center found that "of the 3.3 million children suspended from school each year, 95 percent are sanctioned for nonviolent offenses like disruptive behavior and violating dress codes."[17]

Furthermore, the American Psychological Association (APA) found that zero-tolerance policies do not result in improved school safety but lead to disproportionally high rate of discipline for students with emotional disturbances. According to the NAACP Legal Defense Fund, these policies and practices "harm academic achievement for all students while increasing the chances that those excluded will be held back, drop out, and become involved with the juvenile and criminal justice systems."[18]

Speaking of the school-to-prison pipeline, Kevin Gilbert, a National Education Association Executive Committee member, said, "My eyes were opened by a young man I met who had spent 21 days in a juvenile detention center, basically for talking back in class." Gilbert continued to say, "As educators, we need to step back and look at our discipline structures. We need to make sure they're going to help, not hurt students." Statistically, black and Hispanic students are most severely hurt.[19]

Nevertheless, zero-tolerance policies are not the only culprit in the school-to-prison pipeline. The ACLU also identifies failing public schools, implicit bias, police in school, and juvenile detention as primary factors affecting a student's chance of entering the school-to-prison pipeline. This pipeline is also the byproduct of funding cuts, high-stakes testing, and removing art and music programs from schools.

These decisions create a system that most adversely affects students with special needs, impoverished kids, students of color, and children who have endured trauma or abuse. Foster, homeless, and LGBTQI students are also disproportionately affected.[20] For example, even though students with disabilities make up only 12 percent of students nationally, the US Department of Education found that they represent 25 percent of students arrested. Additionally, these special-needs students receive out-of-school suspensions at more than twice the rate of their peers without a disability.[21]

RACIALIZED PERCEPTIONS AND TRAUMA

Alvin Ailey, the renowned African American choreographer, said, "One of the worst things about racism is what it does to young people."[22] As someone who endured racism as a child and has pastored young people for over a decade, this is profoundly true. The psycho-emotional scarring of racism indelibly marks young people. It breeds a wound that scars, festers, metastasizes, and, if untreated, becomes terminal.

Systemic racism is one of the most common and tragic expression of racism young people are subjected to. While systemic racism can be overt, it is often expressed covertly; insidiously ingrained within institutional culture. Systemic racism is thereby commonly reinforced by well-intentioned people (system employees) in unconscious ways. Implicit bias is a chief expression of institutionalized racism.[23]

Implicit bias is also a prime example of how students are profoundly affected by adults' inability to interrogate our own prejudices and cultural blind spots. When adults do not do this, statistics illuminate that young people suffer grave consequence. While we often believe that our inner thoughts have no bearing on our actions, science proves this untrue. For example, Ohio State University's Kirwan Institute for the

Study of Race and Ethnicity found that implicit bias is "an unconscious yet powerful contributor to school discipline disparities."[24] Additionally, in *Price Waterhouse v. Hopkins* (1989) it was determined that implicit bias affects our behavior and moral judgements.

IMPLICIT BIAS, RACIALIZATION, CRIMINALIZATION, AND SCHOOL PUNISHMENT

Michelle Alexander details the evolution and impact of the racialization of African Americans:

> Arguably the most important parallel between mass incarceration and Jim Crow is that both have served to define the meaning and significance of race in America. Indeed, a primary function of any racial caste system is to define the meaning of race in its time. Slavery defined what it meant to be black (a slave), and Jim Crow defined what it meant to be black (a second-class citizen). Today mass incarceration defines the meaning of blackness in America: black people, especially black men, are criminals. That is what it means to be black.[25]

This analysis helps make sense of what is transpiring in our schools. The criminalization of blackness starts in preschool. While black children bear the most punitive punishments, Hispanic and Native children are also disproportionately punished in punitive ways. The school-to-prison pipeline manifests racial disparities that translate into the racial disproportionalities within our juvenile and adult correctional facilities.

Implicit bias haunts students throughout their education. The US Department of Education found that even as early as preschool, while black children constitute 18 percent of all students nationally, they account for 48 percent of preschoolers who receive more than one out-of-school suspension (see fig. 5.1). Black children are also tracked, profiled, and disciplined at more severe rates than their peers in kindergarten through twelfth grade education. Annually, 40 percent of students expelled from school are black, and black students are suspended three times more often than their white peers. Black girls are suspended at rates 12 percent higher than girls of any other race or ethnicity, and most boys. Collectively, black students make up 19 percent of the students served by the Individuals with Disabilities Education Act but make up 36 percent of the students who are physically restrained with devices intended to restrict movement.[26]

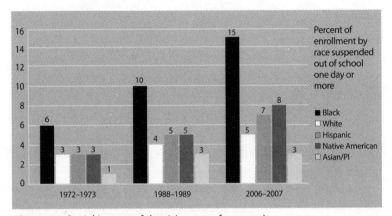

Figure 5.1. Racial impact of the rising use of suspension

Note: School suspensions have risen steadily since the early 1970s, and racial disparities have grown considerably as well.

Source: Daniel J. Losen, "Discipline Policies, Successful Schools, and Racial Justice," University of Colorado Boulder, October 2011, 4, http://files.eric.ed.gov/fulltext/ED524711.pdf.

Nationally, black youth are five times more likely to be incarcerated than their white peers, and Latino and Native American youth are two to three times more likely.[27] In 2009, for example, the Los Angeles Unified School District, one of the more diverse districts in the country, found that 77 percent of the students that were expelled were Hispanic. The district also found that racially, the percentage of their out-of-school-suspensions were 62 percent Hispanic, 33 percent black, 2 percent white, and 2 percent Asian.

INTERRELATED AND CONTRIBUTING FACTORS

How we choose to discipline students is so important because suspensions have become the chief predictor of high school dropouts. The correlation between suspensions and dropout rates is strong, and the relationship between dropout rates and incarceration is undeniable. Youth who do not graduate from high school are eight times more likely to go to prison.[28] Within federal and state prison populations, 41 percent do not have a high school diploma or GED. In local jails, 31 percent have not completed high school or its equivalent. And 68 percent of those in prison do not have a high school diploma.[29]

There is also a strong correlation between foster care and incarceration. This correlation intensifies when they are students of color or LGBTQI. Those in the foster-care system are three times more likely to be suspended or expelled than their peers. Fifty percent of children within the foster-care system are black or Hispanic. Twenty-five percent will end up behind bars within a few years of turning eighteen.[30] Former foster-care children represent one of the largest incarcerated populations. For example, in California 70 percent of the incarcerated populace is former foster-care youth.[31]

For many students the pipeline begins with their enrollment in failing public schools. These schools are distinguished by inadequate resources, overcrowded classrooms, and insufficient funding. Many of these schools do not have or have an inadequate number of counselors, speech and language specialists, and special education services. They are generally located in impoverished communities. The rate of teacher turnover is alarmingly high, and students are frequently taught by less-experienced (and sometimes less-qualified) teachers.[32] These schools struggle to meet the demands of test-based accountability initiatives (like No Child Left Behind), and this high-stakes assessment approach to education incentivizes these schools to oust low-performing students to improve test and performance scores.[33]

Homeless students are also disproportionately affected by this pipeline. There are more than one million homeless K-12 public students. The past decade has seen a doubling in their number. These students are disproportionately people of color and LGBTQI. Forty-sixty percent of homeless youth have experienced physical abuse, while 17 to 35 percent have experienced sexual abuse.[34]

POLICE PRESENCE IN SCHOOLS

One of the most underexplored contributors to the school-to-prison pipeline is the presence of police in schools. As the *Atlantic* reports, in 2015 there were around nineteen thousand sworn police officers in K-12 schools. Three-fourths of high schools had armed security staff. While there was only a slight difference between the number of urban and suburban schools who employed armed security officers, there was a significant difference in how many of these officers were employed based on the racial and socioeconomic composition of the school. The *Atlantic* found that "schools where at least half of the children are nonwhite, as well as high-poverty schools (meaning those where at least 75 percent of students are eligible for free or reduced-price lunch) are home to the highest percentages in the country of K-12 campus law enforcement."[35]

School-employed police—also known as "school resource officers" (SROs)—originated in the 1950s in Flint, Michigan. SROs originated out of a desire to foster healthy relationships between police and students. This idea inspired cities nationwide to implement similar programming, and during this period of rapid growth, SROs saw an expansion of their roles and responsibilities in schools. By the 1960s, SROs were providing services ranging from counseling and coaching to tutoring and mentoring.[36]

In the 1990s the Justice Department initiated a new program called "COPS in Schools," which fundamentally altered the mission and function of SROs. There was a 45 percent increase in the number of SROs between 1997 and 2000, supported by a $68 million governmental allocation.[37] After Columbine, SROs saw their role in schools shift yet again, and this time they were asked to become more involved in policing campuses in ways that officers police society at large: patrolling hallways, intervening in student misbehavior, and enforcing a culture of law and order within schools. From 1999 to 2005 the Justice Department awarded over 750 million dollars in grants through its "Cops in Schools" program, ultimately resulting in the hiring of 6,500 new SROs. While these officers were in schools full time, they were overseen by outside police departments.[38]

Therefore, the officers who occupy our schools play a fundamentally different role from the one envisioned when SROs came into being. This new, enforcement-oriented role was prompted by an increase in campus gun violence. This shift began with Columbine and intensified after the Sandy Hook massacre—which resulted in twenty-eight casualties—in 2012. These two tragedies incited anxiety and provoked concerned parents to advocate for an increased police presence in schools.

In 2016, ABC News conducted a study on mass shootings since Columbine. They found that in schools during that time span (April 1999– February 2016) there were fifty attempted mass shootings, amounting to 141 people killed. Seventeen of the students who attempted a mass shooting were age fifteen or younger. There have been 270 campus shootings since. This amounted in 2015 to one shooting per week.[39]

These tragedies paved the way for increased federal funding earmarked for SROs. Most of these officers were drawn directly from local police departments. Montgomery County, Maryland, an adjacent suburb to Washington, DC, is a prime example of how these tragedies affected the number of SROs in schools. In this region the number of SROs doubled the year after the Sandy Hook mass shooting.

According to a survey conducted by the Department of Education, 43 percent of public schools employ security persons, including SROs, and 28 percent involve law enforcement carrying firearms.[40] This influx of police within our schools is therefore best explained by the furious expansion of zero-tolerance discipline, an increase in campus gun violence, and parental advocacy aimed at creating safer schools.

While many parents believe more SROs make schools safer, research illustrates that students who are disciplined and apprehended by law enforcement are more likely to be incarcerated.[41] A report titled "Education Under Arrest: The Case Against Police in Schools" concluded that SROs exaggerate how school misbehavior is interpreted, leading to juvenile mischief being treated as a criminal offense. This approach to school discipline results in unnecessary arrests.[42]

Schools with SROs have a disproportionate number of students arrested for minor offenses, and since youth with records drop out of high school at higher rates, schools with SROs have higher dropout rates. In many schools the new role of SROs has shifted the atmosphere from an environment of adolescent learning to that of a quasi-correctional institution.

SROS, RACIAL BIAS, AND EXCESSIVE FORCE

On June 5, 2015, a neighborhood pool party in a gated community spiraled out of control in McKinney, Texas. McKinney police officers were called to intervene, and one officer—Eric Casebolt—was recorded using excessive force on a teenage girl. Casebolt repeatedly grabbed Shashona Becton, a fourteen-year-old black girl, by her hair, using it to yank her to the ground. Casebolt then proceeded to mash Becton's face into the ground and knelt on her back, restraining and handcuffing her. Casebolt also drew and pointed his handgun at two other youth.[43]

The incident sparked protests in McKinney and prompted investigations into the relationship between black youth and McKinney police. These investigations revealed that SROs in McKinney schools targeted and profiled black students at a disproportionate rate. While black students made up 13 percent of the school system, they received 39 percent of the arrests by SROs.[44]

This study, and others like it, illustrates flaws in SRO training or a lack thereof. The McKinney studies also reveal that the SROs did not receive special training before being dispatched to serve in schools.[45]

SROs are not typically taught about adolescent psychology or trained to understand and contextually respond to the behavior of students, particularly students with mental illness or other special needs. In most states juvenile justice issues fill just 1 percent of the training hours at police academies.[46] Nationwide, only twelve states mandate SROs to receive student-specific preparation before working in schools.[47]

The National Association of School Resource Officers (NASRO), a large provider of student-specific training for law enforcement, instructs about 1,500 officers each year. This organization has trained SROs for more than two decades, but because this training is optional in most states, the director has said, "We only train the ones that come to us."[48]

Therefore, most SROs are not trained to police adolescents, and this lack of training shows in their overzealous use of excessive force against students. A prime example of this occurred on October 26, 2015, in Columbia, South Carolina, at Spring Valley High School. Senior Deputy Ben Fields was called into the classroom to help settle a disciplinary situation. After speaking with the student for a few moments, Fields was recorded placing a sixteen-year-old girl in a chokehold, lifting her desk off the ground (while she was still in it), flipping the desk over, jerking the student from her desk, dragging her across the classroom floor, and then applying the full weight of his body on her back as he handcuffed her. The student, who was non-violently refusing to leave the classroom after being instructed to by her teacher several times, suffered injuries to her arm, face, neck, and back. While the student should have followed instructions, her non-violent dissent did not warrant this level of aggression or force.

While other cases have not garnered the same headlines, they are no less troubling. There is a glaring problem with SROs. They are prone to using excessive force, establishing a corporal environment where students are treated as criminals rather than children, and police brutality is too commonplace.

The examples are rampant. Whether it is the seven-year-old special-needs student—Yosio Lopez—who was beaten with a baton, shocked with a taser, and put in handcuffs by an SRO in Dallas;[49] Ahmed Mohamed, the Muslim student in Irving, Texas, arrested for building a "hoax bomb" after he proudly showed the clock he built to his science teacher (believing it displayed his scientific ingenuity); or the Round Rock, Texas, SRO who grabbed a fourteen-year-old boy by his neck, forcing him to the ground while choking him, there is a glaring problem with how SROs patrol our schools.[50]

Another specific problem with SROs is the nature of physical force exerted by male officers in interactions with female students. In addition to the incident at Spring Valley High School, there was Jasmine Darwin and Mariana Benton.[51] Benton, a twelve-year-old, was involved in a fight at Piedmont Global Academy School in Dallas. An SRO was called to help break up the fight. After the officer separated the two girls involved in the altercation, he is shown on video picking up Benton and body slamming her to the ground. He then pepper sprays her. Benton's mother says this resulted in her daughter having a "clavicle fractured." The Dallas Independent School District issued a statement saying that "his actions do not appear to represent the type of response we want our officers to display."[52]

SROs have also been fired for stalking teachers, arrested for immoral conduct, and charged with statutory rape of students. For instance, Jacob Ryan Delgadillo, a Houston SRO, forced a fourteen-year-old girl to perform oral sex, and Jamil Hall, a South Carolina SRO, was charged with sexual battery and misconduct in office for having sex with a student on school grounds.[53]

The school-to-prison pipeline has fostered a punitive environment within our school system. Armed officers and retributive punishments have created an atmosphere where kids are no longer allowed to learn from making juvenile mistakes. Adolescent behavior must be corrected, but it also needs to be done in a redeeming manner. Instead, kids are being expelled, arrested, and incarcerated for things that used to be handled within schools in a more restorative manner without involving law enforcement. Furthermore, it is irresponsible to employ officers who have not been educated in childhood and adolescent development to function as disciplinarians or reinforcement within schools. Without this contextual education, officers present a potential danger to students because they are not able to contextually respond to adolescent misbehavior.

JUVENILE JUSTICE SYSTEM

Our juvenile justice system is fundamentally broken, riddled with racial and class biases.[54] For many, criminal justice boils down to "If you do the crime, you do the time," but most people are completely unaware of the inner workings of our justice system. For instance, most do not know that our nation has an elongated history of sentencing juveniles to the death penalty and life in prison. Minors, 365 of them, have been sentenced to capital punishment, with twenty-two of these cases occurring since 1985.[55] The death penalty was not outlawed for juvenile offenders until 2005.

Moreover, per the United Nations, the United States is the only country that imprisons children for life.[56] Consequently, there are currently over 2,500 individuals serving a life sentence without the possibility of parole for crimes they committed as children. Seventy percent of these life-without-parole convictions, for kids fourteen or younger, were of children of color.[57] Mirroring our larger criminal justice system, black juveniles are far more likely than their peers to receive life sentences. Many of these kids were sentenced to life in jail for nonhomicidal offenses. Not until 2010 was it declared unconstitutional for juveniles to be sentenced to life without parole for *nonhomicidal* offenses.[58]

Almost one hundred thousand children are incarcerated in adult jails and prisons annually.[59] Over two hundred thousand are tried as adults yearly. Incarcerating children with adults has been proven to put kids at risk. Children incarcerated with adults are at great risk of being sexually assaulted and are more likely to die by suicide during or after their incarceration. Nevertheless, most states continue to house juveniles in adult facilities.[60]

Children as young as eight years old have been prosecuted as adults. Some states continue to permit juveniles as young as ten and twelve to be tried and sentenced as adults. When juveniles are convicted as adults—as opposed to as juveniles—it increases sentencing severity and permanently mars their criminal record. In many instances, something as simple as trying juveniles as minors could prevent youth from being prohibited from voting, receiving financial aid for college, and qualifying for other important governmental subsidies. This small reform would have enormous implications, enabling youth who have learned from their mistakes to return to their community as productive members of society.[61]

Solitary confinement is another problem. This oppressive practice can cause neurological and psychological damage bringing on a wide range of mental disorders, including panic attacks, hallucinations, depression, and many other issues.[62] Out of all suicides in juvenile facilities, half occurred in solitary confinement, and 62 percent of all juveniles who died by suicide had a history of solitary confinement.[63] Solitary confinement can last for months on end.[64] A 2012 Texas survey found that most jails held juveniles in solitary confinement for six months to more than a year.[65]

Juveniles are especially scarred by solitary confinement because their brains are still in crucial stages of development.[66] The attorney general found that "nowhere is the damaging impact of incarceration on vulnerable children more obvious than when it involves solitary confinement."[67] We need reform, and we need it now. We have been negligent in holding our judicial system accountable, and thus these oppressive practices have become normative.

The attorney general also found that

the vast majority of children involved in the juvenile justice system have survived exposure to violence and are living with the trauma of that experience. If we are to fulfill the goals of the juvenile justice system—to make communities and victims whole, to rehabilitate young offenders while holding them accountable, and to help children develop skills to be productive and succeed—we must rethink the way the juvenile justice system treats, assesses, and evaluates the children within it.[68]

In Cook County, Illinois, for example, nearly all of the children in juvenile detention had been exposed to traumatic violence in the past.[69] Additionally, studies have shown that of all children kept in juvenile detention, nearly 70 percent have been diagnosed with a mental health disorder, and 25 percent have attempted suicide.[70]

Those accountable for supervising juvenile detention facilities have found that "between 2004 and 2007 there were roughly 12,000 documented reports of physical, sexual, or emotional abuse by staff members—nearly 10 assaults a day, on average."[71] Dr. Lauren Abramson says, "If our aim is to nurture healthy children within safe communities, we need to change our approach and the values that drive our responses to violence. The reliance on highly punitive approaches [is] not working—they make people more alienated and angry, they feed cycles of revenge, and, as if that is not enough, they are costly."[72] The juvenile justice system is destroying our next generation. The church must speak up and advocate for new, restorative legislation.

Deconstructing this pipeline will require our time, resources, advocacy, and votes. We need to see ourselves as connected to people we thought we were estranged from. It will require becoming more involved in local schools, supportive of teachers, and collaborative with educational nonprofits. Let us turn now to the church's historic engagement with mass incarceration.

PART **2**

THE CHURCH'S WITNESS AND TESTIMONY

6

PROTESTANT REFORMERS

Prophetic Activism, Nonviolence, and God's Wrath

SCRIPTURE COMMISSIONS THE CHURCH into prison ministry, and because of this Christians have been engaged in ministry behind bars since the days of the early church. In fact, four books of the Bible were composed in prison. Colossians, Philemon, Ephesians, and Philippians are all "prison epistles," or "captivity letters."[1] Whether all four of Paul's prison epistles were written within a single prison sentence or over the course of his numerous incarcerations is debated.[2]

The church has the book of Colossians because a Christian visited Paul during his incarceration. When Paul wrote this letter, he had not visited the church in Colossae.[3] Thus, the letter's inspiration was rooted in a second-hand account by one of the church's leaders, Epaphras. Paul discipled Epaphras, who informed Paul about the spiritual state of his church.[4] The Christians in this region faced many dangers, particularly the potential to backslide into old paganisms. The strongest temptation was syncretism, mixing what they had come to know about Christ with unorthodox teachings they were exposed to both inside and outside of the church.[5] Thus, Paul's letter was to serve as a corrective to the unorthodox manifestation of Christianity being exhibited and embraced in Colossae.

Paul, through this letter, provided discipleship to both the leaders and congregants. He taught the community how and why their beliefs and practices were missing the mark.[6] He then encouraged them to realign themselves with a proper understanding of who God is to them individually and in relation to the world at large.

Colossians illuminates the importance of communing with the incarcerated. Paul's canonized words testify to the fact that God at times chooses to speak through "criminals." Their words and teachings can possess timeless wisdom. Paul's prison epistles turn the tables on how we think about prison ministry. All too often we try to "bring Jesus to prisons," but Jesus is already there. And in this biblical example we see the good news emanating from behind bars.

THE EVOLUTION OF PRISON MINISTRY

The criminal justice system of North American colonies was modeled on the European system, where prisoners were not typically criminals. In the essay "Well Ordered Prison," historian Randall McGowen explains that few incarcerated people were locked up because of crime. Historian Jennifer Graber corroborates this, writing, "What is important to notice about both England and the colonies is that governments did not use imprisonment as a form of punishment."[7]

Prisons, therefore, were filled with debtors and "social undesirables"; most had not broken the law but were paupers, debtors, and idlers. These impoverished, marginalized prisoners were the "least of these": widows, orphans, and the disabled.[8] Criminals, conversely, were punished more harshly. Instead of imprisonment, criminals were publicly humiliated, tortured, and killed. Punishments ranged from being locked in stocks to floggings and capital punishment. Often, the bodies of criminals who were not killed were mutilated.

In the seventeenth and eighteenth centuries England's criminal justice system became increasingly punitive. Prior to the Revolutionary War, English officials expanded the list of crimes warranting capital punishment. The number of capital crimes grew from fifty in 1688, to 165 by 1765, and exceeded two hundred by 1815. During this rapid growth, English ministers preached "condemned sermons" in prison chapels before executions. On execution day clergy offered prayers and the sacraments to offenders before they were hung.[9]

Ministers also traveled with the condemned to executions. Upon arriving at the gallows, they prayed psalms of penitence and would encourage the condemned to recite Christian creeds while they awaited their execution.[10] The American colonies emulated England's increasingly punitive penal code, and its ministers also ceremonially participated in state-sanctioned violence, therein legitimating it.

In New England, for example, when the gallows were used, Puritan ministers liturgically guided crowds through executions. Jennifer Graber says they "reminded the crowd that civil government served as God's institution for keeping social order. According to these ministers, capital punishment served as a sign—one of many—that reminded Puritans to keep their part of the covenant with God. Furthermore, other colonies that were not as religiously oriented as New England still had magistrates and ministers who used capital punishment to support their quest for social order and God's favor."[11] Therefore, ministers consecrated colonial vengeance and declared it divinely ordained.

While colonies mimicked England's punitive culture, retribution was also motivated by a desire to establish order within a country that leaders believed could easily spin out of control. Therefore, colonies used public punishment as a tool, wielding its power and making clear who was in charge. Christianity undergirded this coercive culture of fear and violence. Communities hung not only violent criminals but also first-time offenders who committed sexual crimes.

TURNING THE TIDE

As criminal justice became progressively retributive, a humanitarian countermovement swelled. Activists petitioned humanity's moral consciousness, calling the masses to reconsider society's treatment of the poor, disabled, and incarcerated. Citizens were asked to examine their hearts to discern "if their treatment of these marginalized groups was truly civil, ethical, and humane." The moral awakening generated abolitionist, suffragist, prohibitionist, and penal reformers. Criminal justice activists in Europe and the colonies rode this wave, halting the rising tide of penal retribution.

One of the most significant reformation voices in this movement was Cesare Beccaria, an Italian criminologist. Beccaria wrote a treatise in 1764 titled *On Crimes and Punishments*, condemning the use of torture and the death penalty. He advocated for a recalibrated criminal justice system. Beccaria highlighted the need for an alternative definition of justice; he called for a justice system not predicated on vengeance or on punishment as atonement for crime. Beccaria wrote, "By 'justice,' I understand nothing more than that bond which is necessary to keep the interest of individuals united. . . . All punishments which exceed the necessity of preserving this bond are, in their nature, unjust."[12] Beccaria profoundly influenced some of the most prominent Protestant prison reformers.

EARLY EVANGELICAL PRISON REFORMERS

John Howard, who was once briefly incarcerated, was one of the first Protestant criminal justice reformers. Though he was an English reformer, he profoundly influenced colonial reformation.

As a sheriff, Howard toured England's jails and documented what he experienced. His reflections exposed the unsanitary conditions of prisons and the dehumanizing treatment of prisoners. Howard leveraged his platform to expose prisoners' suffering. In 1773, Howard went before the House of Commons and petitioned them to investigate and improve prison conditions. Garber writes, "Howard successfully petitioned for the overhaul of the British penal code. . . . His work soon inspired change on the other side of the Atlantic."[13]

In addition to Howard, several Quakers served as significant early Protestant prison reformers. Like Howard, the Quakers' activism grew—at least in part—out of their own prison experiences. Quakers were commonly persecuted and jailed in both England and the colonies.[14] Quakers like William Allen and Elizabeth Fry set the standard for Protestant prison reformers. Allen and Fry played significant roles in paving the way for future prison ministries.

William Allen was one of the founders of the Society of Diffusing Information on the Death Penalty in 1808. Allen advocated for criminal justice reform within *The Philanthropist*, a journal he launched in 1811. In 1813, both Allen and Fry began their formal prison ministry at Newgate Prison.

Fry was the quintessential Protestant prison reformer. At the age of eighteen, she was compelled to dedicate her life to serving "the least of these" by a sermon given by American Quaker William Savery.

Sometimes referred to as the "angel of prisons," Fry preached the gospel in prisons, publicly exposed the inhumane conditions prisoners were subjected to, and created new programs focused on the rehabilitation of female prisoners and their children.[15] Quaker historian Margret Bacon details the conditions Fry sought to reform: "prisoners were supposed to pay the jailers for their food, and to endure whatever whippings or other punishment the jailer saw fit to inflict. There was no privacy for women, and lice were a common problem."[16]

In 1817, Fry helped found the Association for the Reformation of the Female Prisoners. This ultimately led to the creation of the British Ladies' Society for Promoting the Reformation of Female Prisoners, which was the first national women's organization in Britain. Fry also introduced education, discipline, and Bible studies into halfway houses women were released to before they reentered society.[17]

Fry believed in the power of proximity and purposeful narrative. She lodged in prisons and invited monarchs to visit so they could see and experience firsthand the inhumane conditions of prisons. Fry's activism was aided by her social capital; her brother-in-law, Thomas Fowell Buxton (an abolitionist), was elected to Parliament. This gave Fry the political clout to expedite reforms. In 1818, Fry spoke before the British Parliament on the conditions in women's prisons, becoming the first woman to present a case in the House of Commons. Angela Davis writes, "Following the tradition established by Elizabeth Fry in England, Quakers were also responsible for extended crusades to institute separate prisons for women."[18]

PAVING A NEW PATH

After the Revolutionary War, many US Protestant prison reformers wanted to distinguish their new nation's penal codes, polices, and punishments from "Bloody England." Zealous to do this, reformers began reexamining legislation and reimagining the penal institution. For example, in 1785, Massachusetts imprisoned convicted criminals in separate spaces from debtors and idlers. A year later, Pennsylvania "authorized public labor, rather than capital and corporal punishments, for crimes such as robbery, sodomy, and horse stealing."[19] Protestant reformers were significant players in these and ensuing prison reforms.

Quakers led the way as the most significant antebellum Protestant prison reformers. Thomas Eddy, a wealthy merchant and philanthropist, proved to be one of the most significant Quaker reformers. Eddy was a leading voice in a collection of Quakers who were profoundly concerned with the punitive nature of prisons. His sensitivity derived in part from his time behind bars. Eddy became a tireless advocate for a more restorative system. He said that "the peace, security, and happiness of society depended on a new penal system 'devised for the prevention of crimes.'"[20]

In the early 1790s, Eddy began a campaign to end the branding, whipping, and hanging of prisoners. Eddy instead advocated for nonviolent and reform-oriented consequences like incarceration, simple labor tasks, and inmate solitude. Due in large part to Eddy's advocacy, in 1796 a law was passed forbidding the keepers (guards) from carrying arms inside prisons and from striking prisoners. After this law passed, the only permissible punishment in prisons was solitary confinement, but even this was on a restricted basis. While these reforms may not sound particularly progressive today, they were significant during this retributive era. Subsequently, while these reforms were desperately needed, Eddy writes that they were not always well received.

> It is to be lamented, that many good citizens, feeling a just abhorrence at crimes, consulting the suggestions of virtuous indignations, rather than the principles of justice, become impatient that the alteration of the penal code has not yet produced greater and more decided effects, and diminished the number of the

guilty. They, sometimes, even express a regret at the change which has been wrought in our laws, and returning to a system of accumulated severity and terror, wish to see every offense against life and property punished with death; as if crimes, would cease with extermination of the criminal.[21]

In 1796, Eddy helped New York state senators draft a bill that established the penitentiary system. Eddy was then appointed to the commission that put the drafted bill into practice. Eddy was also chosen to oversee the construction of the first state prison in the United States, located in Greenwich Village and known as the old Newgate Prison. Eddy served as Newgate's initial prison director from 1797 to 1801.

Eddy believed that the US prison system needed to be markedly different from England's, and he dedicated his life to ensuring that it was. Eddy upbraided the European criminal justice, writing,

> While civilization and refinement were changing the condition and manners of social life, the criminal codes of the nations of Europe retained a vindictive and sanguinary spirt, the growth of rude and barbarous age. Benevolent and virtuous men saw and deplored the evils produced and perpetuated by unequal and cruel punishments; but the mild voice of reason and humanity reached not the throne of princes and the halls of legislators. While the State was aggrandized by conquest, enriched by commerce, or ornamented by the productions of art, they thought not of the unhappy beings who suffered under the numerous oppressions of tyrannical laws.—While every object which encompassed them wore the aspect of spender and fidelity, their dazed eyes were not tuned to those gloomy abodes where the victims of injustice languished in misery and despair.[22]

Protestant reformers and ministers involved in New York penal reform argued that prisoner reformation constituted the prison's primary purpose. They declared that a Christian nation demanded penal institutions with humane practices and reformatory disciplines.

They believed criminals could and should be redeemed. Protestant reformers in New York led the way in lobbying for, designing, and administering the state's first prison.

EVANGELICAL REFORMERS AND THE FIRST PRISONS

While Quakers played a fundamental role in prison reform throughout the new nation, their most prominent impact was in New York and Pennsylvania. Throughout the eighteenth century, Quakers lobbied for legislative change within the criminal justice system, advocated for institutional reform, and pushed for nonviolent supervision within prisons. These Quakers' reform work was rooted in their belief that the proper environment allowed wayward individuals to experience God's presence within.

In 1800, under Eddy's tenure as the director of Newgate, fifteen inmates broke out of the New York prison. The state legislature responded to the prison break by calling an armed guard to surveil and patrol the surrounding area. The prison's agent, also a Quaker, protested the deployment of the armed guard, saying supervising the guard required duties that those "who are of the people called Quakers, cannot with proprietary discharge."[23] While the armed guard was still sent, this story serves as an early example of how Protestant reformers tried to shape the ethics of early US prisons.

For Eddy and most other early Protestant reformers, prisons represented a new mission opportunity. In prisons they believed they could save wayward souls in mass and begin to institutionally inform the cultural ethos of a burgeoning nation. Graber writes that Eddy "believed that prison would put an end not only to state sanctioned afflictions at the stocks and whipping post but also to sufferings create by social factors such as poverty, alcoholism, and urban decay. The prison provided an escape from the gallows and the slum. It was designed not to terrify but to edify."[24] While his vision was never actualized, it yet again demonstrates how reformers saw their faith informing their activism.

Quakers were also strongly represented in the Philadelphia Society for Alleviating the Miseries of the Public Prison. As employees and reformers, Quakers used their influence to inform the culture and values of colonial prisons; inmates were separated to create space for private time with God, assigned simple labor tasks to promote a strong work ethic, and encouraged to meditate and study the Bible.

According to Graber, "Evangelical Protestantism dominated early national American life—in debates about the antebellum prison."[25] Graber describes how strategic Protestant reformers were, initially maximizing their influence by tactically aligning themselves to articulate a uniform message regarding the imperative role religion played in reformative incarceration for both inmates and the moral foundation of penal institutions. Considering this, state and prison officials initially embraced Protestant reformers' and ministers' recommendations, particularly their ideas about inmate discipline, suffering, and redemption.

Over time, however, officials became less amenable to reformers' suggestions, and prisoners became more resistant to them as well. This shift occurred because the reformers' work behind bars frequently proved ineffective as judged by the state's reform metrics. When reformers were welcomed into prisons, their message commonly fell flat with internees and failed to reduce prisoner's violence, and many administrators felt their presence was too partisan. Consequently, by 1804, the watershed moment in which Protestant reformers had the greatest impact on the New York's prisons, their reforms came to an abrupt halt.[26]

The reformers' fall from favor strained relationships between themselves and prisons as well as with state officials and inmates. Over time, tensions grew, and this led to disagreements over religion's place and role within prisons. This argument bred larger debates about the separation of church and state, which in many ways fostered lasting divisions. Over time, this stress inspired calls for a greater diversity of religious expression within prisons and created religious competition to provide spiritual services within governmental institutions, like prisons. Ultimately, the Protestant reformers failed to realize their mission of mass conversions and creating a prison system that reflected their values.

To maintain a presence and voice within prisons, Protestant reformers were told to tone down their evangelical terminology and practices. They were encouraged to instead embrace a more generic, secular prison religion that emphasized American morals, virtues, and good citizenship. Graber writes,

> These rejections created a new problem. If the Protestant reformers could not control religion's content, a new set of negotiations was necessary. In response, politicians and prison officials, along with some of the Protestant prison activists, articulated a religiosity of citizenship focused on ethical behavior and obedience to secular authority. Or, as theorist of religion John Lardas Modern has observed, they "shifted their referents" from Christian creeds to living daily life. . . . While the Protestant reformers supported a furnace of affliction to transform inmates, they found their own religion remade inside the nation's prisons.[27]

When reformers consented to the pressure from prison and state officials, they domesticated the gospel, distorting what it teaches regarding atonement, reconciliation, and redemption.[28] Graber says, "They stressed a Christian faith realized most significantly as moral living and obedience to governmental authorities."[29] In the end, Protestant reformers "sensed that the prison changed them as much or even more than it had transformed inmates. They concluded that America was not the sort of Christian country they once imagined."[30] The reformers lamented this as a tragic loss. Prisons did not prove to be the conversion warehouse they hoped it would be.

Protestant reformers initially hoped prisons would be a controlled atmosphere where they could cultivate conversations and steer the nation toward godly behavior among individuals and government. Historian Mark Noll writes, "The reach of Evangelicals has always exceeded their grasp."[31] In the end, the project to Christianize the populace and its governmental institutions had a secularizing effect on the reformers' religion, which stripped the good news of its prophetic and restorative voice.

EVANGELICALS, ATONEMENT, AND PRISON MINISTRY

In the 1810s and 1820s a new set of Calvinist reformers—many aligning with the Prison Discipline Society of Boston—prescribed more rigorous disciplines intended to break the spirit of prisoners so they could rebuild and shape it. Graber writes, "They turned to the prophet Isaiah and spoke of the prison as a furnace of affliction which God-ordained suffering paved the way for receiving grace and reforming behavior. Consequently, the prison became increasingly harsh in the late 1820s and into the late 1830s."[32]

The increasing retribution was, in part, a response to the crime surge that occurred after the war of 1812. As discipline became more severe, the increasing violence behind bars needed to be justified. Graber explains, "Partisans appealed to religion to underwrite their approaches to inmates and institutional life. Whereas observers once invoked religion to abolish corporal punishment, they soon used it to defend its reinstatement."[33]

The 1822 pamphlet *Sword of Justice Wielded by Mercy* is a primary example of how reformers used Christianity to legitimate state violence. This pamphlet, published by an evangelical press, was an anonymous dialogue between Newgate prison inspectors and an internee about to be released. In reflecting on his time behind bars and the punishments he endured, the internee quoted Proverbs 19:29, saying, "I experienced the truth of the declaration that 'judgements are prepared for scorners, and stripes for the backs of fools.'" Graber writes,

> In response to the inmate's reference to the whip, the inspectors explained that they found it "painful" to administer such severe sanctions. The convict assures them, however, that he understands their position, that stripes were "inflicted in mercy" and "designed for my good." Acknowledging the inmate's contrition, the inspectors offer "forgiveness of [his] trespasses." Before venturing out into the city, the ex-convict replies: "I accept pardon as a gift from heaven."[34]

This pamphlet demonstrates the role religion played in validating, championing, and resuscitating corporal punishment in prisons. It also illuminates how Protestant reformers saw physical punishment as part of the salvific process of redemption, largely because of their flawed atonement theology.

CHUCK COLSON AND PRISON FELLOWSHIP: FOCUSING ON THE SPIRITUAL

From 1969 to 1973, Charles (Chuck) Colson served as special counsel to President Richard Nixon. Colson was one of the Watergate Seven arrested for political corruption. Colson ultimately pleaded guilty to obstructing justice and served seven months in federal prison. While in prison, Colson vowed to serve prisoners and their families on his release. As a result, Prison Fellowship was created. It has now grown into the world's largest family of prison ministries.[35] In 2015 alone, around five thousand prisoners gave their lives to Christ through Prison Fellowship, and more than twenty-three thousand prisoners have participated in more than two hundred evangelism events hosted by Prison Fellowship.[36]

Toward the end of 1973, as Colson was under investigation—facing arrest—a beloved friend, Tom Phillips, CEO of Raytheon, gave him C. S. Lewis's classic text *Mere Christianity*. After completing it, Colson became a Christian. Colson became a profoundly influential evangelical leader; he served as the seminal voice of evangelical prison ministry for four decades.

Colson has a complex history regarding criminal justice advocacy. He commonly called attention to the injustice in our criminal justice system and the politics sustaining it. In "Reconsidering Evangelicals and 'Tough on Crime' Politics," Aaron Griffith highlights three important examples of Colson's activism.

> In 1981, he called U.S. prison conditions "revolting" and its unfair sentencing laws "insane" and "ludicrous." In 1983, he wrote approvingly of two courageous judges who bucked callous trends in their state by declaring mandatory minimums unconstitutional and who attempted to grant leniency to a reformed

convict. According to Colson, those who are willing to fight the cruel overreaches of American penal practice are heroes; in contrast, "Lady Justice, blindfolded to avoid partiality, is sometimes just plain blind." . . . In the early 1990s he decried politicians' use of law and order tropes to further their own agenda. "Willie Hortonism" (a reference to the George H. W. Bush race-baiting campaign commercial) and pandering to the public via support of the death penalty were in Colson's eyes absolute moral scandals.[37]

These examples are vital because Colson can be depicted as a "conservative evangelical" who remained silent on prison reform issues that mattered for marginalized communities.

Nevertheless, it must also be noted that Colson was leery of sociological assessments of crime and punishment. Crime, for Colson, was strictly a sin problem, and its injurious manifestations were exclusively the result of hearts not aligned with God. In a speech on criminal justice reform, Colson said, "The problem is not education, the problem is not poverty, the problem is not race; the problem is the breakdown of moral values in the American life, and the criminal justice system can respond."[38]

Colson also saw punishment as strictly a spiritual matter. Quoting C. S. Lewis's "The Humanitarian Theory of Punishment," he wrote about "just deserts," saying "to justify punish by whether it 'cures or deters' is the triumph of sociology over justice."[39] Colson believed the church got sidetracked from its missional purpose when Christians strayed from "what the Bible teaches" is the only cause of crime: sin. He conveyed that sociological analysis distracted Christians, leading believers down a rabbit hole that inhibited the church from fulfilling the Great Commission: winning wayward souls for Christ. In an interview, Colson said, "I want to stop crime, but I want to stop it by the only way that it will ever be stopped, and that's changing the human heart."[40] In reducing sin to a matter of an individual's heart, Colson— and other evangelicals—ignore corporate and institutional sin.

Moreover, they invalidate analyses that factor in the toxic consequences of structural sin by rendering these analyses as secular and not biblically based. Decontextualized analyses of sin, our criminal justice system, or society at large is unfaithful; it leads to flawed conclusions—more important, it is unbiblical!

Colson, a public advocate of the death penalty "in extreme cases" believed inmate punishment—irrespective of its severity—was necessary, and this belief was rooted in meritocracy.[41] He said previously, "there can be no mercy where justice is not satisfied. Justice entails receiving what we in fact deserve; we did in fact know better. Mercy is not receiving what we in truth deserve. To be punished, however severely, because we indeed deserve it, as C. S. Lewis observed, is to be treated with dignity as human beings created in the image of God." Colson therefore believed that "abandon[ing] the criteria of righteous and just punishment, as Lewis also pointed out, was to abandon all criteria for punishment."[42]

Colson saw this as a potentially disastrous decision, saying, "I am coming to see that mercy extended to offenders whose guilt is certain yet simply ignored creates a moral travesty which, over time, helps pave the way for collapse of the entire social order." Colson turned to the book of Romans to justify this conclusion.

> This is essentially the argument of Romans 13. Romans 12 concludes with an apostolic proscription of personal retribution, yet St. Paul immediately follows this with a divinely instituted prescription for punishing moral evil. It is for eminently social reasons that "the authorities" are to wield the sword, the ius gladii [high justice or the "right of the sword"]: due to human depravity and the need for moral-social order the civil magistrate punishes criminal behavior. The implication of Romans 13 is that by not punishing moral evil the authorities are not performing their God-appointed responsibility in society.[43]

This divine sanctioning of our criminal justice systems' right and responsibility to enact punishment marks Prison Fellowship.

PRISON MINISTRY TODAY

Very few churches today work for criminal justice reform, even though many support various prison ministries. In a 2016 survey of mainline and evangelical pastors, only one out of five claimed involvement in advocacy efforts. Among this number, African American pastors are more than two times more likely to be actively involved in reform, advocacy, or activist work regarding the criminal justice system.[44]

A 2016 LifeWay research study found that only 26 percent of evangelical and mainline pastors had acknowledged incarceration rates during the previous six months. Around the same number of churches were involved in any ministry surrounding incarceration, from the families of prisoners to those reentering the world outside. But this involvement varied between races. A third of black pastors had mentioned mass incarceration in the previous month, but among whites it was almost unheard of. White pastors were most likely of any racial group to say that they had never addressed mass incarceration in a sermon. That is at least partially due to their congregations being less impacted by this oppressive system. About one-third of African American pastors estimated that 10 percent or more of their church's attendees currently had an incarcerated family member.[45]

BLIND SPOTS IN EVANGELICAL PRISON MINISTRY

Prison Fellowship has been critiqued for embracing a theology that ignores the sociopolitical implications of embodiment and systemic sin. While I hope Prison Fellowship will shift toward a more holistic and restorative ministry approach—it did mobilize a Faith & Justice Fellowship in 2016—its historic engagement has been through compassion ministries, not advocacy.[46] This would be a vitally important shirt within Prison Fellowship, and there is reason to believe that it's beginning. James Ackerman, CEO of Prison Fellowship, has said, "Our country's overreliance on incarceration fails to make us safer or to restore people and communities who have been harmed."[47]

Jennifer Graber writes, "Operating in a prison allows Prison Fellowship to rely on state structures of authority to enforce discipline of their utopian Christian community."[48] Winnifred Fallers Sullivan, author of *Prison Religion*, highlights some theological problems inherent within Prison Fellowship's InnerChange Freedom Initiative (IFI) started in 1997 to provide educational, values-based services to help prisoners prepare to reenter society. Sullivan writes,

> IFI uses King David's hymn to a merciful God, and the story Luke tells of Jesus consorting with ordinary people like Zacchaeus, to underwrite the program's message that "crime is sin. . . . The Bible tells us that crime is *sin*" (emphasis in the original). Throughout PFM's materials, this equivalence, crime = sin, is to confer legitimacy on both the U.S. criminal justice system and PF's role in it, in a kind of mutual reinforcement. . . . The criminal justice system is just because it punishes sinners, and PFM is godly because it reforms criminals and brings them to reconciliation with their victims.[49]

In this way, Prison Fellowship, particularly through IFI, sustains a long legacy of Christians who uphold the retributive nature of incarceration by endorsing, legitimating, and actively participating in our nation's punitive system of criminal justice. While Prison Fellowship has done much good and has introduced a multitude of people to Christ, this too is a part of the organization's legacy.

But, even here, there is reason to believe the tide is slowly turning. Leith Anderson, president of the National Association of Evangelicals, has said, "The time has come to fix our criminal justice system." Anderson, in conjunction with Prison Fellowship, helped initiate the Justice Declaration, which summons evangelicals to "concerted action." The Justice Declaration begins,

> Because the good news of Jesus Christ calls the Church to advocate (or "be a witness") for biblical truth and to care for the vulnerable, we, His followers, call for a justice system that is fair

and redemptive for all. The Church has both the unique ability and unparalleled capacity to confront the staggering crisis of crime and incarceration in America and to respond with restorative solutions for communities, victims, and individuals responsible for crime.[50]

The shortcomings of evangelical prison ministries are summed up well by Aaron Griffith in the article "Prisoners and the Least of These in American Protestantism." Griffith, while acknowledging this is an oversimplification, eloquently explains the difference between how evangelical and mainline ministries have responded throughout our criminal justice crisis.

American evangelicals and mainliners often seem worlds apart when it comes to engagement with social issues. Take prisons as a case in point. The rhetoric diverges along the lines that one might expect: mainliners rail against the American mass incarceration system, the new Jim Crow that locks away minorities and the poor and is sustained by in-prison private labor and for-profit facilities. They want to fight this sinful system through activism (protests and petitions), academia (lectures and scholarly books), and artistic endeavors (photo essays and poetry).

Evangelicals seek inmate conversion. Though they may share mainliners' views on the systemic issues at stake, the goal is to save inmates' souls and to bring them peace with God. Indeed, prison is in some ways an ideal mission field: the evangelical prison chaplain or volunteer doesn't have to work too hard to convince their inmate audience that they are sinners in need of salvation. The Romans' Road takes a nice downhill grade when it begins in prison.[51]

Protestant prison ministry is grounded in Matthew 25:31-46, Jesus' discussion of "the least of these." Matthew 25 has profoundly shaped our understanding of the church's relationship to the incarcerated. It was quoted in reference to incarceration in the United

States as early as 1787, in the constitution of the Philadelphia Society for Alleviating the Miseries of Public Prisons. In recent decades, while mainline churches have turned to Matthew 25 to encourage activism, evangelicals have used the passage to encourage prison ministries focused on evangelism.[52]

Both mainline and evangelical churches tend to see prison ministry as an exercise in mission, but few have seen prisoners and prisons as a people and a place already close to the heart of the crucified Christ, who was himself incarcerated, ethnically profiled, and brutalized before being executed by the state.

Considering this, Aaron Griffith writes,

> If Karl Barth is correct that the first Christian community was the criminals crucified beside Jesus, then perhaps we would do well to ask ourselves what God might already be doing inside these shut-away places. Remembering that God is already in the spaces of the incarcerated, and loves those behind bars, might teach us all something new. It might remind evangelicals to look for ways that prisoners can preach the gospel to them. It might remind the mainliner to seek the blessing of fellowship with a person in prison. These are lessons worth learning as part of our worship of the holy criminal whose death and resurrection we remember this Easter season.[53]

The church has profoundly informed our nation's criminal justice system. While its legacy is deeply variegated, its impact is undeniable. Many modern criminal justice historians criticize early Christian reformers, connecting Quaker activism, which promoted the need for inmate solitude for quiet time with God, to later proposals for solitary confinement, and some Calvinist support for the continued use of the death penalty with the doctrine of original sin. While there is surely some merit to these critiques, any analysis of the church's impact on our nation's criminal justice system that does not simultaneously recognize the role of Christians in making prisons more humane, dignified, and reformative is inadequate. In recent years there have been improvements in how evangelicals approach prison ministry. TUMI is a primary example of this improved approach.

THE URBAN MINISTRY INSTITUTE

Dr. Don Davis understood the necessity of being present with our incarcerated brothers and sisters, and he saw the wisdom secluded within many of those behind bars. Davis founded The Urban Ministry Institute (TUMI) in Wichita, Kansas, in 1995. TUMI is a national training arm of World Impact focused on identifying, training, and equipping leaders for the urban church.

In an interview about TUMI's evolution, Davis says, "Before I meet the Lord, I really walked the streets and slung dope."[54] He explains how the Word of God transformed his life and helped him realize the restorative power of God not just for himself or for individuals but for entire communities. Davis says he always saw and believed in the potential of leaders from disenfranchised communities, but all too often the church has been unable to see their potential.[55] Consequently, Davis says TUMI "really staked everything upon our belief that leaders from the city who are well equipped in the Word of God, whose character and commitment to Christ is clear, they can be used in dramatic ways. Regardless of their background, or where they were from, or their academic training."[56]

As Davis launched TUMI, he clung to a belief that in order to advance the kingdom of God in marginalized neighborhoods, the church needed to intentionally cultivate leaders from these communities. Davis notes, "God repeatedly instructs the church to be present with, and concerned about the poor," and this profoundly shapes TUMI's missiology.[57] Led by Davis and others, twenty-two years later TUMI has grown to the point where it now has 263 satellite locations in nineteen countries. It has more than 2,949 students taking classes worldwide; 1,375 of those students are incarcerated, and 382 of them are international.

Testimonies like Davis's and models like TUMI illustrate why it is imperative for Christians to be involved in prison ministry. While we never take God into prisons—because God is there before we enter— we are divinely commissioned to go behind bars, boldly bearing witness to the kingdom by humbly partnering with God's ongoing work in prisons, jails, and detention centers. Scripture is explicitly clear: the church is called to actively pursue holistic evangelism and reconciliation behind bars. Matthew 25 and Hebrews 13:3 convey that prison ministry is not only for a segment of the body of Christ; we are all called to participate in it.

Over time, Christians have zealously served as some of the most prominent advocates for prisoners' civil rights. However, in many ways this legacy has been undermined by the church's theological articulation of redemptive suffering behind bars. This theology and the belief that prisons are furnaces of affliction are rooted in poor atonement theologies, particularly penal substitution. These tensions are best exemplified in the historic legacy of prison chaplains, to which we will now turn our attention.

THE PRISONERS' PASTOR

Chaplaincy and Theology's Institutional Impact

CHRISTIAN PRISON CHAPLAINS are not just preachers who proclaim the good news, they are prisoners' pastors. Chaplains meet the spiritual needs of their congregants and the context-specific concerns within their parish. They provide pastoral care, psycho-emotional support, and promote a peaceful environment where the religious rights of prisoners are respected. This entails everything from processing the offense(s) a person was sentenced for to walking with people as relatives die and relationships end, and lamenting with prisoners when they cannot attend their loved ones' celebrations—birthdays, graduations, marriages, and so on.

Chaplains have many other responsibilities. Figure 7.1 reveals where prison chaplains spend their time.

Despite the challenges, the majority of prison chaplains report they are well satisfied with their jobs. Sixty-four percent report they are very satisfied, and 30 percent report they are somewhat satisfied.[1]

WHAT DOES FAITHFUL CHAPLAINCY ENTAIL?

Responsible chaplaincy entails holistic ministry: caring for the soul *and* body. The best chaplains take time to learn about the systems and structures funneling people into their parish. They educate themselves about systemic injustice—not to condone or encourage a victim mentality, nor to excuse criminal behavior—because this equips them to do contextualized ministry.

Percent of chaplains saying they perform each of the following

	%
Administer/organize religious programs	93
Personally lead worship and other services	92
Work with external faith-based groups	92
Advise correctional staff on religious issues	92
Supervise/train volunteers	91
Provide support/counseling for staff	85
Supervise inmates to help maintain safety and security	78
Facilitate interfaith dialogue	74
Administer educational or other secular rehabilitation services	42
Follow up with former inmates after release	33

Q6a-j. Percentage saying no and no answer not shown.

Figure 7.1. What chaplains do
Source: Pew Research Center Religion & Public Life, "What Prison Chaplains Do . . . and What They Think They Should Do," Polling and Analysis, Religion in Prisons—A 50-State Survey of Prison Chaplains, March 22, 2012.

Learning about systemic injustice is a spiritual discipline, a formational practice of social energies. This deep study of society gives chaplains a better understanding of the institutionally neglected communities most of their flock comes from and will return to. Understanding the system also elucidates the trauma and brokenness many parishioners bear upon entering their parish. These wounds are often undetected and have therefore gone medically undiagnosed and untreated. The best chaplains understand that taking time to learn about the system equips them to faithfully and holistically care for their parishioners.

Chaplains are not called to preach at prisoners. They are commissioned to authentically love, listen to, disciple, equip, and empower prisoners. The best chaplains literally impart courage into their flock, believing in them, and seeing, naming, and affirming their untapped potential. They walk alongside their parishioners, reassuring them that redemption and restoration are not only possible but more important are God's desired outcomes for them.

Healthy chaplains create leadership development opportunities for prisoners. Chaplains are called to curate spaces where those who have decided to follow Christ have opportunities to make disciples of their peers. In these spiritual spaces—Bible studies, preaching opportunities in chapel, and the like—they can share their testimonies of revelation, restoration, and redemption. Chaplains also disciple their congregants by helping them to realize the ways their innate talents can be used for God, instead of the things that they may have previously used them for.

FATHER DAVE

Maura Zagrans has written about Father David T. Link, who was an exemplary chaplain. Link, a former lawyer and dean of the University of Notre Dame, became a chaplain after his wife died. Tracing Link's impact, Zagrans writes,

> Going into maximum-, medium-, minimum-, and re-entry prison facilities taught me that every life has potential. I learned that no life should be tossed aside, abandoned or thrown away, as is currently the practice in our prison empire. When I began working on this book, I was like Father Dave in that I assumed the criminal justice system was doing the job we taxpayers believe it should do. Tragically, this is not so. I came to understand that prisons are a new kind of ghetto. Michelle Alexander views the American crisis of over-incarceration as the "new Jim Crow" and she is correct. Father Dave goes even further: he sees it as a new form of feudalism. When I went to prison, I saw that redemption flourishes in fields that would appear on the surface to be fallow. Many of the 2.3 million incarcerated people in this country have themselves been victimized by the great divide of poverty, or by an educational system that is weak in communities where strength is most needed, or by culture and by legislative policies that ensure there will be an ample number of

scapegoats for generations to come. We dump our scapegoats into prisons and declare that they are being rehabilitated. But the fact is that very few prisoners have access to education, substance abuse programs, counseling, training, therapy, drug therapy and treatment for mental illnesses, and just simple human-to-human contact.[2]

Chaplains are called into this crisis. Through their faithful witness—and the presence of concerned, informed, and humble Christian volunteers—the church breeds hope where death and destruction have all too often reigned. Chaplains like Link, who selflessly accept God's call on their lives while genuinely holding firm to the core Christian belief that no one—irrespective of their crime—is beyond redemption, illustrate what Christian chaplaincy is at its best.

One of the men Link walked with says, "He is living proof that God is still in the business of making miracles."[3] Another man, Dickie, who was in the Indiana State Prison sixteen years prior to Link's arrival, says Father Dave's ministry and presence literally changed his life.

One thing I can say: Father Dave *is* what most Christians talk about being. For me personally, Father Dave has been salvation—not the eternal life salvation but the everyday salvation that most of us need in here. Out of the dire circumstances of our lives, there is a brick wall, and it is right there. No one else can burst through it. Somehow, from the other side, that brick wall began to crumble. For me it was Father Dave who crumbled that brick wall. And then he helped me to get on over to the other side. . . . God used him as a vessel of salvation for me.[4]

Another person Father Dave walked alongside of was a Native American man named Bear. Bear was a Lakota who had previously served in the US Marines. Father Dave encouraged Bear, who was a Christian, to do contextualized ministry within the prison as he was serving his time behind bars. Father Dave supported Bear as he held weekly Native American worship gatherings. During these gatherings,

Bear led the group in practicing Native expressions of Christianity, burning cedar, sage, and sweetgrass as they spoke prayers to the Creator through a sacred smoke trail of incense they blazed to honor God. These men sang praise and worship songs in their Lakota language and participated in Bible studies led by Bear, who culturally recontextualized his messages after hearing Father Dave's homilies.[5]

Father Dave illustrates that prophetic prison chaplaincy is not content with creating a peaceable atmosphere; it is intent on raising up leaders from behind bars for the benefit of the broader church and world. These chaplains understand they are stewarding a parish with the potential to change the world just as much as the churches that you and I attend.

These chaplains embody the gospel they proclaim, treating each prisoner with dignity, advocating for their integrity within the larger institution, and partnering them with believers who will do the same on their release. While Father Dave embodies these virtues, unfortunately, many Christian chaplains have not. As facilitators of prison religion, chaplains are the primary source for assessing the church's role and theological impact within prisons. Let us now explore the theological legacy of chaplains.

THE EMERGENCE OF CHAPLAINCY

In the United States, early Protestant reformers envisioned the penitentiary as a place where prisoners would demonstrate penance and remorse for their crimes through prayer and reflection. Institutionally, this vison revolved around a pastoral figure who would provide spiritual direction and clerical care. Prison chaplains emerged to fulfill this need, becoming the stewards of spirituality behind bars.

In the first few years of the 1800s Newgate Prison was desperately searching for a way to reform its prisoners. They tried increased workloads, mandated silent times, and in extreme circumstances solitary confinement. After these things failed to produce the desired change, Newgate began a lecture series on religion, which was deemed a success. Then sporadic sabbath preaching was instituted in 1805. In

1810 a request for regular Sunday services was made, and in 1812 New York changed its prison visitation rules to allow ministers that "reside in the city of New-York, and have charge of a church or congregation therein" to habitually visit Newgate to minister to prisoners. Later that year, inspectors officially requested Newgate administrators to hire a prison chaplain. They settled on the Reverend John Stanford.

Stanford, who first visited Newgate in 1807 and began writing prison tracts in 1808, set the tone for prison chaplaincy.[6] Stanford's theological understanding of atonement profoundly shaped his ministry behind bars. His first sermon text was "Behold, I have refined thee, but not with silver; I have chosen thee in the furnace of affliction" (Is 48:10). Jennifer Graber writes that within this sermon Stanford "noted that the prison hosted the fullness of divine action, including the suffering necessary for redemption. He believed that criminals necessarily experienced state-imposed physical and psychological pain. While humiliating and awful, such torments were necessary."[7]

In this, Stanford laid the initial groundwork for a repressive theology of redemptive suffering, which would become normative within prisons, legitimating abuse, state sanctioned violence, and torture. The great irony of Stanford's pastoral consecration of prison retribution and the violation of inmates' civil rights is that it emboldened a punitive system that he and other ministers should have counteracted.

Stanford was a Baptist minister who embraced Calvinism. He was ordained in London in 1781, and a few years later he sailed to the United States because he "became dissatisf[ied] with his situation."[8] Stanford arrived in New York and planted a church in 1795. After the turn of the century his ministry honed in on the social outcasts, particularly orphans, the mentally impaired, and incarcerated.

Stanford articulated his philosophy of ministry in one of his tracts. Quoting Job 36, he wrote,

If they be bound in fetters, and beholden in cords of affliction; then [God] sheweth them their work, and their transgressions that they have exceeded. He openeth also their ears to discipline, and commandeth that they return from iniquity. If they obey and serve him, they shall spend their days in prosperity, and their years in pleasures. But if they obey not, they shall perish by the sword, they shall die without knowledge.[9]

In this, Stanford depicted the state's violence as an extension of God's will and as a necessary part of an internee's transformation.

While chaplains' primary responsibility has been theologically framing Christianity for incarcerated individuals, chaplains have also profoundly shaped how the public views prisoners. Chaplains have frequently been tasked with conveying to the broader populace what happens behind bars, giving a glimpse into what the spiritual reformation of incarcerated people entails. This tradition dates to England, where prison chaplains began a tradition of hearing confessions from condemned prisons and publishing them for public consumption.

One of the most popular examples of this was the eighteenth-century *Ordinary of Newgate's Account*. This account, and others like it, presented prisoners as recognizing their violation, coming to terms with their guilt, and taking steps toward reconciling with God in pursuit of conversion and salvation. These chaplain anthologies contained biographies and last dying speeches of prisoners who were in line to be executed. These recorded accounts were extremely popular; the *Ordinary of Newgate's Account* sold over four hundred editions. These chaplain testimonials played a paramount role in forming the public's perception of what prisoner transformation looked like.

SING SING

One of the most prominent examples of Christianity's theological influence on prison culture is the retributive nature of punishment that has evolved behind bars. New York's Sing Sing Prison epitomized this. Elam Lynds, a former agent at New York's Auburn prison, was selected as the initial director of the Sing Sing Prison. Lynds was an ardent advocate of prison punishment and discipline but was also

notorious for blurring the fine line between harsh discipline and brutality. Nevertheless, Lynds was chosen to direct Sing Sing despite
having a violent record of brutalizing inmates, accentuated by his
termination from his previous role as a prison agent at the Auburn
penitentiary. He was removed because a female inmate abruptly died
after he "disciplined" her.[10]

Lynds had friends in high places, and his social capital—particularly
his close relationship with the soon-to-be president Martin Van Buren—
allowed him to secure this appointment in lieu of his transgressions.
Sing Sing took on Lynds's persona, swiftly becoming infamous for its
harsh disciplinary measures. Lynds unequivocally believed that the
whip was the "most efficient" means of disciplining prisoners and that
agents had to be given "absolute and certain power" over prison discipline.[11] This mindset fostered a spirit of retribution within the prison,
and this ethos was only exacerbated by Lynds's belief that adult prisoners were unredeemable.

Lynds did not believe in the potential for comprehensive rehabilitation for adult internees. In an interview Lynds expressed that this
logic led him to concluded that "all society could ask for—and all that
a prison could ever hope to produce—were internees trained to obey
orders and made fearful of disobeying them."[12] Lynds therefore saw
all efforts, programs, and resources dedicated to prisoners' reformation as a complete waste of energy, time, and money.

The violence and torture that prisoners endured at Sing Sing
prompted a crusade in which survivors committed to letting the world
know what was transpiring inside the prison's walls. Returning citizens, beginning in 1833, wrote books exposing the dehumanization,
torture, and abuse that they experienced and witnessed in Sing Sing.
Over a six-year period, three former Sing Sing prisoners wrote books
indicting the penitentiary's administration, detailing human-rights
violations and grotesque barbarism. They implored the broader citi-
zenry to step up, intervene, and advocate for change. One of the most
damning testimonials came from a veteran of the War of 1812, who
served a three-year sentence at Sing Sing.

A VOICE FROM SING SING

In *A Voice from Sing Sing*, Levi S. Burr described the prison's toxic culture. Burr methodically detailed the routine assaults prisoners endured. Describing the instruments of violence used by agents within the prison, Burr reveals how guards used "the cat," a stick with strands possessing sharp wires on its tail. They also used "the cudgel," a short, thick cane with metal spikes, to beat prisoners into submission. In addition to his own suffering, Burr told stories of fellow internees who were starving and sometimes beaten for things like sharing food with other hungry prisoners. He described inmates being worked to death in the quarries, and men who froze to death during the winter due to a lack of provisions.[13]

The greatest injustice that Burr and other prisoners describe was the use of corporal punishment. Burr recollects seeing an prisoner flogged with the cat 133 times. He said the agents whipped him until he was "crying and writhing under the laceration, that tore his skin in pieces from his back." Following this, a keeper pummeled him with "a blow across the mouth with his cane, that caused blood to flow profusely."[14] Burr indicts the Sing Sing administration as being "a Cat-ocracy and Cudgel-ocracry . . . where there is no eye of pity, no tongue to tell, no heart to feel, or will or power to oppose." Burr concludes that Lynds's leadership bred a culture that emboldened dehumanization, torture, and violence.

Burr's narrative was supported and bolstered by Horace Lane's and James Brice's accounts. Brice writes, "If you could but once witness a state prison flogging. The victim is stripped naked and beaten with a cruel instrument of torture called a cat, from neck to heels, until as raw as a piece of beef." Brice recounts the brutality of Sing Sing, saying prisoners were beaten to the point that "they smelled of purification." Brice also shares his own experience of getting flogged twice, and he says that during one of these experiences, an agent threatened to shoot him at gunpoint. Brice pointedly asks his readership, Can such tactics be "permitted in a Christian land, where the gospel is sounded?"[15]

Given Sing Sing's barbarity and Lynds's cynicism regarding prisoner rehabilitation, chaplains were in a precarious position at Sing Sing. Due to this, the first three chaplains tasked with framing Sing Sing's spiritual services—Louis Dwight, Gerrish Barrett, and Jonathan Dickerson—are good illustrations of three roles prison chaplains have played over time.

AN ADVOCATE OF THE LEAST OF THESE

Louis Dwight, one of the most significant chaplains in our nation's history, committed his life to prison reform and ministry after visiting a jail in Washington, DC, in 1825. Dwight was traumatized by the suffering he saw behind bars, particularly that of children. His distress spurred him into activism. Dwight returned home from DC and promptly transcribed a letter to the American Bible Society expressing his grave concerns and advocated for the church to intervene. Dwight shared how he traveled throughout the country spending time in prisons. He noted that Philadelphia's prison did not have a chaplain, Delaware's prison was marred by "great abuse," and Baltimore's prison suffered from "disgraceful management." Furthermore, he complained that prisons south of Pennsylvania lacked institutional accountability, and he highlighted how this severely threatened the health, safety, and potential reformation of prisoners throughout this region of the country.[16]

Dwight frequently ministered in prisons, passing out Bibles and preaching the good news. However, he soon concluded that this outreach, in isolation, was an inadequate response to prisoners' needs. For chaplains to holistically meet the needs of prisoners, Dwight determined he and his fellow ministers must do more than preach good sermons and distribute Bibles.

Prisoners, Dwight believed, also needed institutional reform and accountability as well as ethical leadership. They needed advocates who would give voice to their sufferings outside the four walls of the prison. Jennifer Graber writes that during this period, Dwight increasingly "understood himself as a witness to the church on behalf of prisoners. . . . Dwight's southern journey functioned as a conversion moment, bringing him into reform campaigns to alleviate others' suffering."[17]

While touring prisons throughout the South, Dwight wrote a letter to his wife, which in part reads, "When I shall bring before the church of CHRIST a statement of what my eyes have seen, there will be a united and powerful effort in the United States to alleviate the miseries of prisons."[18] In accordance with this letter, when he returned to Boston, Dwight embarked on a campaign to educate Christians about the suffering of prisoners and the dire need for prison reform. Over time, Dwight particularly advocated for humane discipline behind bars.

Dwight became one of the most prominent activists in the nation, serving as a leading voice within the Prison Discipline Society of Boston. This coalition of Christian leaders—which also included the presidents of Williams, Amherst, and Brown universities, as well as Andover Theological Seminary professors and local ministers—was the primary source of institutional accountability for prisons during this era. Dwight, a graduate of Andover Theological Seminary, served alongside Elam Lynds as the chaplain at Auburn Prison. Dwight fundamentally disapproved of Lynds's philosophy and tactics and was therefore profoundly disappointed when Lynds was named as Sing Sing's director.

As a chaplain, Dwight represented a broader change that was occurring within Puritanism. In the seventeenth century, Puritan ministers facilitated large crowds gathered to witness public punishments and executions, and Dwight was now advocating, because of his faith convictions, against physically punishing offenders with violence. Instead, he advocated for incarceration and, when necessary, measured levels of solitary confinement. Dwight also opposed Lynds's and others' rhetoric, which questioned the redemptive capacity of adult prisoners, both morally and spiritually.[19]

THE FURNACE OF AFFLICTION:
PRISON PUNISHMENT AS GOD'S WRATH

The second chaplain, Reverend Gerrish Barrett, was hand-selected by Dwight to serve as Sing Sing's initial chaplain. Dwight, who served as the spiritual adviser for Sing Sing, selected Barrett in part because he shared his revivalist Calvinist convictions. However, as Jennifer Graber writes, while Barrett "affirmed classic Calvinist tenants such as original sin, he also considered evangelistic work as the means God used to save the lost. . . . The young chaplain considered himself not just a state employee but also the church's missionary to inmates."[20] Barrett was assigned this post at Sing Sing in 1825, his first job after graduating from Princeton Theological Seminary. As an inexperienced, young minister, Barret was asked to create a brand-new program at Sing Sing, and he was expected to do so on a shoestring budget. When Barrett began at Sing Sing, the prison's chapel was still under construction. He lacked a team to work with and the trust and support of Lynds (the prison's director).

Moreover, Barrett did not have any spiritual formation resources to work with, draw from, or build on. Consequently, Barrett had to be innovative and canny. He led Sunday services in the prison courtyard, read Scripture and prayed for people in darkened hallways, and counseled prisoners by whispering wisdom through cell doors. Barrett also had to create his own educational curriculum and discipleship resources because Lynds diverted the funding and support allocated for prisoners' reformation from Barrett's budget; he saw prisoner reformation as futile.

Theologically, the hallmark of Barrett's ministry at Sing Sing was his articulation of a theology of redemptive suffering. Barrett, who was profoundly influenced by John Stanford, took Stanford's theology—which stated that the prison was a furnace of affliction where suffering was imperative for redeeming lost prisoners—and expounded on it. Barrett buttressed Stanford's foundational text, Isaiah 48:10, with his own principal text, Psalm 88. He loved Psalm

88, particularly verses 6-9, which he would quote in his sermons, teachings, and curriculum; it in many respects was the bedrock of his ministry.[21]

> Thou hast laid me in the lowest pit, in darkness, in the deeps.
>
> Thy wrath lieth hard upon me, and thou hast afflicted me with all thy waves. Selah.
>
> Thou hast put away mine acquaintance far from me; thou hast made me an abomination unto them: I am shut up, and I cannot come forth.
>
> Mine eye mourneth by reason of affliction: LORD, I have called daily upon thee, I have stretched out my hands unto thee.
> (Psalm 88:6-9 KJV)

This, according to Barrett, was the perfect description of his parishioners' life behind bars. To Barrett, prisoners' hardships and punishments flowed from God's wrath. Prisoners were severed from their communities because they broke the laws of both God and humanity. Therefore, Barrett believed state-authorized retribution was both a legally legitimate and theologically justified consequence for their crime(s).

Furthermore, Barrett believed violent punishment was not only allowed but biblically sanctioned. Barrett understood the prison's violence, torture, and retribution as part of God's mysterious plan. He saw physical retribution as a fundamental piece of what ultimately helped foster prisoners' reformation, conversion, and salvation. He therefore framed his theology of redemptive suffering within Psalm 88.

This Scripture exemplified what Barrett and other ministers meant when they referred to prison as "the furnace of affliction." He believed internees deserved punishment, and even severe retribution was justified. Barrett thought God used prisoners' sufferings—including those inflicted by the state behind bars—to open their wayward eyes and liberate their shackled souls. Barrett clung to Psalm 88 because he believed it not only demonstrated divine wrath but also God's unyielding love. He highlighted the silver lining of hope he saw within

Psalm 88, lifting it as a sacred promise for downcast, estranged, and otherwise hopeless prisoners.

Barrett attempted to illuminate the hope he believed was ensconced within Psalm 88. He declared that verses 10-18 were the point of contrition that inmates needed to reach before they were truly open to the transforming work of God. Psalm 88:10-12 says,

> Wilt thou shew wonders to the dead? shall the dead arise and praise thee? Selah.
>
> Shall thy lovingkindness be declared in the grave? or thy faithfulness in destruction?
>
> Shall thy wonders be known in the dark? and thy righteousness in the land of forgetfulness? (KJV)

Barrett believed God sovereignly met and transformed prisoners once they arrived at this level of remorse. Upon being humbled, Barrett thought prisoners had their eyes opened to God's truth and redemptive promise enveloped within these verses.

Accordingly, for Barrett Psalm 88 represented God's faithfulness to prisoners, a point of divine revelation where God showed up and answered the solemn questions that shackled the hearts and tormented the minds of repentant prisoners. He felt that verses 10-18 gave voice to prisoners' deepest fears and anxieties. He believed that God responded to these worries in this passage with grace, love, and redemption.

However, when formerly incarcerated people like Levi Burr described their time at Sing Sing, they did not experience prison as a furnace of affliction but described it as a chamber of torture at best and hell on earth at worst. These previously incarcerated citizens exposed life behind bars, and their testimonials caused the public to wrestle with whether it was possible for reformation to occur within a dungeon of torment, whips, and bloodshed. Burr recounted that Lynds directed Sing Sing guards to "lacerate the body, spill the blood, and starve the subject."[22] Surely this nature of suffering was neither redemptive nor just, but Barrett's theology initially hindered him from realizing this.

In the preface to his book, Burr explains that he wanted to expose Sing Sing's savagery to illustrate that Lynds's leadership contradicted any claims made about prison being a place of reformation. Sing Sing, he wrote, invalidated our nation's proclaimed "benign sentiments of mercy."[23] Barrett, as Sing Sing's chaplain, witnessed all the brutality firsthand, and he nevertheless failed to defend the dignity of those being brutalized behind bars. His flawed theology of redemptive suffering made him complicit in their suffering, but this all abruptly changed in 1830, when an administrative scandal broke out in the prison.

A SPIRITUAL AWAKENING

Prisons were routinely neglected when they were not being exploited and abused. Many Sing Sing prisoners developed frostbite during the winter because of inadequate clothing and a lack of heat within the facility.[24] The brutality and negligence was so severe and pervasive that some prisoners ate clay and dirt to stave off hunger. In 1830 all internees were forced to eat innards because prison agents began stealing the money earmarked for prisoners' food. Prison employees regularly lined their pockets at the expense of prisoners' health. When Barrett found this out, he had a spiritual awakening.

Outraged by these administrative crimes, Barrett's eyes were opened to the injustices at Sing Sing. From this moment on Barrett became a fierce advocate for prison reform. He reported to the Board of Prison Inspectors the administrative abuses he witnessed, and he served as an active participant in their investigation into Sing Sing's corruption. Consequently, Barrett became a threat to Sing Sing's oppressive status quo. And as a consequence, Lynds attacked Barrett. On finding out the details of Barrett's whistleblowing reports, Lynds accosted and assaulted Barrett. Lynds threw him out of the prison.[25] Lynds's attack represented the first time a prison chaplain had been battered by a prison director, and this encounter ended chaplaincy services at Sing Sing for a brief period.

Jennifer Graber informs us that "despite evidence that Lynds starved and beat prisoners, defrauded the state, and bodily assaulted a Presbyterian minister, he kept his job."[26] This outraged Louis Dwight! Not only could Lynds not be trusted to ethically direct Sing Sing, but due to his expulsion of chaplains, prisoners now had no pastoral presence to rely on or counsel to turn to in their time of need.

In the 1830 annual report to the Prison Discipline Society, Dwight explained how prisoners were now abandoned—without recourse— to the wrath, barbarity, and inhumanity of Sing Sing. After Lynds's expulsion of chaplains, Dwight asked the society, "What refuge or redress is there for mangled, sick, or starving prisoners . . . when [the prisoner] is held to his task, and then lashed, when he cries out from weakness and hunger? I know he is a felon," Dwight said, "but is he not also a human being?"[27] Despite Dwight's plea, Lynds remained in power until he retired a few years later.

SING SING'S NEW REGIME

Upon retiring, Lynds was replaced by his nephew, Robert Wiltse. Under Wiltse the unthinkable happened: Sing Sing became even more punitive. Wiltse intensified Lynds's severe punishment and endorsed penal theories that questioned the humanity and redemptive potential of prisoners.

Observing Sing Sing under Wiltse's reign, French researchers Alexis de Tocqueville and Gustave de Beaumont determined that "in America, [a criminal] is an enemy of the human race and every human being is against him."[28] Under Wiltse's tenure, internees were beaten with any available weapon by prison staff and private contractors. Historian W. David Lewis details how legislative reports illustrate that under Wiltse, keepers used whips, canes, cat-o'-nine-tails, red-hot pokers, and pistols to curtail the slightest form of inmate resistance. Prisoners were forced to labor in the prison quarry daily, moving huge slabs of marble. When agents felt that internees were working too slowly, they beat the prisoners with a whip used to motivate them to pick up the pace and work harder.

Wiltse also ordered prisoners to be fed with slop buckets. Frequently, their "meal" sat in buckets overnight, drawing mice and other rodents into prisoners' cells. A New York congressman, who also served as a state prison commissioner, lambasted Wiltse for his inhumane treatment of prisoners, saying that Wiltse sanctioned inmates' being "used like oxen in quarries" and struck with "walking staves."[29]

Throughout his tenure as director of Sing Sing, Wiltse saw reformers and ministers as a hindrance to his work because of what he called their misguided sympathy for inmates. Wiltse maintained that prison ministers undermined the necessary authority structure of Sing Sing. He also felt that chaplains "deceived themselves" regarding the potential redemption of prisoners, especially regarding the "supposed good qualities of convicted felons."[30] Explaining his philosophy of disciplining prisoners, Wiltse said, "Criminals must be made to submit through corporal punishment." He went on to say, "They can feel nothing but that which comes home to their bodily suffering."[31] Under Wiltse, prison discipline was no longer legitimated as redemptive suffering but as the state's exclusive tool for producing citizens who feared returning to prison so much that their fear would prohibit criminal activity. Therefore, the discipline had to be unforgiving and unyielding.

Consequently, Wiltse saw chaplains' moral, theological, and pastoral care of internees as a complete waste of time and resources. Due to this opinion, Sing Sing went without a chaplain for years. However, Wiltse finally acquiesced to the will of the public. He reinstituted a chaplain in Sing Sing, but when he did, he was only willing to hire a minister who would theologically underwrite the inhumane treatment, barbarism, and ruthlessness that he desired within his prison. Because of this, Jennifer Graber says, "Wiltse's position signaled an unprecedented level of physical and physiological violence against lawbreakers." She continues, "Wiltse did not cut out religion, but he appropriated it for his own purposes. Suffering became a means to a different end, and he wanted chaplains with theologies heavy on judgement and light on mercy."[32] Wiltse searched far and wide for his ideal chaplain and finally found Jonathan Dickerson, a Presbyterian minister and graduate of Princeton Theological Seminary.

BAPTIZING PHYSICAL VENGEANCE

Unlike Gerrish Barrett, Jonathan Dickerson was not mentored by Louis Dwight but by Charles Hodge. Hodge believed in total depravity, unconditional election, and limited atonement, and he discipled Dickerson to hold these same doctrinal beliefs. Dickerson therefore arrived at Sing Sing opposed to evangelistic revivals, volunteer societies, and educational reform.

Dickerson believed that all people deserve judgement, but only a few were chosen for salvation by God, and criminals were not among God's elect. For Dickerson, criminals' lives of sin exemplified their separation from God, and while he believed that God could redeem criminals, he said that this was extremely rare and unlikely. Jennifer Graber writes that "Dickerson performed his ministerial duties but with little hope of seeing the fruits of his labor. . . . [Dickerson's] theology found a fitting environment in Wiltse's approach to inmates."[33]

As a chaplain, Dickerson called inmates a "great moral waste."[34] He also said that the aim of his discipleship was to make sure Wiltse's "discipline is aided, strengthened, sanctified." With this collaboration, Dickerson wrote, "the whole machinery will co-operate" and produce "amazing effects." Graber says, "Indeed, the Reverend Dickerson began to see Wiltse's 'humane, though firm and ridged discipline,' as the 'handmaid and assistant' to the gospel he preached."[35] With this religious consecration of brutality masquerading as prison punishment, the partnership between state officials and clergy shifted yet again.

Chaplains have generally followed the footprints of one of these three chaplains, with the overwhelming majority emulating Dwight and Barrett. Prison chaplains have been on the frontlines of the church's engagement with the incarcerated, and most have faithfully borne witness to the love, mercy, grace, and redemption the gospel offers. Chaplains have brought many into the body of Christ, helping to renew hope, transform lives, and cultivate reconciliation.

However, the story is incomplete without also acknowledging how some chaplains have served as accomplices in the construction of the dehumanizing, exploitative, punitive system we have today. In order to faithfully move forward as the church and as a nation, we must learn to hold the good with the bad as opposed to denying the shameful elements of our past. Only then can we lament and turn back to God.

CHAPLAINS TODAY

Prison chaplaincy has evolved in some important ways. An interview with Kelly Raths of the Oregon Department of Corrections serves as an example. In an interview with *The Atlantic,* Raths says, "People who come to custody in prison, while they have been the offender, they almost without fail have also been the victims themselves." She continues, "Understanding that often has to come first, but the real, challenging question [for prisoners] was: Can I forgive myself?" Later in the interview, Raths confesses, "I'm not so keen on what we do in our country around prisons. . . . It can and does go both ways. There are some folks who will go through our corrections system and leave it traumatized; they will leave it as a much more savvy criminal than they ever were before."[36]

While Raths correctly points out that not every prisoner serving time will be reformed, nor does every internee see a need for change, there are many who do, and a number of these individuals get hamstrung by our corrections system. Having chaplains who see and acknowledge this is vital. It goes a long way toward bearing witness behind bars to the love and justice of God. It engenders trust in prisoners, which opens them up to trusting chaplains in ways that breed transparency, intimacy, and transformation.

A recent survey illustrates that many chaplains who work within prisons agree that our present corrections system is broken. Thirty-four percent of chaplains say the system needs major change, and 5 percent say it needs to be completely rebuilt.[37] Given these numbers, our system is clearly failing on some level.

The survey also produced some good news. The results reveal that our brothers and sisters behind bars are actively and faithfully living into the Great Commission. The chaplain survey found that 73 percent of state prison chaplains say that incarcerated believers in their facility are actively trying to share the gospel with their peers. Thirty-one percent say that believers sharing the gospel with other prisoners is very common, and 43 percent say it is somewhat common.[38] This fruit is in large part due to the faithful witness and discipleship of prison chaplains, and it is aided by church volunteers who have taken the time to learn what doing holistic ministry entails.

The study also revealed nearly 75 percent of chaplains believe their counseling and faith-based programs have been imperative to rehabilitating prisoners.[39] These programs not only help individuals understand their need for God, but they also encourage them to seek holistic treatment that aids internees in accepting responsibility for their crimes, considering what restoration entails, and realizing crime is always a communal offense, never simply an individual violation.

The survey also illuminated that 78 percent of chaplains consider support from churches and religious groups as imperative for returning citizens. Fifty-seven percent of prison chaplains providing faith-based rehabilitation or reentry programs said the quality of such programming has improved over the last three years, and thus most said participation in such programs has increased.[40]

THE SPIRIT OF PUNISHMENT

Atonement, Penal Substitution, and the Wrath of God

*While Yahweh may have said, "Vengeance is mine, I will
repay" . . . it would seem that our society . . . considers
itself to be God. . . . And nowhere is the spirit of punishment
more visible and more virulent than in our prisons.*

T. RICHARD SNYDER, *THE PROTESTANT ETHIC
AND THE SPIRIT OF PUNISHMENT*

WHENEVER WE THRUST OURSELVES into a role exclusively reserved for God, we sin. God is the lone just judge (Genesis 18:25;
Romans 3:5-6). When we forget this, we are prone to mistake punitive responses to crime for justice. Justice is not seeking legislative
vengeance, issuing retributive sentences, or condemning to the death
penalty those who commit violent offenses. Our Creator is the only
magistrate and jury who should possess the power to end life. Capital
punishment then is antithetical to the gospel of Jesus Christ, which
is predicated on reconciliation, redemption, and restoration.

During an interview with *Ebony* magazine in 1957, Dr. Martin
Luther King Jr. was asked, "Do you think God approves the death
penalty for crimes like rape and murder?" King responded, "I do not
think that God approves the death penalty for any crime, rape and
murder included. . . . Capital punishment is against the better judgment

of modern criminology, and, above all, against the highest expression of love in the nature of God."[1] Since most people are given the death penalty for a violent crime, it is also noteworthy that a few years later King also said, "The ultimate weakness of violence is that it is a descending spiral, begetting the very thing it seeks to destroy. Instead of diminishing evil, it multiplies it. . . . Returning violence for violence multiplies violence, adding deeper darkness to a night already devoid of stars. Darkness cannot drive out hate; only love can do that."[2]

Christopher Marshall—chair of Restorative Justice at Victoria University of Wellington, New Zealand—affirms King's conclusions, writing, "capital punishment is incompatible with a gospel of redemption and reconciliation."[3] Since the church is called to think alternatively about justice, what should we do?

DIVINE JUSTICE

Marshall correctly insists that understanding God's justice begins with humility and a recognition of our own sinfulness.

> Just as our human capacity to know God and the truth about God is limited by sin, so too is our capacity to know fully the nature of God's universal justice. Our ability to grasp the meaning of justice is constrained by our creaturely finitude. It is also constrained by historical circumstance. Our experience of justice and of reality in general is always mediated through particular cultural and historical traditions. It is therefore unavoidably contextual. It can only be partial, fallible, and provisional.[4]

Marshall's concluding sentence points to a harsh yet essential reality for Christians. Justice—until Jesus returns—is partial and limited. While this is a difficult truth to submit to—especially amid oppression—it is nevertheless foundational for our faith. The reality of imperfect justice here and now reminds us that justice is a divine act. It also contextualizes the reconciling work that God has invited us into as colaborers with Christ. It situates our struggles within the broader mission and movement of God in the world, which ultimately reassures us that our labor in the Lord is not in vain. Therefore, the imperfect nature of justice is not an impediment to people of faith. It cannot dissuade us from radically and sacrificially pursuing justice here and now. After all, Scripture tells us that the Lord requires this of us. God's biblical promises anchor and embolden us as we partner with God. So, what is biblical justice?

BIBLICAL JUSTICE

Scripture consistently reveals that restoration, not punitive punishment, is at the heart of God's justice. Biblical justice does include retribution, but not exclusively. Biblical justice cannot be solely defined by it. The more accurate description of biblical justice is restorative justice. Biblically, justice is a divine act of reparation where breached relationships are renewed and victims, offenders, and communities are restored. Justice, therefore, is about relationships and our conduct within them. Justice asks, How is righteousness embodied and exuded in how I live in relation to God, neighbor, and creation? In fact, Scripture could be read as the narrative of God's restorative justice unfolding in the world.

Defining justice in everyday terms is difficult. Many biblical scholars agree that Scripture nuances justice in at least two distinct ways. There is *distributive* justice, which focuses on how material possessions and resources are justly distributed in society between individuals and groups. Then there is *corrective* justice, what is called criminal justice, which deals with how crime and lawlessness are both identified and dealt with.

Christopher Marshall declares that the church must not misunderstand the biblical distinction regarding these two types of justice as license to separate them, because these two forms of justice are interdependent. History illustrates what happens when they are uncoupled: when corrective justice is analyzed apart from distributive justice, statistics are used to pathologize and stigmatize people, groups, and communities. Therefore, distributive justice ultimately provides the context for understanding and authentically analyzing corrective justice. Marshall writes,

It is vitally important the two domains [social and criminal justice] are not viewed in splendid isolation, especially when seeking to apply biblical insights and priorities to our context. Much of what the Bible says about social justice has direct relevance to the criminal justice domain. If we took more seriously the biblical imperative to care for the poor and dispossessed, to avoid the unjust accumulation of wealth and power in the hands of the few, and to set at liberty those who are oppressed by debt or exploitation, we would have less cause to employ criminal sanctions against those on the margins of the community who feel they have no stake in society.[5]

Therefore, while justice is about relationships, it is not simply about personal relationships. Justice is primarily about how systems, structures, and institutions relate to people. Justice, like faith, is both individual and social.

Accordingly, biblical justice requires the church to protect the dignity and livelihood of "the least of these," ensuring that government, systems, and structures are not preying on or exploiting the weak, lowly, and marginalized. Justice thereby requires Christians to be socially engaged advocates for righteousness in public, social, personal, and private places. Justice summons the church to social stewardship, to the toilsome work of cultivating communities where communal flourishing and *shalom* are not infringed by systemic injustice, institutional greed, or legislation that dehumanizes people, groups, and neighborhoods.

RIGHT(EOUS) RELATIONSHIPS

Biblical justice is established and worked out within the confines of relationship. The relational working out of justice is righteousness. This is why Scripture calls us to pursue right(eous) relationships with God, neighbor, and creation, and through our realigned relationship with God, in Christ, empowered by the Holy Spirit, we become the righteousness of God (2 Cor 5:21).

While most people think about God's holiness, private morality, or spiritual prudence when they see the word *righteousness*, scripturally *righteousness* is most commonly used to define those who conduct themselves uprightly in all of their relationships. A righteous person treats all people—whether rich, poor, or condemned—with justice, generosity, and equity.[6] The two ancient words translated as "righteousness" in Scripture, *tsedeq* (Hebrew) and *dikaiosynē* (Greek), are used to define someone who has "lived uprightly and behaved justly before God and their neighbor."[7] Righteousness also entails the omission of actions that cause any kind of damage to one's neighbor.[8] This is why we liturgically pray for God's forgiveness, for both the things we have done and the things we have left undone. Inaction, silence, and indifference are also relational failures. They breed injustice, oppression, and death. God finds these lukewarm responses to be unfaithful repulsive (Revelation 3:14-22).

Christopher Marshall expounds on righteousness as the relational working out of just relations: "The biblical notion of righteousness refers broadly to doing, being, declaring, or bringing about what is right. Righteousness is a comprehensively relational reality. It is not a private moral attribute one has on one's own. It is something that inheres in our relationships as social beings. To be righteous is to be true to the demands of a relationship, whether that relationship is with God or with other persons."[9]

Since this is what righteousness entails, unrighteousness (e.g., criminal activity) is outside the boundaries of a covenantal relationship. Given this, when we think about criminal justice we should ask question like, What happens when people are unrighteous? How do we respond when someone violates the confines of right relationships? The church is uniquely equipped to answer these questions, which are integral to our faith. We must not continue to ask the same questions of our justice system that the broader population does. And we certainly cannot cling to the same punitive "solutions" of the world at large.

Marshall explains that when criminal violation occurs, the offender(s) stand in need of restoration, spiritually and communally.

He writes that "biblical law often prescribes punitive counter-measures that are intended to denounce the wrong, arrest its power, and rectify its damage. Penalties may be imposed on the guilty party. But the goal of the punishment is not to maintain some abstract cosmic balance, but to put right what has gone wrong, to protect the community, and to restore the integrity of its life and its relationship with God." This sharply contrasts with our criminal justice system. Marshall concludes that "justice is satisfied by the restoration of peace to relationships, not by the pain of punishment."[10] This biblical understanding of justice is what the church is called to relentlessly pursue in the world today.

BIBLICAL JUSTICE: FLOWING THROUGH GOD, CHRIST, AND THE CHURCH

The Hebrew word for "justice" is *mishpat*. It occurs more than two hundred times in the Old Testament. *Mishpat* means impartially and equitably punishing people for relational violations, and ensuring people's rights.[11] It means giving people what they are due.

Mishpat involves advocating for the vulnerable and giving them care and protection. Widows, orphans, immigrants, and the poor were some of the most vulnerable and impoverished groups mentioned in the Old Testament. God is described as their primary defender. God is "a father to the fatherless, a defender of widows" (Psalm 68:4-5). God identifies with these groups to the point where God says that when we neglect, disrespect, or forsake the least of these, we are doing the same to God. Referencing passages like Proverbs 14:31 and Proverbs 17:5, biblical scholar Elsa Tamez says that "God identifies himself with the poor to such an extent that their rights become the rights of God himself."[12]

God makes no such proclamations about any other group. God's intimate identification with the oppressed is an irrevocable sign of his particular union with "the least of these." The church cannot ignore this. Scripture proclaims that God identifies with the broken and poor.[13] Throughout Scripture, justice is consistently referenced in relation to the vulnerable.

The Bible links justice to taking care of and taking up the cause of "the least of these" (widows, orphans, immigrants, and the poor). Israel's inability to care for this quartet of the vulnerable led to exile. In fact, biblical scholar Donald Gowan writes that as Zechariah identifies the reason for the exile, he offers a single thought: "Administer true justice; show mercy and compassion to one another. Do not oppress the widow and fatherless, the foreigner or the poor. Do not plot evil against each other" (Zechariah 7:9-10).[14]

Gowan continues:

> In the healthy community, that is, the people Israel as it lives according to the standards God has established for it (the Torah, 7:12), there will be no defrauding of widows and orphans, sojourners, and the poor. This negative criterion has become the Old Testament's regularly used distillation of the essence of social justice (and it reappears in the New Testament in James 1:27). Individuals can be judged righteous or wicked by how they treat widows, orphans, and sojourners (e.g., Job 31:16-32; Ps. 94:6), and a community's health can be determined by how well these groups fare in its midst (e.g., Ezek. 22:7).[15]

Therefore, biblically we see that "the mishpat, or justness, of a society, according to the Bible, is evaluated by how it treats these groups. Any neglect shown to the needs of the members of this quartet is not called merely a lack of mercy or charity but a violation of justice, of mishpat. God loves and defends those with the least economic and social power, and so should we. That is what it means to 'do justice.'"[16]

In agrarian societies, widows, orphans, immigrants, and the poor were powerless. Without a measure of self-reliance, they were dependent on the community. Day to day they lived at risk of starvation. Any instability within the community—famine, war, social upheaval— wiped these groups out first. Today, we might expand our definition of the vulnerable to include refugees, migrant workers, day laborers, the homeless, the elderly, the formerly incarcerated, the mentally and physically impaired, single parents, and veterans plagued by PTSD.

Since God so intimately identifies with "the least of these" and intentionally takes up the cause of the socially vulnerable, what should God's people be like? When pondering this question, especially in relation to our criminal justice system, two things become crystal clear: the vulnerable are being preyed upon continuously, and our relationship with the socially vulnerable has failed to reflect God's protection, love, and justice.

Many people think that God's concern for the vulnerable is limited to the Old Testament, but God intimately identifies with the hungry, thirsty, stranger, naked, prisoner, and sick in Matthew 25. These are not descriptions of spiritual impoverishment; they speak to the physical and material reality of poverty, oppression, and social marginalization. Christ ardently takes up the cause of the vulnerable in the Gospels, constantly healing the sick, restoring the social outcast to community, and defending the interest and dignity of "the least of these." Furthermore, the ascended Christ entrusts the church—his hands and feet in the world today—with the both Holy Spirit and the task of taking up this cause.

Theologian Daniel Groody writes that "God's concern for the poor and oppressed is one of the most central themes of the Bible. In the New Testament one out of every sixteen verses is about the poor. In the Gospels, the number is one out of every ten; in Luke's Gospel it is one out of every seven, and in James, one out of every five." He concludes, "From a Christian perspective, whenever a community ceases to care for the most vulnerable members of society, its spiritual integrity falls apart."[17]

RIGHTEOUSNESS AND JUSTICE: INHERENTLY CONNECTED

The Hebrew and Greek words for justice and righteousness often occur together. In fact, the prophet Amos never speaks of righteousness without justice. Righteousness, therefore, cannot be experienced without justice. Justice is the foundation of righteousness.[18] Justice and righteousness are the indispensable presuppositions for Israel's worship and existence (Amos 5, 7, 15, 21-24). Theologian Jorge Jeremias writes that "justice and righteousness are the most precious gifts of God to his people."[19]

What justice and righteousness mean for the people of God is exemplified in Amos 5:21-24. Jeremias summarizes what God says: "hatred of any worship of men among whom justice and righteousness are absent. If justice and righteousness are missing, Israel in its worship does not celebrate God but celebrates itself. God is no longer present in its worship and its festivals ('I hate, I despise your festivals'). God does not accept the offerings, songs, and prayers of such a congregation, because its worship means self-deception: It pretends that it is 'righteous,' i.e., that its relation to God is intact."[20]

Theologian Dave Doty explains what this means for the church:

> Justice and righteousness emanate from the nature and character of God. That the people of God are called to abide in that character is presented throughout the Bible. "Learn to do good; seek justice, reprove the ruthless; defend the orphan, plead for the widow" (Isa 1:17). And in Isaiah 16:5 we find, "A throne (seat of honor) will even be established in loving-kindness, And a judge will sit on it in faithfulness in the tent of David; Moreover, he will seek justice And be prompt in righteousness." Micah 6:8 says, "He has told you, O man, what is good; and what does the Lord require of you but to do justice, to love kindness, and to walk humbly with your God?" And James 1:27 explains, "This is pure and undefiled religion in the sight of our God and Father, to visit orphans and widows in their distress, and to keep oneself unstained by the world."[21]

Christopher Marshall says that "it is particularly important to recognize the justice connotations of the righteousness language of the New Testament, which is pervasive and significant."[22] Marshall highlights Paul's description of the gospel as the "revelation of God's righteousness" to explain this point. He writes that Paul "is depicting it (the 'revelation of God's righteousness') as the definitive manifestation of God's saving justice. The death and resurrection of Christ is, for Christians, the controlling frame of reference for comprehending the true meaning of divine justice."[23] Marshall then declares that on the cross Christ demonstrates that "what ultimately 'shows' or 'proves' God's justice (Romans 3:26) is not the ineluctable imposition of retribution on wrongdoers but the restoration of right relationship made possible by 'his grace as a gift, through the redemption that is in Christ Jesus (3:24).'"[24]

Dave Doty writes that "to speak of the righteousness of God seems redundant. Righteousness is *mishpat*, the justice of God, enacted."[25] Jeremias says, "Righteousness is the outcome of a functioning justice."[26] The concepts of righteousness and justice are intended to pattern the lives of God's people, governing the church's relational ethics. When righteousness and justice are wed, as they are about forty times in Scripture, the surest implication is social justice.[27] For a life built on Scripture, the call to social justice is inescapable.[28] Doty notes that "the four vital relationships in which we live—with God, with others, with our environment, and with ourselves—remain under the microscope of mishpat and tsedeq."[29]

GETTING WHAT ONE DESERVES

Christianity is predicated on the belief that we are saved by grace alone through faith—not by our merit. While faith without works is indeed dead, we all have sinned and fallen short of the glory of God. We are all sinners—individuals who have violated right relationships with God, our neighbor, and creation.

Thus, within a framework of retributive justice, we all deserve—based upon our merit—to die.[30] Yet we are given unmerited grace through our Lord and Savior Jesus Christ. If it were not for this gift of grace, we would all be destined for destruction and eternal separation from God. Hallelujah, for grace and God's desire to restore us in spite of our merit.

Therefore, should not the grace that was first extended to us—despite our relational violations—inform how we respond to our neighbors when they violate relationships? Unfortunately, it often does not. Historically, our nation—the church included—has not only responded punitively to other's violations but also elected to define people by the worst things they have done. Once a person steals, they forever become a thief; once someone kills, they are branded a murderer; and once someone crosses the border without documentation, they are deemed illegal. The church must realize that these are relational violations, not things that define people or their identities.

When we define people by what they have done—particularly the worst thing they have ever done—we dehumanize them. Imagine what it would feel like for everyone to not only know the most frightening skeleton in your closest but to also be forever defined and identified by it. As Bryan Stevenson says, "Each of us is more than the worst thing we have ever done."[31] The scarlet letter of "felon" and "excon" we engrave on returning citizens stigmatizes, restricts, and shames them for the rest of their lives.

In *Just Mercy* Stevenson reminds us that "we have all hurt someone and have been hurt. We all share the condition of brokenness even if our brokenness is not equivalent." He continues:

> There is a strength, a power even, in understanding brokenness, because embracing our brokenness creates a need and desire for mercy, and perhaps a corresponding need to show mercy. When you experience mercy, you learn things that are hard to learn otherwise. You see things you can't otherwise see; you hear things you can't otherwise hear. You begin to recognize the humanity that resides in each of us.[32]

When we lose sight of the grace and mercy exemplified on the cross of Christ, people who have violated right relationship become irredeemable "criminals" to fear, avoid, and quarantine. When "criminals" are viewed as the social cancer infecting our communal health, safety, and thriving, we cease to see and affirm their humanity. Rather than fellow image bearers, we see "criminals" as hazardous elements contaminating our neighborhoods, and they thus must be purged by any means necessary.

Michelle Alexander writes, "Criminals, it turns out, are the one social group in America we have permission to hate. In 'colorblind' America, criminals are the new whipping boys. They are entitled to no respect and little moral concern."[33] This pejorative and discriminating view of people who have served or are serving time for criminal activity is often more prevalent within the church than in society at large. The great irony in that is that Christianity revolves around Jesus, a falsely convicted criminal who was falsely charged, punitively convicted, mercilessly tortured, and unjustly sentenced to death. Given this, I would think the church would understand the necessity of thinking more restoratively about criminal justice.

Rooting our response to crime—and its subsequent punishment—in the grace first extended to us is not to be soft on crime. It means responding to crime in a christocentric way. Crime must be addressed, and punishment needs to be issued, but as followers of Christ our response must be different from the broader world.

Biblical justice does not exclude retribution. In what many refer to as just deserts, there are undoubtedly consequences for immoral human deeds. Christopher Marshall writes that there is even "a kind of inbuilt law of recompense in the universe that means people 'reap whatever they sow' (Galatians 6:7, cf. Ecclesiastes 10:8; Proverbs 1:32; 26:27; Psalm 7:15-16). In addition, the basic retributive concepts of guilt, desert, proportionality, and atonement are widely attested in the Old Testament legal and cultic system, and undergird moral and theological teaching in the New Testament as well."[34]

Nevertheless, Marshall writes that

biblical justice is retributive justice insofar as it turns on the principles of moral culpability, measured recompense, and the rule of law. It would be a mistake to conclude, however, that biblical teaching on justice is wholly or solely controlled by some impersonal metaphysical principle of measure for measure. Instead it has a distinctively personal and relational character. Justice in ancient Israel involved doing all that was needed to create, sustain, and restore healthy relationships within the covenant community. Criminal offending was considered wrong, first, because it breaches the relational commitments that hold society together and, second, because the wrongful deeds themselves unleash a disordering power in the community that threatens to trigger a chain-reaction of ruin and disaster unless it is arrested.[35]

The church's inability to respond to crime in a biblically rooted way that testifies to the restorative nature of God has emboldened a system of retribution. Our system asserts that justice has been actualized when a sentence is handed down; communal reintegration as part of justice is not even considered. The church has abided by this same flawed logic. This ecclesial failure to understand God's justice is crystallized is in our atonement theologies. Let us now turn to making connections between our atonement theologies and our historic response to crime.

ATONEMENT AND SANCTIFYING RETRIBUTION

CHRISTOLOGY AND THE ATONEMENT are inherently connected.[1] God was in Christ reconciling the world to himself. Christ reveals that God is self-giving, relational, merciful, restorative, and just. Moreover, in restoring the world through Jesus, we see that God consistently chooses to work from within creation, pointing and moving it toward salvific redemption. To redeem the world, God became contextual and intimately relatable—incarnate.

Jesus, the archetype of self-giving love through the redemptive power of the Trinity—made manifest in the resurrection—affords us access to reconciliation with God, liberating us from the shackles of sin, death, and subordination to the powers and principalities that breed material oppression in the world. Jesus thereby makes right relationships possible. The undeserved grace that has given us a new identity and purpose in life is accessible to all equally, indiscriminately, and exclusively through Jesus Christ.

While some biblical passages explain how God enacted cosmic redemption, the atonement remains a great mystery. Despite countless theologians and ministers using Scripture and various analogies in an attempt to make sense of what occurred, the atonement remains an enigma. The most affirmed theories of atonement revolve around Jesus taking our place and enduring divine wrath—to appease God—on our account. While several atonement theologies exist within this frame, penal substitution has evolved as the Western church's preeminent atonement theory.

PENAL SUBSTITUTION

Penal substitution holds that sin separated Creator and creation. Sin, which entered the world through the first Adam, created a chasm between God and creation. Sin enslaved humanity and led us down the path of death and destruction. The relational chasm between God and us caused by sin bred divine wrath, and God's pent-up wrath needed to be released for reconciliation to transpire. While God's ire should have been poured on us—slaves to sin—God, in grace and mercy, sent Jesus—the second Adam—to sacrificially be a substitute for us.

On the cross Jesus endured the divine wrath we inspired, and in bearing the punishment we deserved to endure, Christ became creation's "ram in the bush" (Genesis 22:13). Jesus was able to serve as humanity's sacrificial substitute because he lived in the flesh as one of us, but he was different from us in that he was, is, and will be the only sinless person to walk the earth. Jesus therefore was the incarnate, spotless lamb.

AUGUSTINE'S CONTRIBUTION TO PENAL SUBSTITUTION

While penal substitution has been challenged by many scholars (some refer to it as "divine child abuse"),[2] it nevertheless remains the prevailing atonement theory in the West. In many ways, penal substitution is predicated on meritocracy. Meritocracy is the belief that we get what we deserve based on our merit. Augustine of Hippo was one of the first theologians to articulate a meritocratic understanding of God's justice. He said that God "both rewards the good and punishes the bad" and that "these punishments are evils to those who suffer them."[3] Punishment was thus seen as a byproduct of God's judgment; it was a fundamental element of divine retribution. From Augustine's perspective, vengeance was a necessary and inherent component of God's justice. This will prove important as we trace the evolution of penal substitution.

Augustine's understanding of God's justice shaped many Christians', particularly later Protestant Reformers', understanding of Anselm of

Canterbury's atonement theory of satisfaction. Anselm used *satisfaction* in the theological sense; that is, making restitution as the way to signify gratification. Satisfaction for Anselm required reestablishing what was lost.

SATISFACTION THEORY

Anselm articulated his satisfaction theory in response to the most popular atonement theory of his time, the ransom theory. The ransom theory stated that Jesus' death paid a ransom to Satan, and this ransom allowed God to rescue all the sinners who were under Satan's control. Anselm found this theory heretical. Why would God owe anything to Satan? Moreover, why would God be willing to barter with the evil one? Anselm believed that the ransom theory was a gross misreading of the atonement, and he therefore set out to articulate a more faithful explanation.

Anselm concluded a debt was indeed owed and needed to be atoned for. However, it was humanity who owed the debt, which was owed to God, not Satan. For Anselm, humanity owed a debt of honor, not of punishment or a penalty. Anselm said, "This is the debt which man and angel owe to God, and no one who pays this debt commits sin; but everyone who does not pay it sins. This is justice, or uprightness of will, which makes a being just or upright in heart, that is, in will; and this is the sole and complete debt of honor which we owe to God, and which God requires of us."[4] Anselm declared that disobedience inhibited humanity from giving the appropriate honor due to God.

Since creation could not do what it was created to do—give honor to God—God intervened. However, rendering satisfaction to God was complicated by the fact that for satisfaction to avail for humanity, honor had to be given by a human. This, according to Anselm, is what led to the incarnation. Jesus, the only God-man, was the only human capable of redeeming humanity because he is the only human who has not dishonored God by being disobedient. In obedience, Christ went to the cross on our behalf and offered himself as a worthy sacrifice, satisfying God by rendering the proper honor due. However, Jesus' willingness to endure crucifixion on our behalf went beyond his duty, and therefore his radical obedience produced even more honor than he was obliged to give. Thus, Anselm believed Christ's surplus of honor was able to repay all of creation's honor deficit.

AQUINAS'S CONTRIBUTION TO PENAL SUBSTITUTION

Thomas Aquinas took Anselm's theory of satisfaction and shifted its ethos. Aquinas believed that instead of deficient honor being the hindrance to right relationship with God, humanity's sinful nature was the cause. Aquinas believed humanity was corrupted by and enslaved to sin, and it would remain shackled by sin until divinely liberated. Aquinas, like Augustine before him, stated that punishment and divine judgment were intertwined, but Aquinas taught that both function to move humanity toward redemption.

Aquinas concluded that punishment is good, appropriate, and—most important—a morally appropriate response to sin. He believed that punishment aided in ridding sin and fostering the restoration of right relationships, particularly between violators and victims. Aquinas said, "Christ bore a satisfactory punishment, not for His, but for our sins."[5] This signified his belief that Christ's substitution (for us) was permissible (and sufficient for our sins) if we (the offenders) joined in will to the one (Christ) enduring the punishment on our behalf. Therefore, while Aquinas used Anselm's language of satisfaction, he did not actually build upon his theory. Aquinas did not believe that honor would appease God's wrath, nor would it produce satisfaction. Aquinas departed from Anselm's theory, stating that Christ endured the punishment that we should have, divine judgement and wrath, and in doing so paid the penalty that we could not, making reconciliation possible.

THE EVOLUTION OF PENAL SUBSTITUTION

In the *Summa Theologiae*, Aquinas said that Jesus' death satisfied the penalty owed by sin and that only Christ's Passion could have covered humanity's sin debt. Aquinas believed that Christ's Passion provided the merit humanity needed to pay its debt. He said, "Christ by His Passion merited salvation, not only for Himself, but likewise for all His members."[6] The most significant point of agreement between Anselm and Aquinas is their belief that Christ gave God more than what was required on the cross, and because of this his atonement was able "to compensate for the offense of the whole human race."[7]

The satisfaction theory depicts Jesus' death as substitutionary in the fact that he pays the honor instead of humanity, but his payment is not penal. Anselm said that Jesus' death pays our honor, not our penalty. Despite this and other significant differences between penal substitution and Anselm's satisfaction theory, much of Western Christianity has conflated these two theories. While penal substitution states that Jesus was substituted for us, enduring our penalty for sin, Anselm's satisfaction theory states that humanity's disobedience defrauded God of the honor that was due, and Jesus' sacrifice, as the supreme act of obedience, compensated for our deficit.

According to an article outlining the satisfaction theory,

> The Protestant reformers shifted the focus of this satisfaction theory to concentrate not merely on divine offense but on divine justice. God's righteousness demands punishment for human sin. God in his grace both exacts punishment and supplies the one to bear it.
>
> This is an important difference. For Anselm, Christ obeyed where we should have obeyed; for John Calvin, he was punished where we should have been punished.[8]

Therefore, while the satisfaction theory and penal substitution are similar in ways, they each emphasize different principles in regard to what motivated the atonement and the divine exchange that took place. Consequently, it is inappropriate to synchronize them.

In many ways, John Calvin's articulation of penal substitution is an even better example of how different penal substitution is from Anselm's satisfaction theory. Calvin, a lawyer with a criminal law background, reinterpreted Anselm's theory to fit more specifically within a legal context. In his *Institutes* Calvin wrote,

> The Son of God has become man and has stood in man's place to bear the immeasurable weight of wrath, the curse, and the condemnation of a righteous God. He was made a substitute and a surety in the place of transgressors and even submitted as a criminal, to sustain and suffer all the punishment which would have been inflicted on them.[9]

Calvin's language reveals the influence of a court-based system of justice as well as a change in terminology regarding the atonement. The substitution of Jesus was no longer about preserving the honor of the Father but specifically about enduring the legal penalty for sins. Language that formerly emphasized repentance and restitution now focused on retribution. Thus, the notion of satisfaction in Anselm's context, which was based on fulfilling obligations to loyalty and honor, was converted into fulfilling certain demands of the law. With this shift in both language and metaphors, the penal substitution theory came to life, focusing not merely on satisfaction but on retribution—paying a legal penalty for sin. The image of a court became an all-encompassing image that changed the rhetoric surrounding the atoning work of Christ. Theologian Norman Kraus observes,

> Post-Reformation atonement theory assumes that God's righteousness demands retributive justice, and Christ's death paid the retributive penalty, or "debt to justice." These seventeenth-century theologians pictured God in the metaphor of a just-yet-merciful judge rather than an honorable-yet-kind lord. This moved the concept of substitution well beyond Anselm's satisfaction theory.[10]

As the satisfaction theory evolved more specifically into the penal substitution theory, the notion emerged within Protestant orthodoxy that the atonement was an act of God meeting the demands of his own legal justice. Jesus' act of satisfaction became his satisfaction of the legal penalty for disobedience by bearing the violent punishment for our sins—death on the cross. With this shift in language, the Reformers began to focus on salvation as a type of acquittal from our own guilt, a transfer of punishment from our own bodies to that of Christ. Consequently, the Protestant church began to speak of the atonement primarily in these legal terms.

PENAL SUBSTITUTION AND CRIMINAL JUSTICE

The ethos of penal substitution has been inscribed within the United States criminal justice system. Early in our "Christian" nation's history, penal substitution was understood to mean that *all* crime is generally understood as sin, and sin is an affront to God. Therefore all crime must be both punished and atoned for. Penal substitution therefore emphasizes the need for penalties, retribution, and recompense. This is the standard approach within our criminal justice system; justice comes through indictment, sentencing, and punishment. Punishment is seen as something that will correct unrighteousness and lead to the restoration of individuals and reconciled relationships.

Theologically, Augustine, Aquinas, and Calvin each contributed to the logic of legal retribution by proclaiming that sin and crime must be punished without exception. Penal substitution, which uses law-court metaphors, conceals a call for punishment within a Christian framing of justice. Christopher Marshall explains, "God's justice is retributive inasmuch as it is never prejudiced, arbitrary, or impulsive, and is always morally attuned to human deeds and deserts. Yet it focuses not on imposition of retribution on wrongdoers, but the restoration of right relationship."[11] Penal substitution theologically substantiates the notion that justice is served when someone suffers and pays the penalty for a relational violation. Within a penal substitutionary framework, punishment is not only necessary, it is seen as a virtue because it breeds reform, transformation, and restoration.

Largely because of this penalty-centered view of justice, Western Christianity's understanding of justice has become intrinsically intertwined with state law. Due to the complex and historic relationship between church and state in our nation, there is little distinction between committing a sin against God and committing a crime against the state. Christians largely see the state as morally obligated to punish offenders, exclusively responsible for criminal justice, and divinely ordained for human governance. Our criminal justice system has thereby become an ordained agent of "divine" retribution. Passages such as Romans 13:1-7 and 1 Peter 2:13-14 are integral in this divine sanctioning of our government and sequentially its criminal justice system. We therefore have emboldened the state to enforce whatever nature of castigation they discern is appropriate, given the nature of the violation.

C. S. LEWIS AND PUNISHMENT

In 1949 C. S. Lewis penned an important essay on punishment titled "The Humanitarian Theory of Punishment." In this essay, Lewis critiques the humanitarian theory, saying, "Those who hold it think that it is mild and merciful. In this I believe that they are seriously mistaken." Lewis rebutted this theory, writing, "I urge a return to the traditional or Retributive theory not solely, nor even primarily, in the interests of society but in the interests of the criminal."[12]

Lewis believed the humanitarian theory held that "to punish a man because he deserves it, and as much as he deserves, is mere revenge, and, therefore, barbarous and immoral. It is maintained that the only legitimate motives for punishing are the desire to deter others by example or to mend the criminal."[13] This was extremely problematic in Lewis's eyes: "When this theory is combined, as frequently happens, with the belief that all crime is more or less pathological, the idea of mending tails off into that of healing or curing and punishment becomes therapeutic. Thus, it appears at first sight that we have passed from the harsh and self-righteous notion of giving the wicked their deserts to the charitable and enlightened one of tending the psychologically sick. What could be more amiable?" However, Lewis warns that things are not always as they appear, especially at first sight. Lewis's thesis is,

One little point which is taken for granted in this theory needs, however, to be made explicit. The things done to the criminal, even if they are called cures, will be just as compulsory as they were in the old days when we called them punishments. . . .

My contention is that this doctrine, merciful though it appears, really means that each one of us, from the moment he breaks the law, is deprived of the rights of a human being.

The reason is this. The Humanitarian theory removes from Punishment the concept of Desert. But the concept of Desert is the only connecting link between punishment and justice. It is only as deserved or undeserved that a sentence can be just or unjust.

Lewis concludes, "When we cease to consider what the criminal deserves and consider only what will cure him or deter others, we have tacitly removed him from the sphere of justice altogether; instead of a person, a subject of rights, we now have a mere object, a patient, a 'case.'"[14] Therefore, Lewis, like Augustine, Aquinas, and Calvin before him, saw punishment not only as a virtue but also the key to justice, accountability, and transformation in the offender. This meritocratic view of justice insists that punishment and reconciliation are codependent, that when wed they induce justice and right relationships.

This theology has arrested the evangelical mind. We have been discipled to think that crime is sin, and sin fosters unrighteousness and separation from God, provoking God's wrath. God's wrath then necessitates punishment, and punishment leads to accountability, transformation, and ultimately reconciliation. This is what evangelicalism, broadly speaking, understands biblically based justice to be. In accounting for this, Winnifred Fallers Sullivan, in *Prison Religion: Faith-Based Reform and the Constitution*, says, "Whether one can conclude that dominant contemporary Christian theologies of punishment actually contributed directly to the increased punitive nature of U.S. society, there is no question that the two are culturally congruent and mutually recognizable."[15]

WHY PENAL SUBSTITUTION IS PROBLEMATIC

Our atonement theology is important because it expresses what we truly believe about God. Therefore, penal substitution is problematic for a multitude of reasons. First, it declares that punishment was needed for reconciliation to transpire. It then says that Christ took on flesh not because of love (as John 3:16 says) but to endure punishment in our stead. This is significant because it not only disputes a foundational biblical truth—God's love inspired the incarnation—it reduces or eliminates the significance of Jesus' incarnation and emboldens penal substitution to covertly function as gnosticism (a disembodied faith which teaches that our spirits alone truly matter).

Penal substitution is a reductionist theory that forsakes the embodied life, ministry, and relationships of Jesus, reducing Christ's body to punitive surrogacy. Penal substitution says Jesus merely came into the world to clean up our mess. Outside of establishing the possibility of reconciliation (not by love), nothing else about Jesus matters, not the Spirit descending on him after his baptism, his inauguration of the kingdom of God, or his calling and sending of the disciples.

Penal substitution also fails to hold in tension the wrath and love involved in God's justice. Retribution, in isolation, is incapable of breeding true transformation; it merely induces vengeance and retaliation. However, when issued within the context of relational accountability, and done with a restorative paradigm, Scripture shows that measured retribution can be an important part of holding individuals accountable who commit relational violations. However, we must not lose sight of the fact that justice is ultimately manifested in the restoration of righteousness within relationships, not in the pain inflicted or the time served behind bars because of a punishment.

As Christians, the cross undoubtedly frames our understanding of divine justice. Christopher Marshall writes, "The logic of the cross actually confounds the principle of retributive justice, for salvation is achieved not by the offender compensating for his crimes by suffering, but by the victim, the one offended against, suffering vicariously on behalf of the offended—a radical inversion of the *lex talionis* [the law of retaliation, whereby a punishment resembles the offense committed in kind and degree]."[16]

Thus, penal substitution is most problematic because it makes God's response to sin too much like our own. It is a sort of recasting of God in our own image, as opposed to allowing the divinely inspired Scriptures to speak for God's motives. Marshall also writes that "restoration, not retribution, is the hallmark of God's justice and is God's final word in history."[17] Restorative justice must be the aim of God's people. God's intent to restore all things and all people must inform and transform our understanding and pursuit of justice.

JUSTICE AS THE PROTECTION OF INDIVIDUAL RIGHTS

Atonement theologies have also distorted our understanding of justice by encouraging us to understand justice in individualistic ways. Most Christians understand justice to be the upholding of individual rights and securities by the state. John Heagle, author of *Justice Rising*, writes, "We think of justice as protecting our rights, our possessions, and our personal safety. Consequently, our idea of justice is focused on creating laws, keeping laws, and punishing those who transgress them. The assumption is that those who transgress the law ought to pay the consequence."[18] Thus, when someone's rights are violated, we believe that justice is served when the state hands down a retributive sentence to the offender.

In this framework, the victim and perpetrator submit themselves to the state's will, trusting that both parties will "get what they deserve." Viewing justice in this way perpetuates the flawed notion that crime is a violation against the state and not a relational transgression, one that causes a relational chasm and communal breaches. When we subscribe to this view, the state becomes responsible for conflict mediation, resolution, and transformation. The church, therefore, exports to the state its social responsibility to be ambassadors of reconciliation, thereby relinquishing its communal legitimacy and title as a people committed to repair, redemption, and transformation in the face of brokenness, harm, and violation.

Furthermore, when we surrender the responsibility of facilitating communal conflict to the state, history illustrates that Christians become disengaged citizens seduced into believing communities can rid themselves of social ills by simply identifying, weeding out, and quarantining deviant individuals. We think we can banish the source of our social sickness by extracting the people we see as a *cancer* among us; thus we become a fundamental part of the problem plaguing our nation.

Angela Davis says, "According to this logic the prison becomes a way of disappearing people in the false hope of disappearing the underlying social problems they represent."[19] Not only is it delusional to believe that we can simply remove the criminal element from society by purging, expelling, and incarcerating it, but this response to relational violations fails to live up to the church's biblical commission. The church is commissioned to wade into the waters of conflict, the throes of communal crisis, and the trenches of division until we find the source of what plagues our neighborhoods. We have the insights, reconciliatory practices, and disciplines our communities desperately need. We are not meant to fix every problem—we are not capable of that—but we are called to be actively engaged citizens who sacrificially put the interest of others before our own as we seek the peace and prosperity of our communities.

In Galatians, Paul instructs the church, "Brothers and sisters, if someone is caught in a sin, you who live by the Spirit should restore that person gently. But watch yourself, or you also may be tempted" (Galatians 6:1). The Spirit inspires us to participate in restoring offenders while we recognize our own inclination toward transgression. Christopher Marshall declares that Paul's words make it clear that "Christian justice focuses normatively on solidarity with sinners and their restoration, not on harsh punishment and rejection."[20] Therefore, Scripture calls the church to actively engage in being involved in the muck and mire of communal transgressions, civic harms, and the restoration of broken relationships.

The church, therefore, through its hands-off approach, has allowed people who have committed relational harms to become pilloried, denounced as contaminated individuals who are not only cast from society but also stripped of their civil liberties, often for the rest of their lives. Once someone is branded a criminal, society, including the church, usually ceases to relate to them as fellow citizens. We no longer see them as people in need of love, care, and community. When individuals are held accountable exclusively by the state with no accountability from the church, incarceration becomes a way to isolate "undesirable" individuals from the rest of society without taking full responsibility for their rehabilitation and reintegration.

When we view the formerly incarcerated as defiled people, we extend their sentences, and in doing so we fail to bear witness to the faith we proclaim. When we cannot see the redemptive potential within people because we fear them and their potential to reoffend, we not only doubt the redemptive power of God but create a stumbling block for those who desire to know Jesus.

Many Christians—given our individualistic society—disengage because they believe justice is merely the protection of individual rights. A fair number of Christians cling to this belief, even when guarding the rights of an individual comes at the expense of another person's freedoms (think "stand your ground" laws). However, theologians such as Walter Burghardt argue that as covenant people, our definition of justice must differ from mainstream society's. Burghardt explains that for Israel, justice and sin were both relational, and therefore the church today must realize that "biblical justice is making things right, not simply recognizing or defining individual rights. Its concern is the right relation of human beings to God and to one another."[21] The rightness of relationships, on every level, is *shalom*.

Burghardt highlights that biblical justice is radically different from our nation's criminal justice system. In embracing the biblical vision of *shalom*, Christians can begin envisioning, pursuing, and working to cultivate a criminal justice system predicated on mutual accountability rather than individual rights. We have the potential to assume responsibility not only for our own liberties but also for the life, dignity, and interests of others, especially "the least of these." Within this biblical framework the church can come to understand that our identities are ultimately bound to one another, and that even those labeled as criminals are our brothers and sisters. Biblical justice calls us to make reconciliation tangible, costly, and personal. It asks us to begin the process of forgiving those who have hurt or wronged us, just as we have been forgiven by God.

PURSUING SHALOM

When we unpack God's desire for *shalom*, our criminal justice system's reliance on punishment as the catalyst for change becomes exceedingly problematic. Within the biblical framework of *shalom*, justice is not reduced to distributing punishment. Punishment cannot satisfy the demands of justice. Justice is ultimately satisfied when repentance, restoration, and renewal occur.[22] Therefore, while punishment sometimes leads to outward changes, lasting transformation requires more than retribution.

Similarly, biblical justice is rooted in the rectification of relationships, not in isolation and punishment. Incarceration, as currently practiced in our nation, violates important expressions of biblical righteousness. While wrongdoers must be held accountable for their violations, a covenant community seeks to restore harms together.[23]

As the people of God, we are called to be committed to each other's welfare, collectively seeking the flourishing of our communities. Burghardt writes that the church must do this by seeking "new approaches that understand crime as a threat to community, not just a violation of law; that demand new efforts to rebuild lives, not just build more prisons, and that demonstrate a commitment to reweave a broader social fabric of respect for life, civility, responsibility, and reconciliation."[24] Rather than supporting a system that merely punishes, the church must pursue a justice system that builds community, affirms human dignity, and seeks God's *shalom*.

These shifts will lead us to consider alternative forms of justice, expressions seeking healing, forgiveness, and reconciliation amid relational violations. While most of us are familiar only with retributive responses to crime, a framework called restorative justice is predicated on bringing "victims, offenders, and the community together with government in repairing injuries caused by crime . . . [and] emphasizes repairing all the injured parties . . . understand[ing] that all the relationships among the parties implicated in the circle of crime are in need of healing and restoration."[25] Such restorative justice practices may be applied differently in various contexts but ultimately focus on pursuing *shalom*, fostering right relationships, and dealing holistically with the damage caused by relational violations.

Within the matrix of racial injustice, moving from individualized notions of justice to justice understood within the parameters of covenant community will necessitate confessing the foundational role racism has played in the creation and sustaining of disproportionate numbers of racial minorities warehoused behind bars. The church has misused theology to legitimate racial violence (genocide, slavery, internment, segregation, and mass incarceration). But within every race a remnant has understood that Scripture consistently speaks of God's people actively participating in the ministry of reconciliation. They boldly confront injustice, sacrificially fight to end oppression, and diligently work to restore things to God's original intent.

Christopher Marshall writes, "The 'advent on earth of God's eschatological justice' is 'a redemptive and reconstructive action more than a retributive or punitive one.'"[26] Jesus, God with us, knows the stress and strain of living under systemic oppression. Christ came into our context, taking on marginalized flesh, and upon his birth (to impoverished parents) Herod placed a bounty on his head. He faced ethnic profiling and social stigma (because of the community he came from), and he was a refugee who was falsely convicted as a criminal and sentenced to the death penalty.

Through of all of this, Jesus embodied relational righteousness and justice. He remained faithful to the call on his life. He never lost sight of his mission, which was to tear down the "dividing wall of hostility," bringing peace to the enemies of God. The trajectory of

God's justice is continuous with the Hebrew conception of righteousness as "comprehensively relational."[27]

Biblical justice is not easy or simplistic. It is not contained within the four walls of the church or constrained within the homogeneity of our friendships or congregations. Biblical justice summons followers of Christ to consider what right relationships entail across lines of difference—racial, ethnic, class, gender, human sexuality, national origin, and so forth.

These social stratifications shape a person's life chances, access to opportunities, and the severity of punishment received when standing before our criminal justice system. Bryan Stevenson says we currently "have a system of justice that treats you better if you are rich and guilty than if you are poor and innocent. Wealth, not culpability, shapes outcomes. We have gone from 300,000 in 1972 to 2.3 million today. We've never had more innocent people in jails and prisons than we do right now."[28] He notes, "A system that denies the poor the legal help they need, that makes wealth and status more important than culpability, must be changed."[29] With a system having such glaring flaws, the church must reimagine a more faithful way. We must reexamine the biblical text to see anew what God is calling us to in this seminal moment.

THEOLOGICALLY JUSTIFYING RACISM

Therefore, as we move toward restorative justice, we must confess that our criminal justice system is, and has been, inextricably bound to race and class. Our justice system has legislatively stripped some citizens of their civil and human rights and bestowed unearned benefits on others. Racism has been legislatively sanctioned, sustained, and enforced. Nevertheless, it must be noted that the racial declarations of the state would ring hollow if they were not ultimately undergirded and legitimated by coded theological justifications of racism.

Therefore, when the church acquiesced to the state, allowing it to decide what justice entails, we increased the state's power to further shape racial outcomes. Richard Snyder, speaking to the convergence of racist theology and legislation, writes,

When we take a close look at the penal system in our country, most especially the prisons, we discover an entire system based upon the classification of persons as wretches. The fact that a majority of the wretches are people of color is not an accident. It fits fundamental assumption of white racism that people of color are fundamentally inferior, prone to criminal behavior, and lacking in responsibility. By building our prison system on the notion of punishing wretches, our country has been able to systematically label and criminalize entire classes of people as inferior.[30]

Rima Vesely-Flad, a religious studies professor, traces the theological development of the classification Snyder references, particularly for African Americans. She begins with Puritan New Englanders and their justification for slavery: "Puritan New Englanders viewed the idleness of slaves in light of theological concepts of sinfulness and inhumanity, and determined that enslaved persons of dark hue lacked the inherent qualities . . . that were essential for Christian redemption."[31] Christian concepts of sin and redemption were therefore used to dehumanize African Americans and exclude them from the body of Christ.

Later, in the antebellum years, southerners continued to misuse theology, this time to criminalization blackness. Vesely-Flad writes, "The concept of blackness was loaded with theological meaning— blackness evoked baseness, evil, danger, and repulsion, as opposed to white purity, virginity, virtue and godliness."[32] These judgments were then used to justify the harsh treatment and inhumane punishment of those of African descent.

Vesely-Flad writes that even in the postbellum and civil rights era, many conservative Christians believed "that the cause of crime lies in the human 'propensity towards evil' . . . [and they] elevated images of black men in particular and fueled fears of racial integration."[33] Reluctant to accept social progress, many Euro-Americans perpetuated narratives of black "criminality" and "violence" to shackle African Americans yet again (neoslavery and mass incarceration). Most Euro-American Christians silently stood by, complicit.

Bryan Stevenson highlights how antiblackness continues to plague our nation. Racial bias even profoundly informs who is sentenced to the death penalty. According to Stevenson, the decision in the 1987 Supreme Court Case *McCleskey v. Kemp* revealed that there is convincing "empirical evidence that the race of the victim is the greatest predictor of who gets the death penalty in the United States. The study conducted for that case revealed that offenders in Georgia were eleven times more likely to get the death penalty if the victim was white than if the victim was black." Furthermore, Stevenson reveals that "these findings were replicated in every other state where studies about race and the death penalty took place. In Alabama, even though 65% of all homicide victims were black, nearly 80% of the people on death row were there for crimes against victims who were white. Black defendant and white victim pairings increased the likelihood of a death sentence even more."[34]

Speaking of the death penalty, Stevenson says, "It's a way in which we create a world where people can legitimately say black lives don't matter. Because we don't protect people who are poor, we don't protect people of color in the same way we protect other people."[35] The church is called to serve as the social voice that represents the interest and protects the dignity of those society abuses. As Stevenson says, there are alternatives to retribution, vengeance, and capital punishment, so in reality the death penalty "really isn't about what people deserve; it's about us."[36] When the church fails to live up to its calling as a prophetic voice for justice defending the vulnerable and warding off injustice, atrocities like mass incarceration transpire.

Christian theology has emboldened a punitive culture of hyperincarceration, one where our pursuit of justice has manifested a blatant disregard for the dignity of human life, particularly for poor blacks, Hispanics, and Native Americans. We have perpetuated a retributive culture that depends on the state for justice despite the blatant racism our justice system is entrenched in. As more and more people call this out, the church and our nation are at a critical juncture. This watershed moment beckons the church to reassess how we engage our criminal justice system. It should provoke us to recalibrate how we define and pursue justice. There *is* a growing movement to end mass incarceration, and the church must decide if it is going to help lead or prohibit this movement. Choosing to remain silent is an endorsement of the status quo.

DIVINE JUSTICE IS INHERENTLY RESTORATIVE

CHRISTIANITY HAS PLAYED a paramount role in mass incarceration. Mass incarceration's origins, sustainment, and astronomic growth are inherently linked to Christian theology. Our embrace of penal substitution has engendered a retributive culture within our criminal justice system. The church has adopted and supported a meritocratic ethic that declares people get what they deserve. This worldview has subconsciously fostered an unquestioning allegiance to the state, and it has led the church to unwittingly consent to and affirm that crime is primarily a legal offense committed against the state rather than a sin that relationally harms individuals and communities, infringing on the *shalom* that God intends for us all.

Our understanding of God's wrath colors our response to crime. We have read of God's vengeance toward sin and legislatively translated it into zero-tolerance policies. There are many problems with this; primarily, we need to understand God is perfect, and we are fallible. God is the only righteous, impartial, and just judge. Only God can purely define, respond to, and legislate sin while also knowing the nature of a person's heart. As fallen people, our judgment is never completely pure; everyone is embedded in culture and has conformed to the patterns of this world to some degree. Consequently, when it comes to enforcing no-tolerance policies, the officials commissioned to enforce and govern these policies are often unable to do so without bias— whether conscious or subconscious.

MERITOCRACY'S IMPACT

Christianity is predicated on grace, which opposes meritocracy and the rugged individualism we pride ourselves on. Meritocracy insidiously compromises our vison. It distorts how we see ourselves and perverts how we relate to and interact with our neighbor.

Meritocracy places us in a position of judgment over and against others. It subtly fosters a fear of *the other* by differentiating *us* from *them*. It endows us with a sense of moral superiority in which we indict others and look down upon them. Meritocracy engenders an anxiety that clings to fearmongering and embraces jail cells border walls, and ethnic exclusion as social safeguards that will protect *us* from *them*.

Legislatively, meritocracy seduces us into supporting policies that punish, racially target, and geographically profile. Meritocracy holds that *those* people deserve to be quarantined and caged like animals because their actions prove they are dangerous and immoral. Meritocracy thereby holds that retributively responding to crime is not only right, it is also responsible. It ensures the peace, stability, and safety of moral citizens.

Over time, the church has welcomed a meritocratic ethic, which forsakes the grace our faith is founded on. Christian meritocracy has evolved as the byproduct of syncretizing biblical and nationalistic values. This toxic mixture trivializes grace and promotes the dichotomy of saints and sinners that ignores the fact that we have all fallen short of the glory of God. Meritocracy, sanctified and baptized by the church, breeds stigmatization, disunity, and dehumanization. It therefore serves as a stumbling block to Christian reconciliation and redemption. It hinders lost sheep trying to find their way back to their Shepherd, and blinds those who believe that they have spiritually arrived.

Meritocracy has led professing Christians to endorse and actively participate in the largest prison system in the history of the world.[1] Largely due to meritocracy, the vast majority of us have seen no contradiction between legislatively supporting the policies that bred mass incarceration and bearing witness to the inbreaking kingdom of God.

Christopher Marshall says that when meritocracy is buttressed by the separation of church and state,

> Christians today often suppose that their ecclesial ethics—how believers are called to treat one another within the church and community of faith—have no pertinence to the ethical standards and legal practices that apply in mainstream society. Church and world are assumed to be entirely separate domains with their own distinctive norms. As a result, conservative Christians in America often rank among the strongest supporters of the current, highly retributive penal system, with its galloping rates of incarceration and its enduring, shameful reliance on capital punishment.[2]

This observation helps explain the church's eerie silence during the evolution of mass incarceration, the convict leasing era, the War on Drugs, and the present war on immigration.

According to Marshall, Christians who see the church and world as "entirely separate domains, with their own distinctive norms" are able to "sense no tension between their support for a relentlessly punitive criminal justice system and the incessant call in Scripture to practice forgiveness and reconciliation, a call they conveniently confine to the sphere of interpersonal relationships within the Church." Marshall lambasts this theological schizophrenia, saying that "such incongruity is theologically indefensible." He declares,

> The Church is called to bear witness to the reality of God's saving justice in Christ, both by proclaiming it verbally in the story of the gospel and by putting it into practice in the way it deals with offending and failure in its own midst. Knowing God's justice to be a restoring and renewing justice, the Church is obliged to practice restorative justice in its own ranks and to summons society to move in the same direction.

Even in spite of legislation around the separation of church and state, Marshall concludes that "there can be no justification for saying one thing about God's justice in Church and advocating the opposite in the world."[3]

As followers of Christ, we must be cognizant of how embracing meritocracy impedes our ability to reflect God's gracious character, restorative nature, and missional activity in the world. God is actively restoring all things, including fallible people like you and me, as well as those we sometime mistakenly believe are beyond the point of redemption.

JUSTICE ROOTED IN GRACE AND FAITH

In *Just Mercy*, Bryan Stevenson explains his motive for establishing the Equal Justice Initiative. He was compelled to create it after realizing not all people are equal under our current criminal justice system. One of his mentors encapsulated this by saying, "Them without the capital get the punishment."[4]

Stevenson tells riveting stories about the emotional distress that led to the revelation that changed his life. After working for years as an attorney within the criminal justice system, Stevenson writes, "Finally, I've come to believe that the true measure of our commitment to the rule of law, fairness, and equality cannot be measured by how we treat the rich, the powerful, the privileged, and the respected among us. The true measure of our character is how we treat the poor, the disfavored, the accused, the incarcerated, and the condemned. . . . We all need mercy, we all need justice, and—perhaps—we all need some measure of unmerited grace."[5]

As people who were pursued and saved by Christ while we were yet sinners, we can never lose sight of the grace that restored us. When we support capital punishment, retributive law-and-order polices, and legislation that leads to more prisons and less medical interventions for people plagued by addictions, we disavow the grace that rescued us. Punishment devoid of grace is not justice but vengeance. Christians cannot subscribe to such morally bankrupt social solutions. Our lives are intended to be marked by the grace we first received. Marshall writes that "the truth of God's justice is in Jesus, and that justice is a liberating and restoring justice. The Church fails in its vocation if it fails to proclaim, to embody, and to advocate the principles of restorative justice in every sphere of life."

Marshall continues,

> If Paul were to come among us today, singing of God's amazing grace on Sundays while on Mondays supporting, or being indifferent to, the retributive degradation of the present penal system, he would say what he said to the Ephesians who were being seduced by the standards of wider society: "That is not the way you learned Christ! For surely you have heard about him and were taught in him, as the truth is in Jesus" (4:20-21).[6]

In this moment of crisis, the church must remember its birthright; we cannot nullify the gift that redeemed us. We have to ethically and theologically root ourselves in the grace that sets captives free, becoming ardent advocates for a justice system that restores, transforms, and reintegrates.

RENEWING OUR MINDS AND OUR SYSTEM

I have spent the last fifteen years doing ministry in communities ravaged by mass incarceration, and the last decade working with people directly affected by incarceration. I have worked with juveniles, young adults, and adults trapped in the system, and have walked alongside and ministered to families adjusting to life without their loved ones. I have ministered to individuals in jails, prisons, and detention centers, and to those who are trying to reintegrate into society on the completion of their time behind bars. As I have become more proximate to the torment, injustice, and hopelessness our system breeds, I am haunted by the multitudes behind bars who are concretely affected by the church's support of punitive policies. I am also heartbroken by the church's complacency, all of which undergird mass incarceration.

I think about men like Armando, who has spent twenty years in prison for a crime he committed as a teenager, and how despite his transformation and achievements—he has become a published author, chapel preacher, and influential leader—many of his brothers and sisters in Christ will always see him as only an ex-convict. Armando has tried time and time again to find the love, acceptance, and support inside the church that he found within the prison's chapel. Too often, congregants will only love him from a distance.

I think about young women like Michelle, a mother of three who is in prison for drug trafficking. She was caught serving as a drug mule, carrying drugs for her abusive partner after being physically threatened with assault. Michelle previously tried to flee from her partner, taking her kids in search of refuge, but he tracked her down and brutalized her in front of her children. How does our system account for her circumstances?

I think about young men like Robert, who started stealing drugs at thirteen to help his single mother put food on the table for his younger siblings. Robert was a great kid I met when he was seventeen. He lamented the choice he made to sell drugs, but he felt as if he had no other choice with two younger siblings in need, a mom who was working three jobs that collectively did not pay a livable wage, and an incarcerated father. Robert returned from his time behind bars ready to turn his life around. I went with him as he tried to secure work, but time after time he was denied the opportunity to work because of his criminal record. Luckily for Robert, his record was expunged (wiped clean) because he committed his crime as a juvenile and now had support. But there are thousands of Roberts who are not so lucky.

I think about James, who is continuously denied opportunities to minister in churches because of his criminal record, despite completing an urban ministry leadership certificate during his incarceration and serving as a pastoral leader within the prison's chapel for a number of years. James desperately wants to fulfill his calling as a minster. He yearns to help people avoid the mistakes he made. James's resilience will not let him give up on his dream in spite of its deferment. In the meantime, he has dedicated his life to practicing restorative justice.

These relationships have compelled me to ask, What does God's justice look like for these individuals? How is the gospel proclaimed and experienced as good news amid their circumstances? What would happen if the church saw itself as inherently bound to disenfranchised people such as these? What would it look like for us to be sacramentally linked in covenant community with these individuals?

RESTORATIVE JUSTICE: AN INTRODUCTION

Authentically confronting our nation's culture of mass incarceration must provoke the church to seek alternative forms of justice. We need justice that produces healing, forgiveness, and reconciliation. While most Christians are only familiar with retributive justice, restorative justice is experiencing growing global momentum. Restorative justice began to be applied in legal settings during the 1970s.[7]

Restorative justice never diminishes the significance of a violation (crime); it summons all parties affected to collectively determine how to heal, repair, and restore relationships after the violation. It prioritizes disrupting cycles of harm and violence by creating pathways for healing and restoration. Restorative justice acknowledges that crime damages the perpetrator's relationship with the victim, the victim's community, the perpetrator's own community, and the perpetrator. It also acknowledges the offender's responsibility to help meet the needs of the victim(s) in restoring relationship and community.

Over the past forty years, restorative justice has an impressive global track record in criminal justice reform, educational systems, and addressing broader societal trauma.[8] Restorative justice has created alternatives to traditional legal processes, restoring relationships and creating communal healing. It has helped eliminate juvenile detention facilities in New Zealand and has also been used to address racial conflict and gang violence in Rio de Janeiro.[9] Restorative justice was also used to facilitate national healing in postapartheid South Africa and postgenocide Rwanda.

Restorative justice has been successful within the United States. Major cities have implemented it to disrupt the school-to-prison pipeline, creating alternatives to suspension, expulsion, and incarceration. The Civil Rights and Restorative Justice Project utilized it to catalyze reparations, remediation, and truth commissions for victims of racial injustice in the Jim Crow Era.[10] Restorative justice has been implemented within both the juvenile and adult justice systems, leading to options for alternative sentencing, victim-offender reconciliation, and community healing.

Restorative justice has reduced reincarceration and increased victim satisfaction. A Pew Research study found that normally 43.3 percent of individuals released from prison will return within three years, but only 10.8 percent of inmates who participated in a Texas-based restorative justice program ended up reincarcerated, and only 1.1 percent of those released returned for violent crimes.[11] Moreover, an Indianapolis program for juvenile offenders found that 96.2 percent of victims who participated in restorative processing were satisfied, compared to a 72.4 percent satisfaction rate for those who did not.[12] While we have not institutionally shifted toward restorative justice, these statistics are encouraging.

RESTORATIVE JUSTICE IN ACTION: TAYLOR'S STORY

I have experienced how restorative justice fosters accountability, change, and healing. My community uses restorative justice as an alternative to punitive models of school discipline. Take, for instance, the experience of Taylor, a sixth-grade boy who stole his teacher's keys. In a retributive model of discipline, this student is simply punished. The violating student is "tried" and "sentenced" (generally exclusionary measures: detention, suspension, or expulsion) by the administration.

These punitive measures alienate students from their teachers, classmates, and instructional time, and thus each of these responses fails to encourage or prioritize confession, reconciliation, and restoration. Furthermore, these approaches usually result in the offending student falling behind in their school work. When the offending student is eligible to come back to school, few steps are taken to reintegrate them back into the classroom, and often there is unresolved tension between the student, the teacher, and the rest of the class. This tension has the potential to spark further conflict.

By applying restorative justice principles to Taylor's situation, the administration helped facilitate a healing conversation. Taylor was invited into a circle with several of his classmates, the teacher he stole from, a school counselor, and the vice principal.[13] Through the restorative circle, Taylor was able to hear directly from his peers, the teacher, and school administration about how his actions affected them. He was also able to share his thoughts and confess the underlying fears and assumptions that led to his violation. The group collectively formed a plan for how Taylor would make amends, which included helping his teacher after school to repair trust and writing an apology to the class.

Punishment alone would not have shifted Taylor's thinking; the collaborative care and effort to reintegrate him began his transformation. If Taylor had been suspended, he would not have had to confront how his choice affected others—his peers, teacher, and administrators. He also would not have had the opportunity to hear how much his community cared about him and wanted him to make better choices. Moreover, without this restorative approach, the classroom would have missed an opportunity to learn how to resolve communal conflict.

Taylor's case is not exceptional. A study on the effects of restorative justice for Oakland Unified School District found that not only did restorative practices lead to a 29 percent decline in the rate of African American students suspended, it also led to a doubling of reading proficiency scores in high school freshmen, a 60 percent increase in graduation rates, and a 24 percent decline in chronic absenteeism among middle schoolers.[14] Moreover, over 90 percent of the teachers surveyed reported that restorative practices were helpful in managing difficult behavior in their classroom.

RESTORATIVE JUSTICE: THEOLOGICAL AND BIBLICAL FOUNDATIONS

Restorative justice aligns with the heart of God. It supports that justice is primarily *relational* rather than individual. In the Old Testament, justice and sin were both relational realities, and justice was not about upholding individual rights but protecting the well-being of communities. Walter Burghardt observes, "Biblical justice is making things right, not simply recognizing or defining individual rights. Its concern is the right relation of human beings to God and to one another."[15]

This rightness of relationships on every level is known as *shalom*, which is juxtaposed to the state's understanding of justice. *Shalom* calls Christians to view and pursue justice in light of God's original intent. It summons us to live within the confines of covenantal community, where we actively pursue communal flourishing, consider the interest of others (particularly "the least of these"), and prioritize the restoration of righteous relationships in the face of harm. Crime is never merely an individual breaking the law; it is always a communal transgression that fractures *shalom*.

God's justice is restorative and reconciling as opposed to retributive and isolating. Our criminal justice system quarantines people who cause harm, which subsequently harms them through punitive measures and dehumanizing conditions. Theologically, restorative justice acknowledges that divine justice entails people being reconciled to God, each other, the community, and themselves. While biblical justice often contains aspects of "moral culpability, measured recompense, and the rule of the law,"[16] which retributive frameworks are grounded in, these realities are enfolded within a larger narrative of relationship, redemption, and restoration. Christopher Marshall illustrates this, explaining that while crimes require consequences, "the goal of the punishment is not to maintain some abstract cosmic balance, but to put right what has gone wrong, to protect the community, and to restore the integrity of its life and its relationship with God. Justice is satisfied by the restoration of peace to relationships, not by the pain of punishment."[17]

Thus, while God's story sometimes includes punishment, isolation, and harsh consequences, God's justice moves toward restoration, reintegration, and redemption. God's justice is inherently connected to healing the harmed, restoring what has been lost, and reconciling those who are estranged from God and community. God's heart and justice are inherently restorative.

Restorative justice gives shape to a communal ethic that is conciliatory in spirit and just in nature. It provides a structure for conflict resolution that facilitates truth telling, accountability, forgiveness, and restitution. The restorative nature of God's justice is woven throughout Scripture. Divine justice induces relational rightness between hostile parties, the holistic reintegration of exiled individuals, and economic and systemic restitution in the face of harm. Throughout Scripture, God works amid brokenness, restoring victims, communities, and offenders. The following passages illuminate tenets of biblically based restorative justice.

"O GOD, PLEASE HEAL HER": RESTORATIVE JUSTICE (NUMBERS 12)

One of the most profound examples of restorative justice is found in an unlikely place—book of Numbers. Most people perceive that the God of the Old Testament ruled punitively and the Mosaic Law dictated all interpersonal interactions. In the New Testament, on the other hand, God's grace abounds, and the Spirit guides the Christian community toward compassion and mercy. It is therefore surprising for many to see what unfolds in Numbers 12. In this passage, restorative justice is divinely implemented within a relational context.

Numbers 12:1 says, "Miriam and Aaron began to talk against Moses because of his Cushite wife, for he had married a Cushite." The cause of their animosity toward Moses is clear. But why was marrying such a woman so problematic in their eyes?

Cushites were from the region of Cush.[18] The people of Cush were known for their black skin. There is another reference to the distinctive skin color of Cushites in Jeremiah 13:23, which reads,

> Can the Ethiopian [Cushite] change his skin
>   or the leopard its spots?
> Neither can you do good,
>   who are accustomed to doing evil.

The emphasis this passage places on the hue of the Cushite people's skin is intentional. Cushites were infamous because of their blackness.

Furthermore, biblical scholar Daniel Hays writes that Cush was "where a Black African civilization flourished for over two thousand years. Thus, it [Numbers 12:1] is quite clear that Moses marries a Black African woman."[19]

As Aaron and Miriam slandered Moses because of their prejudice and ethnocentrism, God intervened. God summoned the three stakeholders to the tent of meeting. There God confronted Aaron and Miriam about their sin, calling them to confess, repent, and make amends. It is worth noting that Aaron and Miriam were faith and community leaders who held positions of power and influence in spite of their unaddressed bigotry, but God does not allow this to continue unhindered. As God departed from them, Miriam's skin became "like a stillborn infant coming from its mother's womb, with its flesh half eaten away" (v. 12). Miriam's skin was leprous—a condition notoriously associated with the depletion of skin pigmentation, causing skin discoloration that leaves a person with pale, albino-like white skin. Because of bigotry (racism), Miriam is rendered pigmentless, left with unnaturally white skin by God because of her antiblackness.

If the story were to end here, this would be divine affirmation of a retributive system: a wrong was committed, the violators were confronted, and a punishment was administered (at least to one of the offenders). However, the story does not end here. Upon seeing what happens to Miriam, Aaron turned to Moses, confessed their sinfulness, and pleaded for Moses' forgiveness. Following a meritocratic ethic, Moses could have said, "You got what you deserved." Nevertheless, Moses heard the confession of Aaron and cried out to God in response, saying, "Please, God, heal her" (v. 13). Aaron's confession and repentance moved Moses from harm to healing; Moses shifts from being the victim to being an advocate for those who victimized him. This kind of transformation is only made possible through the power and work of the Holy Spirit. Nevertheless, God's gathering of accountability made room for the Spirit's movement.

Despite Moses' plea, God determined that punishment was warranted for Miriam and Aaron's sin. God replied to Moses, "Confine her outside the camp for seven days; after that she can be brought back" (v. 14). This is important because some critique restorative justice as soft on crime. However, even within restorative approaches, at *times* an offender does need to be removed from the community to reflect, learn from, and change in light of their violation. Nonetheless, as we see here, there must be a reintegration plan.

Restorative justice affirms the biblical truth that as a covenantal community, we cannot truly move forward until everyone is welcomed to reintegrate into community. Though not everyone will accept this invitation, part of our covenantal responsibility as people sacramentally marked and sealed by God is inviting and welcoming people in— especially those the world shuns.

"SALVATION HAS COME TO THIS HOUSE": RESTORATIVE JUSTICE (LUKE 19)

Most Christians know Zacchaeus as a "wee little man," but a closer examination of Luke 19 reveals not only a short man who encounters Jesus but a criminal who is restored to God, his victims, his community, and himself.

Zacchaeus was a criminal. He made his livelihood from immoral and harmful behaviors. He became "very wealthy" (Luke 19:2) by cheating, defrauding, and stealing from others, preying on the poor and vulnerable. As a Jew, Zacchaeus was conscripted by the Roman Empire as a tax collector. He charged his fellow Jews more than what they owed Rome in order to keep the profits for himself. Moreover, as a chief tax collector, Zacchaeus also benefitted from perpetuating a culture of dishonesty, profiting personally from other tax collectors under his leadership. Like many white-collar criminals today, Zacchaeus's flourishing was rooted in institutional injustice; his thriving was predicated on systemic sin that ensured the rich would become richer by oppressing and extorting the public.

Despite his wealth and status, Zacchaeus's community despises him as a traitor. Moreover, Zacchaeus was in intimate contact with the Gentile occupation government, making him ceremonially unclean and thus cut off from the covenant community. When Jesus comes into town, Zacchaeus is not only unable to see Jesus because he's short but also because the crowds refuse to touch or help an unclean and immoral man. Consequently, Zacchaeus was physically and socially isolated from both Jesus and the crowd. In order to see Jesus, he runs ahead of the crowds and climbs a sycamore tree.

In the remaining sections of Luke 19:1-10, we see Jesus embody God's heart for restoration. First, Jesus seeks out Zacchaeus and says, "Zacchaeus, come down immediately" (v. 5). By stating Zacchaeus's name and calling him out of hiding, Jesus signifies that he knows Zacchaeus's identity as a tax collector but that Zacchaeus no longer needs to hide from others. Moreover, by saying, "I must stay at your house today," Jesus challenges both the purity rituals and kinship norms of Near Eastern society, because he would have become both culturally unclean and dishonorable by aligning himself with a criminal like Zacchaeus. By intentionally choosing to dwell in Zacchaeus's home and share in table fellowship with him, Jesus brings Zacchaeus—the criminal—back into fellowship with God. Jesus thus embodies an ethic of belonging to those he was socialized to disdain as contaminated, inferior, and "the other." Zacchaeus welcomes Jesus "gladly." This reveals that Jesus' identification with him restored not only a criminal to God but a sense of worth and joy in Zacchaeus himself. Zacchaeus no longer needs to hide or to live in isolation; he is happy to be welcomed into a life of newfound freedom.

It is important to note, however, that the salvation Jesus enacts in Zacchaeus's life was not purely personal. It was not solely about restoring Zacchaeus's relationship with God, or even restoring Zacchaeus's sense of peace and worth in himself. Instead, by Zacchaeus's actions we see true salvation also involves providing reparations to those harmed by our sins. As Jesus chooses to bind himself to Zacchaeus in relationship, Zacchaeus must also choose to bind himself to those he had oppressed by making amends for his crimes.

Zacchaeus states that "if I have cheated anybody out of anything, I will pay back four times the amount" (v. 8), thereby recognizing the multiplying effect that his crimes had and making reparations accordingly. Such an act requires both honestly naming and facing his victims, acknowledging every person he had harmed and the impact of his dishonest actions. Furthermore, Zacchaeus recognizes that his crimes may have not only hurt his direct victims—those he directly defrauded—but also the broader community, as he states, "Look, Lord! Here and now I give half of my possessions to the poor" (v. 8).

Through this gesture, Zacchaeus acknowledges that the system of tax collection has led to patterns of debt and poverty, constructing a perpetual underclass and hurting more than those he directly cheated. He pays a costly price to acknowledge both the communal and systemic impact his crimes had. He actively chooses to do his part to end generational cycles of sin and oppression by bringing economic transformation to his entire community.

Ultimately, through Zacchaeus's restoration to God, himself, his victims, and his community, Jesus declares, "Today salvation has come to this house, because this man, too, is a son of Abraham" (v. 9). Because Christ embodies a sacramental ethic of love, justice, and restoration, Zacchaeus experiences true, holistic salvation. The man who was once a criminal, cut off from his people and excluded from membership in covenant community, is now reconnected to the family of God.

As a "son of Abraham" Zacchaeus is no longer defined by the offenses and injustices he enacted; he is now known as the one who made reparations for his wrongdoing. He is no longer destined to exist in isolation but invited to participate in covenant community. He is no longer complicit in an unjust system but one who is sacramentally bond to the poor. Jesus transformed a socially invisible, isolated, and despised person into an indispensable member of God's family and a productive member of his community. This is what God's restorative justice is truly about.

JUSTICE THAT RESTORES: IMAGINING A BETTER WAY

Legislative policies like the federal Violent Crime Control and Law Enforcement Act of 1994 incentivize incarceration. Acts like these require a state applying for a federal grant for prison construction to show that it "(A) has increased the percentage of convicted violent offenders sentenced to prison; (B) has increased the average prison time which will be served in prison by convicted violent offenders sentenced to prison; (C) has increased the percentage of sentences which will be served in prison by violent offenders sentenced to prison."[20] These policies are not aimed at rehabilitation but on profiteering.

Furthermore, laws like stop and frisk, the detention bed quotas, and anti-immigration laws like SB 1070 highlight the robust history of racially targeted and profiled legislation our system is rooted in.[21] The church cannot turn its face away from these harsh realities; we must confess our complicity in the legacy of mass incarceration and turn away from a system that dehumanizes people by criminalizing them. We must zealously pursue a system that restores individuals and renews covenant community. As we allow Scripture to light our path and the Spirit to guide our steps, we must discern whether our civic engagement and understanding of justice is more loyal to our nation's cultural ethos or to the heart of God.

The church has the power to help transform our criminal justice system. We have the potential to be a key voice in shifting our system's priorities to conflict resolution, prisoner transformation, and successfully reintegrating people into their communities upon their release. If reconciled communities are ever to become the true aim of our justice system, the church must lead the way in advocating for a system that gives opportunities for authentic rehabilitation, lasting transformation, and healthy reintegration.

The church can begin this process by establishing healthy communal partnerships with the state, providing support, accountability, and hospitality to those who were once hated and despised. Then we can move to bearing witness to our faith by pointing toward redemption and new life in Christ by intentionally communing with the condemned and creating a place for them at our dinner tables, doing life-on-life discipleship rather than evangelism from a safe distance. We must learn about and get trained to facilitate restorative circles in our churches and communities. Next, we can create collaborative spaces that foster authentic healing, reconciliation, and restoration, which we offer to the broader community, intent on meeting the needs of everyone affected by crime and incarceration. Each congregation must ask itself, How are we remembering the prisoner? Are we living into Matthew 25? We are all called to go into prisons, to be present with Jesus there. However, how we will work to deconstruct mass incarceration will differ. Some communities and congregations will be called and best equipped to focus on ministering within the walls of prisons, while others will focus on walking alongside families with incarcerated loved ones. Still others will focus on prevention, and others will prioritize reentry and re-sourcing returning citizens. We are not all called to the same thing, but we are all called to something. Every congregation has a role to play.

A 2014 Pew survey found that more than 60 percent of Americans said providing treatment for drug abusers was more important than prosecuting them.[22] Where is the church's voice in this? The church must galvanize its prophetic voice. Even the federal government has admitted that "we can't arrest our way out of the problem." Instead, Michael Botticelli, the former director of the White House's Office of National Drug Control Policy, declared, "We really need to focus our attention on proven public health strategies to make a significant difference as it relates to drug use."[23]

HOLY INTERRUPTIONS

Dismantling Mass Incarceration

MANY OF THE MOST RESPECTED PEOPLE in the Bible were imprisoned: John the Baptist, Paul, and Jesus—the author and perfecter of our faith. And they are not the only ones: Samson, Hanani the seer, Joseph, Micaiah, Stephen, Jeremiah, Peter, Shadrach, Meshach, Abednego, and Silas were all incarcerated. The truth is, we would not have the Bible without "criminals." These men were all imprisoned for prophetically bearing witness to the kingdom of God within earthly empires. Nevertheless, there are also Christians who committed crimes that warranted incarceration, like Moses and David, who both murdered someone but were not sentenced to time behind bars.

The book of Acts, which most people see as the church in its healthiest expression, details the church at the zenith of its prophetic witness. This book of the Bible records the most incidents of Christians being incarcerated. Therefore, we could rationally deduce a relationship between the church's health, its prophetic witness, and the spread of the gospel.

Many members of the early church understood following Jesus as something that compelled them to countercultural action. Patterning one's life after Jesus, they believed, sometimes meant engaging in nonviolent civil disobedience, which provoked persecution from the powers that be. These leaders prophetically bore witness to the kingdom of God in ways that made many of their contemporaries uncomfortable, and in a manner that led many to denounce them and their actions as disruptive, divisive, and counterproductive to the gospel. Nevertheless, they persisted.

When instructed by earthly authorities to refrain from following the Spirit's prompting (whether preaching the gospel in public, bearing witness to their true citizenship by refusing to bow before idols, or rebuking worldly counsel that advised them to distort the truth to appease kings), they resisted earthly authorities, defied imperial orders, continued their prophetic action, and peacefully endured the consequences their protest provoked. These Christians were willing to be imprisoned for nonviolently resisting earthly authorities who acted unjustly and authorized legislation antithetical to the kingdom of God. They were compelled to resist in this manner because their discipleship reminded them where their true citizenship resided.

Shadrach, Meshach, Abednego, Paul, and Silas all continued their prophetic witness even after being arrested and detained. Shadrach, Meshach, and Abednego were so fervent in their protest that they were sentenced to death. Their civil disobedience was deemed so distasteful and unpatriotic that the king had to witness their audacity firsthand. These three noble, God-honoring men intentionally spurned earthly authorities and the law of the land multiple times. And God was pleased! God affirmed their protest, intervening to rescue them from the flames of death. Since their protest was faithful, God validated their nonviolent civil disobedience. Their peaceful resistance prophetically bore witness to the kingdom of God, and the Lord affirmed their "lawlessness" because it was rooted in giving honor and praise to the one and only true God.

The church, by and large, has forsaken public, nonviolent civil disobedience, which is supposed to be a fundamental component of Christian discipleship. We have thereby forsaken public demonstrations of faith that bear witness to the inbreaking kingdom of God in the midst of worldly empires. The early church saw itself as outside of the confines of empire; it was, instead, a countercultural community marked by the cross of Jesus Christ. Their faith was something that did not align with the political interests, socioeconomic practices, and unrighteous ethics of the powers that be. They understood the empire to be antithetical to the kingdom, and therefore kingdom people were called to prophetically bear witness to their faith through resisting the power of empire.

Daniel Groody, in *Globalization, Spirituality, and Justice*, writes,

> In the Bible, Egypt is the first in a series of empires, including Assyria, Babylon, Persia, Greece, and Rome, that embody power structures that benefit the elite, enslave the poor, and dominate the weak. The notion of empire often describes political entities, but it is not limited to them. Symbolically, the empire represents any power that arrogates to itself the power that belongs to God alone, or any group or institution that subjugates the poor and needy for its own advantage.[1]

Rome was the most powerful and oppressive empire the world had ever know. Many believers in this era understood following Jesus required the church to be set apart—a community called to resist the oppressive underpinnings of empire. Their faith in Jesus commissioned them to imperial resistance to the point of being persecuted, imprisoned, or killed.

Groody writes,

> The opening accounts of the New Testament begins with a clash between the empire and Gospel, between the reign of Caesar Augustus and the reign of God, between a king who seeks to save his own power even at the cost of others' lives (Mt 2:16), and the king who lays down his own power so he might save the lives of all who are open to his reign (Mt 20-28; Mk 10:45). At the heart of the Narrative of the Gospel is Jesus Christ. Through his life, death, and resurrection, God subverts the power of the empire, destroys idols which oppose the God of Life, brings good news to the poor, reveals the undying love of Yahweh, and proclaims a new kingdom of truth and life, of holiness and grace, of justice,

love, and peace. The Narrative of the Gospel not only gives flesh to the liberating story of the Scriptures but it is *the* defining narrative of the Christian faith.[2]

Many early church leaders understood following Jesus meant continuing to subvert the power of the empire; subverting the power of empire was a hallmark of Christianity. They saw this responsibility as a reminder of who they were and whose they were. The charge to subvert the empire's power, therefore, commissioned the early church to a radically alternative lifestyle, witness, and ethic.

Dr. Martin Luther King Jr. addressed this part of the early church's legacy and the church's ongoing responsibility to subvert the power of the empire in his legendary "Letter from a Birmingham Jail," writing,

> Wherever the early Christians entered a town the power structure got disturbed and immediately sought to convict them for being "disturbers of the peace" and "outside agitators." But they went on with the conviction that they were a "colony of heaven" and had to obey God rather than man. They were small in number but big in commitment. They were too God-intoxicated to be "astronomically intimidated." They brought an end to such ancient evils as infanticide and gladiatorial contest.[3]

King continued, "Things are different now. The contemporary Church is so often a weak, ineffectual voice with an uncertain sound. It is so often the arch supporter of the status quo. Far from being disturbed by the presence of the Church, the power structure of the average community is consoled by the Church's silent and often vocal sanction of things as they are."[4] King indicts the church for failing to maintain its prophetic witness, for ceasing to embody a christocentric ethic that subverts imperial power. King wrote this letter as a lament. It was a response to Christian leaders who criticized him for waging a campaign of nonviolent resistance aimed at subverting the power of the US empire. King composed this letter from his jail cell as he peacefully endured the consequences of his nonviolent resistance to imperial power.

Mass incarceration is a byproduct of the church's failure to sustain a witness that subverts the power of empire. It is the rotten fruit of the domesticated discipleship King denounces. It is evidence of what transpires when the church forgets its mission, ceases its prophetic witness, and cowers before imperial power.

RECLAIMING OUR IDENTITY

Christianity cannot fit neatly into partisan politics. Both the left and the right are inadequate. Neither party is God-ordained, and both champion principles antithetical to the kingdom.

Nationwide, right now people are ardently fighting to end mass incarceration. In faith communities, in nonprofits, in reentry centers, in schools, on campuses, on street corners, and in communal forums, people are uncompromisingly pushing for change, asking revolutionary questions, and refusing to settle for pat answers. People are declaring that they are not content with living in a carceral state, and they are building a movement that has the potential to birth something novel, restorative, and transformative.

Michelle Alexander writes,

> I don't view mass incarceration as just a problem of politics or policy, I view it as a profound moral and spiritual crisis as well. I think that racial justice in this country will remain a distant dream as long as we think that it can be achieved simply through rational policy discussions. If we take a purely technocratic approach to these issues and strip them of their moral and spiritual dimensions, I think we'll just keep tinkering and tinkering and fail to realize that all of these issues really have more to do with who we are individually and collectively, and what we believe we owe one another, and how we ought to treat one another as human beings.

Alexander explains that "these are philosophical questions, moral questions, theological questions, as much as they are questions about the costs and benefits of using one system of punishment or policing practice over another."[5] The church must divorce itself from partisan politics, reclaim its prophetic zeal, and renew its commitment to subverting the power of empire. This process begins with recalibrating our vison.

RECALIBRATING OUR VISION

Sight is a central theme of Scripture. Jesus tells Nicodemus that "no one can see the kingdom of God unless they are born again" (John 3:3). In Luke 4:18, Jesus unrolls the scroll in the temple and proclaims his mission statement:

> to proclaim good news to the poor . . .
> to proclaim freedom for the prisoners
>   and recovery of sight for the blind,
> to set the oppressed free.

We also see Jesus physically do this by laying hands on people and literally restoring their vision.

The church has been blind, unable to see the true impact of our criminal justice system. We have not noticed that mass incarceration is predicated on dehumanization, exploitation, and profiteering. We have not understood the communal effects of drug-war legislation, law-and-order politics, and zero-tolerance policies. We have not realized that most people behind bars are nonviolent addicts who need medical interventions, not incarceration. We have been unable to detect that mass incarceration has evolved into a sinister social strategy to quarantine and exploit the most vulnerable, undesired, and stigmatized populations. We fail to see because many of us have circumvented Scripture's call to be present in prisons.

All too often, when we encounter the formerly incarcerated, we do not see them as brothers and sisters who reflect God's image. We usually view them with suspicion and interact cautiously with them. Furthermore, when we do go into prisons and detention centers, we frequently do not believe that people behind bars are capable of returning as citizens who can make our neighborhoods better places.

When we think this way, we limit the ways God can work in us and through our ministries.

Dennis Gaddy, founder and executive of Community Success Initiative, a North Carolina–based organization serving the recently released, asks, "Why is it that the same vans that come to the prison on Wednesday and Sunday nights to take us to Bible study seem hesitant to pick us up from our homes now that we are released?"[6] When we doubt the redemptive power of God to transform returning citizens, we are prone to support restrictive legislation that significantly hinders their future lives, particularly their opportunities and access going forward. When we do not believe all people are redeemable, we support tough-on-crime legislation, which handcuffs many individuals who are sincerely trying to turn their lives around. We often do not realize how this legislation affects these individuals, families, and most notably their children.

God's justice is not soft on crime, but it also not marginalizing, dehumanizing, and retaliatory. Divine discipline must always be understood within the broader context of God's redemption of all things. Our criminal justice system administrates punishment without a plan for restoration. Presently, many individuals serve their time and then cannot successfully reintegrate into communities because they are stripped of their dignity (labeled as ex-cons), deprived of voting rights, and denied the liberties and freedoms that enable them to flourish. Upon completion of their sentence, most continue serving time on the outside, unable to shake the social stigma of incarceration or unable to overcome the barrier posed by a felony record. Many people are never given a second chance in our society.

When Jesus encountered people who would have been labeled as criminal or immoral—Zacchaeus, the adulterous woman, and the woman at the well—he responded to them with grace and truth enfolded in love. He did not jettison these "unprincipled people" into isolation or confinement (which, it can be argued, they deserved), but instead he validated their humanity, affirmed their dignity, and reintegrated them into society, telling them to go and sin no more. In

Jesus, we see God's heart and mission of restoration enfleshed. In him we find our blueprint for our civic engagement. Let us now explore several examples of the hope that we can glean from their models, establish new partnerships, envision new ways of responding in our local contexts, and see the ways God is already at work, both within and beyond the church.

EDUCATION AS REPARATIVE JUSTICE

North Park Theological Seminary (NPTS) is framing education as an act of reparative justice. NPTS offers theological education to prisoners through integrated classrooms where NPTS students take courses alongside incarcerated students. This groundbreaking project for evangelical higher education develops the vocational identity of prisoners and widens the parameters of vocational call for seminarians.

Michelle Clifton-Soderstrom, who directs the program, says, "There is a great need for integrated theological education in prison. Many in prison desire formative courses and vocational development for themselves and to build the church inside prison." She notes that "around 40% of those incarcerated are eligible for college courses, but the sad reality is that the number of college in prison programs in the U.S. has fallen from 350 in 1982 to just 12 by 2005." She goes on to say that "education in prison increases public safety, promotes the economy by creating a stronger workforce, and reduces the chances of recidivism by 40-50%."[7] NPTS is rethinking teaching and pedagogy as it challenges unjust social institutions.

NPTS partners with Stateville Correctional Center, a maximum-security prison housing approximately three thousand men. Due to the fruit these courses have yielded, NPTS created a new certificate in transformative justice. Interest among Stateville students is high, and NPTS receives more than twice the amount of applications than current offerings allow.[8]

Duke Divinity School offers a certificate in prison studies, giving students the opportunity to engage prisoners and the system that imprisons them. In this context of theological education and ministry formation, students take courses in restorative justice and prison studies, and then take a course in a local prison. Students also complete a field education placement in a prison, a church doing prison ministry, or a nonprofit working with prisoners.[9]

Twenty-two years ago, New Orleans Baptist Theological Seminary (NOBTS) was invited into Angola Prison to help change the culture. Angola (see chapter two) was notorious for blood and violence. In the 1970s, court supervision, wardens working for reform, and new educational programs helped curb violence.[10] Nevertheless, the true change began in 1995, when Burl Cain took over as the prison's warden. Facing drastic cuts in educational funding, Cain invited NOBTS to open a Bible college inside Angola. NOBTS agreed, and they also covered the costs. Looking back at this partnership, Cain says NOBTS transformed Angola.

At the twenty-year celebration of this prophetic partnership, NOBTS dedicated a new facility at Angola. The facility was inaugurated with the commissioning of its 278th graduate. Following the graduation, Cain said, "This has been the most spectacular day we could ever have. . . . We have a new seminary building; we doubled our capacity; and, it means less victims of violent crime."[11] Over sixteen thousand churches support the work through the Louisiana Baptist Convention's mission offering.

James LeBlanc, secretary of the Louisiana Department of Corrections, acknowledged the work of thirty-five NOBTS graduates as a significant factor in the drop in repeat offenders. These NOBTS graduates spread the gospel and plant inmate-led churches in prisons. Jimmy Dukes, director of the program, mentioned that NOBTS missionaries were in demand at other prisons. Through the program, inmates can earn a bachelor of arts in Christian ministry and other certificate degrees, and with the new facility masters-level coursework is now offered.[12]

Daryl Walters, forty-five, will spend the rest of his life in Angola, like most of his peers. Of the six thousand prisoners at Angola, 80 percent have a life sentence. Walters nevertheless preaches the gospel weekly to two hundred men in chapel. The *New York Times* wrote that Walters proclaims "salvation and joy to murderers and rapists and robbers who waved their arms to an inmate band's Christian worship music."[13] Walters, a NOBTS graduate, is an assistant pastor of one of the Angola churches.

NOBTS graduates pastor other prisoners. Some graduates become missionaries in other prisons! "Beyond the bachelor's degrees, the college has granted hundreds more certificates or associate degrees, producing a cadre of men who lead churches, provide informal counseling in their dorms and take on what many describe as their hardest task—informing fellow inmates when a loved one on the outside has died. Some 2,500 inmates attend church regularly."[14] NOBTS president Charles S. Kelley Jr. says that the program's mission is to transform prison into "a positive influence and a place of healthy preparation for reentering society. . . . It's not education alone, but a change of heart."[15]

RESTORATIVE COURT

The Department of Justice (DOJ) granted ten jurisdictions two years of funding to explore the effectiveness of restorative justice community courts, which offers young adults charged with nonviolent felonies or misdemeanors an alternative way to reconcile relational violations. The courts will take a holistic approach: "confronting crime—offering mediation between the accused and accuser, and restitution targeted at the local community—will result in fewer young adults going to jail."[16]

The DOJ said these courts "can reduce crime and substance use, increase services to victims, reduce unnecessary use of jail, save money, and improve public confidence in justice."[17] Cliff Nellis, the executive director of the Lawndale Christian Legal Center, who cochairs the court's steering committee, explains, "This court will function so much outside the regular system. You aren't trusting the judge or the prosecutor—you're trusting your neighbor who is sitting in the circle next to you."[18] The court expects to see one hundred offenders annually.

UNEXPECTED ADVOCATES

In 2015, 130 police chiefs, sheriffs, and prosecutors gathered to discern how to end mass incarceration. They launched a coalition—Law Enforcement Leaders to Reduce Crime and Incarceration—aimed at reducing the prison population. "We can do it and protect public safety at the same time," observes Ronal Serpas, former superintendent of the New Orleans Police Department.[19]

The group included many high-profile law officers and was backed by groups such as the NAACP and Koch Industries. Their mission statement reads, in part, "We believe unnecessary incarceration does not work to reduce crime, wastes taxpayer dollars, damages families, and divides communities." The group says locking up too many people for drug and nonviolent offenses can "kick-start a cycle of incarceration that turns first-time offenders into repeat offenders."[20] Leading law enforcement officers have never lent their support like this before. The church must hold these officials accountable to their words, especially amid the new attorney general's recommitment to mandatory minimums. A shift in approach is required. The Los Angeles Police Department chief says he's fought the "war on drugs" and the "war on gangs," and he now realizes that "police departments cannot be at war with communities they serve."[21]

OLD SKOOL CAFE

Old Skool Cafe is a faith-based, youth-run, jazz-themed supper club. Doing innovative work to end mass incarceration in San Francisco, it is yielding amazing dividends. The café works to prevent violence by teaching employment skills to at-risk youth. The café provides these youth with employment, a supportive environment, like-minded community, and mentorship, all of which are needed in order to break cycles of incarceration.

Old Skool is committed to transforming the prospects of formerly incarcerated youth and halting recidivism. At the café, youth create bonds with mentors and peers that encourage them as they work toward communal reintegration. The rate of repeat offense for youth mentored at Old Skool Cafe is less than the national rate by astounding numbers.

The café was launched in 2005 by a former Los Angeles corrections officer. Teresa, the founder, had prayed for a part to play in ending the cycle of incarceration of at-risk youth, and God gave her the vision for the café.[22]

HOMEBOY INDUSTRIES

Homeboy Industries humbly started in 1988. Twenty-nine years later it is the largest gang-intervention program in the world. Homeboy Industries provides employment, training, mentorship, conflict resolution, and discipleship. Annually, more than ten thousand former gang members (many previously incarcerated) come through Homeboy Industries' doors to change their lives. They are provided with a wide array of services ranging from mental health to anger management courses to solar-panel training and certifications—all in a rich community environment. Homeboy Industries has nine social enterprises that provide the formerly incarcerated with meaningful employment at livable wages.

Homeboys Industries is committed to changing lives in Los Angeles. The California Department of Education found "the rate of 9-12th dropping out among black high school students rose to 43.5% and to 36.1% for Hispanic/Latino students in 2009. In East Los Angeles, over 53% of adults never completed high school." In 2010, Los Angeles was named the "dropout epicenter" of the nation. A remarkable 34 percent of California's poor live in Los Angeles County, and 75 percent of youth-involved gang homicides occur there.[23] Homeboy Industries employs and trains men and women who have fallen through society's cracks and provides critical services to fifteen thousand people annually.

The founder of Homeboy Industries, Father Greg Boyle, was named a Champion of Change by the White House, and he received the 2016 Humanitarian of the Year Award.[24]

MINISTRY TO RETURNING CITIZENS BIRTHED A CHURCH

The Promised Land Church (TPLC) grew out the missionary efforts of Urban Youth Alliance (a grassroots parachurch organization in the South Bronx) to adjudicated youth and the formerly incarcerated. This program strove to find churches for these individuals as they reintegrated into the community. However, TPLC leaders found that while the people they ministered to responded to the gospel, they rarely found a church home. Consequently, youth and adults alike usually returned to TPLC leaders with demoralizing congregational experiences. They frequently felt judged and unwelcomed. When TPLC leaders urged them to reconnect with churches, they commonly responded, "Why can't this just be my church?"

TPLC leaders had the relationships, trust, and experience to start a church. They served this population through providing job training, court advocacy, and drug counseling. TPLC leaders also are those who shared the gospel with them. They began to sense that God was calling them to church planting, specifically reaching out to returning citizens and providing a safe place to worship and find healing, free from judgment and condemnation. TPLC held its first service in October 2006. Since then, the church has consistently grown in membership by planting six other congregations throughout New York City with a similar vision and mission.[25]

In this crisis moment, the church—particularly evangelicals—must feel the anguish of traumatized parts of Christ's body. Our theology must be historically rooted, curating a common memory that acknowledges the grave realities of racism, classism, and sexism, particularly as these oppressions intersect. In our reluctance—and sometimes refusal—to do this, the body has allowed these evils to establish footholds within the church. To exorcise these demons, we must boldly confront them.

Amid this racial nadir we find ourselves in, society desperately needs Christians to become Spirit-led ambassadors who sacrificially seek the peace and prosperity of our cities, especially within the most stigmatized parts. We must begin by identifying and renouncing the truncated theologies that prohibit us from authentically embodying God's love. We have to develop the fortitude to have difficult ecclesial conversations about history, racial injustice, and institutional oppression. The truth spoken in these conversations must always be expressed in love; however, the rhetoric of love cannot be strategically deployed by those in power to obscure hard truths. As authentic conversations transpire, we will learn how to mutually trust and submit to one another in true fellowship.

As people marked by God's grace, we must lead the charge in advocating for another way. Michelle Alexander writes, "As a society, our decision to heap shame and contempt upon those who struggle and fail in a system designed to keep them locked up and locked out says far more about ourselves than it does about them."[26] Some Christians are doing amazing work to topple mass incarceration, but most churches are uninvolved. Christopher Marshall writes that "the first Christians experienced in Christ and lived out in their faith communities an understanding of justice as a power that heals, restores, and reconciles rather than hurts, punishes, and kills, and . . . this reality ought to shape and direct a Christian contribution to the criminal justice debate today."[27]

We serve a God whose final word is not retribution but restoration, who desires liberation, reconciliation, and reintegration for those behind bars. God invites the church to participate in setting the captives free, spiritually liberating them and emancipating them from a depraved system that defaces the imago Dei.

ACKNOWLEDGMENTS

I WANT TO THANK THE COMMUNITY who helped birth this project—particularly my family, mentors, and friends who previewed chapters, gave invaluable feedback, and helped refine my words.

I also want to acknowledge the organizations, institutions, and associations—the Evangelical Covenant Church, North Park Theological Seminary, and the Christian Community Development Association— that have fundamentally influenced me, informed my discipleship, and helped to shape this project. Without the spiritual formation and ministry experience I gained in these spaces, this book would not exist.

I also want to thank Ben and Michael McBride, Erina Kim-Eubanks, Michelle Warren, Miea Walker, Shawn Casselberry, and Amy Williams for being collaborators in this work. And I want to give a special shout out to Erica Elan Ciganek who created a beautiful artistic piece to accompany this text, which served as a muse for me at various points throughout my writing process.

I want to thank all my colleagues who wrote blurbs for this book. These cherished peers took the time to preview my words and deemed them worthy of endorsing. I am eternally grateful for your willingness to leverage your social capital on behalf of this project.

Most importantly, I want to thank my mother, Catherine Gilliard. She has affirmed, encouraged, and supported me through every step of my faith journey. She has corrected me when I've gone astray and empowered me to be all that I can be for the kingdom.

I finally want to thank the team at InterVarsity Press, especially Helen Lee and Al Hsu. Helen, this book was originally your vision, and Al, it came into fruition because of your guidance, hard work, and craftsmanship.

NOTES

INTRODUCTION

[1]Lin-Manuel Miranda, "My Shot," *Hamilton: An American Musical*, 2016.

[2]Ta-Nehisi Coates, *Between the World and Me* (New York: Spiegel & Grau, 2015), 18.

[3]Mark Lewis Taylor, *The Executed God: The Way of the Cross in Lockdown America*, 2nd ed. (Minneapolis: Fortress, 2015), xii.

[4]Michelle Alexander, *The New Jim Crow: Mass Incarceration in the Age of Colorblindness* (New York: New Press, 2012), 13.

[5]Ibid., 1.

[6]Ibid., 180.

[7]Ibid., 98.

[8]Ibid., 233.

[9]Bryan Stevenson, *Just Mercy: A Story of Justice and Redemption* (New York: Spiegel & Grau, 2015), 294.

[10]Martin Luther King Jr., *Strength to Love* (Minneapolis: Fortress, 2010), 59.

[11]Toni Cade Bambara, foreword to *This Bridge Called My Back: Writings by Radical Women of Color*, ed. Cherrie Moraga and Gloria Anzaldúa (New York: Kitchen Table: Women of Color Press, 1981), viii.

1 THE WAR ON DRUGS

[1]"Ex-Cops Apologize for Deadly Drug Raid Ahead of Sentencing," CNN, February 23, 2009, www.cnn.com/2009/CRIME/02/23/atlanta.police .sentencing/index.html.

[2]"Ex-Atlanta Officers Get Prison Time for Cover-up in Deadly Raid," CNN, February 24, 2009, www.cnn.com/2009/CRIME/02/24/atlanta.police.

[3]Ibid.

[4]Ibid.

[5]Kevin Sack, "Door-Busting Drug Raids Leave a Trail of Blood," *New York Times*, March 18, 2017, www.nytimes.com/interactive/2017/03/18/us /forced-entry-warrant-drug-raid.html?_r=0.

[6]Peter B. Kraska, "Militarization and Policing—Its Relevance to 21st Century Police," *Policing* 1, no. 4 (2007): 501-13, doi:10.1093/police/pam065.

[7]Michelle Alexander, *The New Jim Crow: Mass Incarceration in the Age of Colorblindness* (New York: New Press, 2012), 74.

[8]"War Comes Home: The Excessive Militarization of American Police," ACLU, June 2014, www.aclu.org/report/war-comes-home-excessive-mili tarization-american-police.

[9]Sack, "Door-Busting Drug Raids Leave a Trail of Blood."

[10]Ibid.

[11]Ibid.

[12]Ibid.

[13]Alexander, *New Jim Crow*, 104.

[14]"DEA History," Drug Enforcement Administration, accessed August 21, 2017, www.dea.gov/about/history.shtml. Read more about the history of the drug war at "A Brief History of the Drug War," Drug Policy Alliance, accessed August 21, 2017, www.drugpolicy.org/facts/new-solutions-drug-policy /brief-history-drug-war-0.

[15]See Alexander, *New Jim Crow*, 49, for a breakdown of the numbers.

[16]Ibid.

[17]"DEA History."

[18]Alexander, *New Jim Crow*, 79.

[19]Ibid., 91.

[20]Ibid., 87.

[21]Ibid.

[22]Ibid., 112.

[23]"Fair Sentencing Act," ACLU, accessed August 21, 2017, www.aclu.org/feature /fair-sentencing-act.

[24]Ibid.

[25]Alexander, *New Jim Crow*, 6.

[26]"History of Mandatory Minimum Penalties and Statutory Relief Mechanisms," p. 25 of "2011 Report to the Congress: Mandatory Minimum Penalties in the Federal Criminal Justice System," accessed August 21, 2017, United States Sentencing Commission, www.ussc.gov/research/congressional-reports

/2011-report-congress-mandatory-minimum-penalties-federal-criminal
-justice-system.

[27]Ibid., 88.

[28]"Conduct of Law Enforcement Agencies," United States Department of Justice, accessed August 21, 2017, www.justice.gov/crt/about/spl/police.php.

[29]R. David LaCourse Jr., "Three Strikes, You're Out: A Review," Washington Policy Center, January 1, 1997, www.washingtonpolicy.org/publications /detail/three-strikes-youre-out-a-review.

[30]Alexander, *New Jim Crow*, 114.

[31]Ibid., 74.

[32]Radley Balko, *Overkill: The Rise of Paramilitary Police Raids in America* (Washington, DC: Cato Institute, 2006), 8.

[33]Megan Twohey, "SWATs Under Fire," *National Journal*, January 1, 2000, 37. See also Balko, *Overkill*, 8.

[34]Christopher J. Coyne and Abigail R. Hall, "Four Decades and Counting: The Continued Failure of the War on Drugs," CATO Institute, April 12, 2017, www.cato.org/publications/policy-analysis/four-decades-counting -continued-failure-war-drugs.

[35]Alexander, *New Jim Crow*, 9.

[36]Ibid., 60.

[37]Ibid., 7.

[38]Loïc Wacquant, "Deadly Symbiosis: Rethinking Race and Imprisonment in Twenty-First-Century America," *Boston Review* 27 (2002): 1.

[39]Ibid., 2.

[40]"Women Behind Bars," *New York Times*, November 30, 2015, www.ny times.com/2015/11/30/opinion/women-behind-bars.html?mcubz=0.

[41]Morgan Lee, "How Churches Change the Equation for Life After Prison," *Christianity Today*, August 22, 2016, www.christianitytoday.com/ct/2016 /september/life-after-prison.html.

[42]Gail L. Thompson, "African American Women and the U.S. Criminal Justice System," *Journal of African American History* 98, no. 2 (2013): 295-99.

[43]Ibid., 236-37.

[44]Bryan Stevenson, *Just Mercy: A Story of Justice and Redemption* (New York: Spiegel & Grau, 2015), 236.

[45]Ibid., 237.

[46]Nate Blakeslee, *Tulia: Race, Cocaine, and Corruption in a Small Texas Town* (New York: Public Affairs, 2006), 409.

[47]Ibid., 22.

[48]"An African-American Community in Texas Is Victimized by the 'War on Drugs,'" NAACP Legal Defense Fund, accessed August 21, 2017, www .naacpldf.org/case-issue/bad-times-tulia-texas. Four of the people arrested were Mexican, and the remaining three were Euro-Americans who had either biracial children or marital ties to an African American.

[49]Blakeslee, *Tulia*, 5.

[50]Pam Easton, "Texas Drug Bust Raises Questions," *Washington Post*, October 1, 2000, www.washingtonpost.com/wp-srv/aponline/20001001 /aponline123942_000.htm.

[51]Ibid.

[52]"Racist Arrests in Tulia, Texas," American Civil Liberties Union, accessed July 3, 2017, www.aclu.org/other/racist-arrests-tulia-texas.

[53]"$5 Million Settlement in Texas Drug Sting: Lone Informant's Testimony Was Later Discredited," NBC News, March 11, 2004, www.nbcnews.com /id/4506032/ns/us_news-crime_and_courts/t/million-settlement-texas -drug-sting. The settlement was based on a formula that took into account prison time and the duration of incarceration.

[54]See "Erma Faye Stewart and Regina Kelly," *Frontline*, June 21, 2004, www .pbs.org/wgbh/pages/frontline/shows/plea/four/stewart.html; and "ACLU Charges Racial Discrimination in Second Texas Drug Bust Scandal," ACLU, November 1, 2002, www.aclu.org/news/aclu-charges-racial-discrimination -second-texas-drug-bust-scandal.

[55]Alexander, *New Jim Crow*, 106.

[56]Ibid., 99.

[57]"Report of the Sentencing Project to the United Nations Human Rights Committee Regarding Racial Disparities in the United States Criminal Justice System," The Sentencing Project, August 2013, http://sentencing project.org/doc/publications/rd_ICCPR%20Race%20and%20Justice%20 Shadow%20Report.pdf.

[58]Stevenson, *Just Mercy*, 18.

[59]Wendell Berry, *The Hidden Wound* (Berkeley, CA: Counterpoint, 2010), 105, 4.

[60]Christopher Ingraham, "The U.S. Has More Jails Than Colleges. Here's a Map of Where Those Prisoners Live," *Washington Post*, January 2015, www .washingtonpost.com/news/wonk/wp/2015/01/06/the-u-s-has-more -jails-than-colleges-heres-a-map-of-where-those-prisoners-live.

[61]David Von Drehle, "More Innocent People on Death Row Than Estimated: Study," *Time*, April 28, 2014, www.time.com/79572/more-innocent-people-on-death-row-than-estimated-study.

[62]"Briefing Paper: The Shackling of Pregnant Women & Girls in U.S. Prisons, Jails & Youth Detention Centers," ACLU, accessed August 21, 2017, www.aclu.org/other/aclu-briefing-paper-shackling-pregnant-women-girls-us-prisons-jails-youth-detention-centers.

[63]"Thirteen States Have No Minimum Age for Adult Prosecution of Children," Equal Justice Initiative, September 19, 2006, www.eji.org/news/13-states-lack-minimum-age-for-trying-kids-as-adults.

[64]"Against Torture and Other Cruel, Inhuman or Degrading Treatment or Punishment," United Nations Convention, accessed August 21, 2017, www.hrweb.org/legal/cat.html.

[65]Elliot Currie, *Crime and Punishment in America* (New York: Picador, 2013), 18.

2 HOW DID WE GET HERE?

[1]Angela Y. Davis, *Are Prisons Obsolete?* (New York: Seven Stories, 2003), 60.

[2]Kali Nicole Gross, "African American Women, Mass Incarceration, and the Politics of Protection," *Journal of American History* 102, no. 1 (2015): 25-33, doi:10.1093/jahist/jav226. Gross's article informs much of this section.

[3]"Primary Documents in American History," Library of Congress, accessed August 21, 2017, www.loc.gov/rr/program/bib/ourdocs/13thamendment.html. Emphasis added.

[4]"Lynching in America: Confronting the Legacy of Racial Terror," Equal Justice Initiative, accessed September 14, 2017, www.eji.org/reports/lynching-in-america.

[5]James Cone, *The Cross and the Lynching Tree* (New York: Orbis, 2011), 7.

[6]Ken Wytsma, *The Myth of Equality: Uncovering the Roots of Injustice and Privilege* (Downers Grove, IL: InterVarsity Press, 2017), 69.

[7]Michael J. Perry, *Human Rights in the Constitutional Law of the United States* (Cambridge: Cambridge University Press, 2013), 9.

[8]Michael Slate, "Slavery by Another Name," interview with Douglas Blackmon, KPFK Los Angeles, June 15, 2008, www.revcom.us/a/132/Blackmon-en.html.

[9]"The Southern 'Black Codes' of 1865-66," Constitutional Rights Foundation, accessed July 5, 2017, www.crf-usa.org/brown-v-board-50th-anniversary/southern-black-codes.html.

[10]Frank Morey, *Condition and Wants of the South—Political, Material, Legislative: Speech of Hon. Frank Morey, of Louisiana, in the House of Representatives, June 15, 1874* (Washington, DC: Government Printing House, 1874), 7.

[11]US Congress, *Senate Executive Document No. 2* (Washington, DC, 1865), 93-94. Also from Louisiana.

[12]Paula S. Rothenberg, *Race, Class, and Gender in the United States: An Integrated Study*, 6th ed. (London: Worth, 2003), 475. From South Carolina.

[13]Mary Ellen Curtin, "The Origins of Black Codes," PBS, accessed August 21, 2017, www.pbs.org/tpt/slavery-by-another-name/themes/black-codes.

[14]Douglas Blackmon, interview by Bill Moyers, *Bill Moyers Journal*, June 20, 2008, www.pbs.org/moyers/journal/06202008/transcript2.html.

[15]Michelle Alexander, *The New Jim Crow: Mass Incarceration in the Age of Colorblindness* (New York: New Press, 2012), 28.

[16]"Black Codes," History Channel, accessed August 29, 2017, www.history.com /topics/black-history/black-codes.

[17]Curtin, "Origins of Black Codes."

[18]Blackmon, *Bill Moyers Journal.*

[19]Matthew J. Mancini, *One Dies, Get Another: Convict Leasing in the American South, 1866–1928* (Columbia: University of South Carolina Press, 1996), 1.

[20]Douglas Blackmon, "American Slavery Continued Until 1941," *Newsweek*, July, 13, 2008, www.newsweek.com/book-american-slavery-continued -until-1941-93231.

[21]Douglas Blackmon, interview by Neal Conan, *Talk of the Nation*, March 25, 2008, www.npr.org/templates/story/story.php?storyID=89051115.

[22]Mary Ellen Curtin, interview by Gwen Ifill, "'Slavery by Another Name' Relays the Forgotten Stories of Post-Civil War Slaves," PBS News Hour, February 13, 2012, www.pbs.org/newshour/bb/politics-jan-june12-slavery_02-13.

[23]Blackmon, *Bill Moyers Journal.*

[24]Ibid.

[25]Douglas A. Blackmon, *Slavery by Another Name: The Re-enslavement of Black Americans from the Civil War to World War II* (New York: Anchor Books, 2009), 7.

[26]There were sheriff, deputy, court clerk, and witness fees.

[27]Alex Lichtenstein, *Twice the Work of Free Labor: The Political Economy of Convict Labor in the New South* (New York: Verso, 1996), 112.

[28]Blackmon, *Slavery by Another Name*, 8.

[29]Ibid.

[30]Lichtenstein, *Twice the Work of Free Labor*, 3.

[31]Alexander, *New Jim Crow,* 114.

[32]Douglas Blackmon, "From Alabama's Past, Capitalism Teamed with Racism to Create Cruel Partnership," *Wall Street Journal,* July 16, 2001, www.hartford -hwp.com/archives/45a/618.html.

[33]"Classification 50: Involuntary Servitude and Slavery," National Archives, accessed August 21, 2017, www.archives.gov/research/investigations/fbi /classifications/050-slavery.html.

[34]Leon Litwack, *Trouble in Mind: Black Southerners in the Age of Jim Crow* (New York: Vintage, 1998), 271.

[35]For more information about the history of Angola, see Krissah Thompson, "From a Slave House to a Prison Cell: The History of Angola Plantation," *Washington Post,* September 21, 2016, www.washingtonpost.com /entertainment/museums/from-a-slave-house-to-a-prison-cell-the -history-of-angola-plantation/2016/09/21/7712eeac-63ee-11e6-96c0 -37533479f3f5 _story.html?

[36]Whitney Benns, "American Slavery, Reinvented," *Atlantic,* September 21, 2015, www.theatlantic.com/business/archive/2015/09/prison-labor-in -america/406177.

[37]"History of Angola Prison," Angola Museum, accessed August 21, 2017, www.angolamuseum.org/history/history.

[38]Ibid.

[39]"Prison Industry Enhancement Certification Program," Office of Justice Programs Bureau of Justice Assistance, March 2004, www.ncjrs.gov/pdf -files1/bja/203483.pdf.

[40]Ibid.

[41]Alex Helmick, "Thousands of Inmates Serve Time Fighting the West's Forest Fires," *All Things Considered,* July 31, 2014, www.npr.org/2014/07 /31/336309329/thousands-of-inmates-serve-time-fighting-the-wests -forest-fires.

[42]"About Us," Texas Correctional Industries, accessed August 21, 2017, www .tci.tdcj.texas.gov/info/about/default.aspx.

[43]Jeff Spross, "Corporate America Has a Secret Slave Labor Force," *The Week,* June 20, 2016, www.theweek.com/articles/630907/corporate-america -secret-slave-labor-force.

[44]"Texas Correctional Industries: Providing Useful Work Skills or Slave Labor?," Prison Legal News, August 7, 2014, www.prisonlegalnews.org/news /2014/aug/7/texas-correctional-industries-providing-useful-work-skills -or-slave-labor.

[45]Alice Speri, "Prisoners in Multiple States Call for Strikes to Protest Forced Labor," *The Intercept*, April 4, 2016, www.theintercept.com/2016/04/04/prisoners-in-multiple-states-call-for-strikes-to-protest-forced-labor.

[46]"Texas Correctional Industries: Providing Useful Work Skills or Slave Labor?"

[47]Vicky Peláez, "The Prison Industry in the United States: Big Business or a New Form of Slavery?," Global Research, August 28, 2016, www.globalresearch.ca/the-prison-industry-in-the-united-states-big-business-or-a-new-form-of-slavery/8289.

[48]Benns, "American Slavery, Reinvented."

[49]Such as the Fair Labor Standards Act or the National Labor Relations Act.

[50]Ibid.

[51]W. E. B. Du Bois, *The Souls of Black Folk* (Mineola, NY: Dover, 1994), 78.

3 BEYOND LAW AND ORDER

[1]Michelle Clifton-Soderstrom, "The Dehumanization of Black and Brown Bodies," plenary presentation, Covenant Justice Coalition Conference, New Rochelle, NY, October 21, 2016. Watch the ad at www.youtube.com/watch?v=EC9j6Wfdq3o.

[2]Ibid.

[3]Michelle Alexander, *The New Jim Crow: Mass Incarceration in the Age of Colorblindness* (New York: New Press, 2012), 40.

[4]Fannie Lou Hamer, quoted in Louis A. DeCaro Jr., *John Brown, Emancipator* (Chicago: Lulu, 2012), 76.

[5]Alexander, *New Jim Crow*, 42.

[6]Ibid.

[7]Michael Fortner, interview by Leon Neyfakh, "Black Americans Supported the 1994 Crime Bill, Too," *Slate*, February 12, 2016, www.slate.com/articles/news_and_politics/crime/2016/02/why_many_black_politicians_backed_the_1994_crime_bill_championed_by_the.html.

[8]Ibid.

[9]Ibid., 170.

[10]Khalil Muhammad, "Power and Punishment: Two New Books About Race and Crime," *New York Times*, April 14, 2017, www.nytimes.com/2017/04/14/books/review/locking-up-our-own-james-forman-jr-colony-in-nation-chris-hayes.html?mcubz=0.

[11]Ibid.

[12]Tony Campolo, "Who Are Red Letter Christians?," *Huffington Post*, February 15, 2008, www.huffingtonpost.com/tony-campolo/who-are-red-letter-christ_b_86887.html.

[13]Billy Graham, interview by Katie Couric, "I Hope They'll Say That He Was Faithful," *Today*, June 23, 2005, www.today.com/news/i-hope-theyll-say-he-was-faithful-wbna8326362.

[14]Jerry Falwell, "Why Jerry Farwell Formed the Moral Majority," *The Day*, April 20, 1982, www.news.google.com/newspapers?nid=1915&dat=19820420&id=CBMhAAAAIBAJ&sjid=QXUFAAAAIBAJ&pg=1824,3727640&hl=en.

[15]Franklin Graham, quoted in Lindsey Bever, "Franklin Graham: The Media Didn't Understand the 'God-Factor' in Trump's Win," *Washington Post*, November 10, 2016, www.washingtonpost.com/news/acts-of-faith/wp/2016/11/10/franklin-graham-the-media-didnt-understand-the-god-factor/?utm_term=.7f81c887d8b6.

[16]Franklin Graham, quoted in Emma Green, "Franklin Graham Is the Evangelical Id," *Atlantic*, May 21, 2017, www.theatlantic.com/politics/archive/2017/05/franklin-graham/527013.

[17]Franklin Graham, Facebook post, March 12, 2015, www.facebook.com/FranklinGraham/posts/883361438386705.

[18]Jerry Falwell Jr., quoted in Sarah Pulliam Bailey, "'Their Dream President': Trump Just Gave White Evangelicals a Big Boost," *Washington Post*, May 4, 2017, www.washingtonpost.com/news/acts-of-faith/wp/2017/05/04/their-dream-president-trump-just-gave-white-evangelicals-a-big-boost/?utm_term=.9b84c46025fa.

[19]Martin Luther King Jr., "Letter from a Birmingham Jail," April 16, 1963.

[20]Ibid.

[21]Ibid.

[22]Martin Luther King Jr., *The Radical King* (Boston: Beacon, 2016), 20.

[23]Willie Jennings, *Acts* (Louisville: Westminster John Knox, 2017), 161.

[24]Ibid.

[25]Ibid.

[26]Ibid., 162.

[27]Ibid., 161.

[28]See Shane Claiborne, *Executing Grace: How the Death Penalty Killed Jesus and Why It's Killing Us* (New York: HarperOne, 2016); and Gardner C. Hanks, *Against the Death Penalty* (Harrisonburg, VA: Herald, 1997).

[29]Ibid., 70.

4 THREE OVERLOOKED PIPELINES

[1]"Forced Internment of Japanese Americans," Equal Justice Initiative, accessed August 22, 2017, www.eji.org/history-racial-injustice-forced-internment-of-japanese-americans.

[2]"Japanese-American Relocation," History Channel, accessed August 22, 2017, www.history.com/topics/world-war-ii/japanese-american-relocation.

[3]University of California, "Relocation and Incarceration of Japanese Americans During World War II," Japanese American Relocation Digital Archive (JARDA), 2005.

[4]Children of the Camps Project, "Internment History," PBS, accessed August 22, 2017, www.pbs.org/childofcamp/history.

[5]Ibid.

[6]Nicole Goodkind, "Top 5 Secrets of the Private Prison Industry," Yahoo Finance, August 6, 2013, www.finance.yahoo.com/blogs/daily-ticker/top-5-secrets-private-prison-industry-163005314.html.

[7]ACLU, "Banking on Bondage: Private Prisons and Mass Incarceration," November 2011, www.aclu.org/banking-bondage-private-prisons-and-mass-incarceration.

[8]Joe Watson, "Report Finds Two-Thirds of Private Prison Contracts Include 'Lockup Quotas,'" Prison Legal News, August, 2015, 42, www.prisonlegalnews.org/news/2015/jul/31/report-finds-two-thirds-private-prison-contracts-include-lockup-quotas.

[9]Ibid.

[10]Marc Mauer, Race to Incarcerate, rev. ed. (New York: New Press, 2006), 68.

[11]Goodkind, "Top 5 Secrets."

[12]Michelle Warren, "Locked in Solidarity: Report on Mass Incarceration Rally," Christian Community Development Association, February 12, 2014, www.ccda.org/locked-in-solidarity-report-on-mass-incarceration-rally.

[13]Ibid.

[14]ACLU, "Banking on Bondage."

[15]Christopher Ingraham, "Private Prison Stocks Collapse After Justice Department Promises to Phase Them Out," Washington Post, August 18, 2016, www.washingtonpost.com/news/wonk/wp/2016/08/18/private-prison-stocks-collapse-after-justice-department-promises-to-phase-them-out/?utm_term=.35ada596f76d.

[16]Goodkind, "Top 5 Secrets."

[17]ACLU, "Banking on Bondage."

[18]Gisgie Dávila Gendreau, "U.S. Criminal Justice System Unfair, Unjust for Hispanics," Michigan State University, October 14, 2004, www.msutoday .msu.edu/news/2004/report-us-criminal-justice-system-unfair-unjust -for-hispanics.

[19]Ibid.

[20]"Immigration Offenses Make Latinos New Majority in Federal Prisons, Report Says," Fox News World, September 7, 2011, www.foxnews.com /world/2011/09/07/immigration-offenses-make-latinos-new-majority -in-federal-prisons-report-says.html.

[21]John Gramlich and Kristen Bialik, "Immigration Offenses Make Up a Growing Share of Federal Arrests," Pew Research Center, April 10, 2017, www.pewresearch.org/fact-tank/2017/04/10/immigration-offenses-make -up-a-growing-share-of-federal-arrests.

[22]Leigh Ann Caldwell, "The U.S. Already Spends Billions on Border Security," NBC News, August 31, 2016, www.nbcnews.com/politics/2016-election /trump-s-wall-would-add-billions-u-s-spends-border-n640251.

[23]Brian Naylor, "Trump's Plan to Hire 15,000 Border Patrol and ICE Agents Won't Be Easy," NPR, February 23, 2017, www.npr.org/2017/02/23 /516712980/trumps-plan-to-hire-15-000-border-patrol-and-ice-agents -wont-be-easy-to-fulfill.

[24]Aimee Picchi, "Prison Inc.: Immigration Busts a Boon for America's Biggest Private Lockup," CBS MoneyWatch, February 16, 2017, www.cbsnews.com /news/trump-immigration-corecivic-private-prisons.

[25]"Immigration Detention Bed Quota Timeline," National Immigrant Justice Center, spring 2015, www.immigrantjustice.org/sites/immigrantjustice .org/files/Immigration%20Detention%20Bed%20Quota%20Timeline%20 2015_03_24.pdf.

[26]Nick Miroff, "Controversial Quota Drives Immigration Detention Boom," *Washington Post*, October 13, 2013, www.washingtonpost.com/world /controversial-quota-drives-immigration-detention-boom/2013/10/13 /09bb689e-214c-11e3-ad1a-1a919f2ed890_story.html?utm_term= .cc760dae79c3.

[27]Jeff Sommer, "Trump Immigration Crackdown Is Great for Private Prison Stocks," *New York Times*, March 2017, www.nytimes.com/2017/03/10/your -money/immigrants-prison-stocks.html?mcubz=3. The three agencies are ICE, Customs and Border Protection, and the Marshals Service.

[28]Ibid.

[29]Matt Stroud, "What Private Prisons Companies Have Done to Diversify in the Face of Sentencing Reform: Corrections Corporation and GEO Group Have Both Invested into Offender Rehabilitation Services," Bloomberg Business, May 12, 2015, www.bloomberg.com/amp/news/articles/2015 -05-13/what-private-prisons-companies-have-done-to-diversify-in-the -face-of-sentencing-reform.

[30]Paul R. La Monica, "Clinton Call for End of Private Prisons Sinks Jail Stocks," CNN Money, September 27, 2016, www.money.cnn.com/2016/09/27 /investing/prison-stocks-hillary-clinton-debate-corrections-corporation -america-geo-group.

[31]"CCA Rebrands as CoreCivic," CoreCivic, accessed August 22, 2107, www .corecivic.squarespace.com.

[32]Picchi, "Prison Inc."

[33]Heather Long, "Private Prison Stocks up 100% Since Trump's Win," CNN Money, February 24, 2017, www.money.cnn.com/2017/02/24/investing /private-prison-stocks-soar-trump/index.html.

[34]Sommer, "Trump Immigration Crackdown."

[35]Carl Takei, quoted in Picchi, "Prison Inc."

[36]Alene Tchekmedyian, "Thousands of Immigrant Detainees Sue Private Prison Firm Over 'Forced' Labor," Los Angeles Times, March 5, 2017.

[37]Bernard E. Harcourt, "From the Asylum to the Prison: Rethinking the Incarceration Revolution," Texas Law Review 84 (2006): 1760, 1780.

[38]Paula M. Ditton, "Special Report: Mental Health and the Treatment of Inmates and Probationers," Bureau of Justice Statistics 3 (1999), www.bjs .gov/content/pub/pdf/mhtip.pdf.

[39]Harcourt, "From the Asylum to the Prison," 1761.

[40]"Emptying the 'New Asylums': A Beds Capacity Model to Reduce Mental Illness Behind Bars," Treatment Advocacy Center, January 2017, 1, www.treat mentadvocacycenter.org/storage/documents/emptying-new-asylums.pdf.

[41]Michel Foucault, Madness and Civilization: A History of Insanity in the Age of Reason (Hove, UK: Psychology Press, 2001), 5.

[42]Ibid., 4.

[43]Ibid.

[44]Ibid., 5.

[45]"The Treatment of Persons with Mental Illness in Prisons and Jails: Summary of Findings," Treatment Advocacy Center, 2014, www.treatment

advocacycenter.org/the-treatment-of-persons-with-mental-illness-in
-prisons-and-jails-2014/findings.

[46]Foucault, *Madness and Civilization*, 5.

[47]Harcourt, "From the Asylum to the Prison," 1781.

[48]Ibid.

[49]Erving Goffman, *Asylums: Essays on the Social Situation of Mental Patients
and Other Inmates* (New York: Anchor, 1961), 352.

[50]"The Treatment of Persons with Mental Illness in Prisons and Jails: A State
Survey," Treatment Advocacy Center, April 8, 2014, www.treatmentadvocacy
center.org/storage/documents/treatment-behind-bars/treatment-behind
-bars.pdf, 6.

[51]Ibid.

[52]Treatment and Advocacy Center, "Emptying the 'New Asylums,'" 1.

[53]Ibid.

[54]Harcourt, "From the Asylum to the Prison," 1783.

[55]Bernard E. Harcourt, "Rethinking the Carceral Through an Institutional
Lens: On Prisons and Asylums in the United States," Champ Pénal, March
21, 2008, 57, champpenal.revues.org/7563?lang=en. This is a translation
of *Repenser le carcéral à travers le prisme de l'institutionalisation: Sur les liens
entre asiles et prisons aux Etats-Unis.*

5 THE SCHOOL-TO-PRISON PIPELINE

[1]"Luzerne County Kids-for-Cash Scandal," Juvenile Law Center, accessed
August 22, 2017, www.jlc.org/luzerne-county-kids-cash-scandal.

[2]Ibid.

[3]Ibid.

[4]Ibid.

[5]Ibid.

[6]"Pennsylvania Judge Gets 28 Years in 'Kids for Cash' Case: State's Top Court
Tosses Thousands of Convictions Issued by Judge Ciavarella," NBC News,
August 11, 2011, www.nbcnews.com/id/44105072/ns/us_news-crime_and
courts/t/pennsylvania-judge-gets-years-kids-cash-case/#.WZyu-lGnIU.

[7]Lauren Ciavarella Stahl, quoted in Mary Claire Dale, "Judge's Daughter,
'Kids for Cash' Teen Join Forces," *Washington Times*, April 6, 2014, www
.washingtontimes.com/news/2014/apr/6/judges-daughter-kids-for-cash
-teen-join-forces.

[8]Hillary Transue, quoted in ibid.

[9]Stahl, quoted in "Judge's Daughter, 'Kids for Cash' Teen Join Forces."

[10]Ibid.

[11]Mark Ciavarella Jr., quoted in Ronald K. Fried, "'Kids for Cash': Crooked Judge, Damaged Teens, and the Perils of Zero Tolerance," *Daily Beast*, February 25, 2014, www.thedailybeast.com/kids-for-cash-crooked-judge-damaged-teens-and-the-perils-of-zero-tolerance.

[12]Matthew Henry, "Proverbs 31," Bible Study Tools, accessed September 15, 2017, www.biblestudytools.com/commentaries/matthew-henry-complete/proverbs/31.html.

[13]"Locating the School-to-Prison Pipeline," ACLU, accessed August 22, 2017, www.aclu.org/files/images/asset_upload_file966_35553.pdf.

[14]Thalia González, "Keeping Kids in Schools: Restorative Justice, Punitive Discipline, and the School to Prison Pipeline," *Journal of Law & Education* 41, no. 2 (2012): 3.

[15]James Duran, quoted in Mary Ellen Flannery, "The School-to-Prison Pipeline: Time to Shut It Down," NEA Today, January 5, 2015, www.neatoday.org/2015/01/05/school-prison-pipeline-time-shut.

[16]Laura Finley, ed., *Crime and Punishment in America: An Encyclopedia of Trends and Controversies in the Justice System* (Santa Barbara, CA: ABC-CLIO, 2016), 1:510.

[17]Daniel J. Losen, "Discipline Policies, Successful Schools, and Racial Justice," National Education Policy Center, October 5, 2011, 8, www.nepc.colorado.edu/publication/discipline-policies.

[18]"School-to-Prison Pipeline," NAACP Legal Defense and Educational Fund, accessed August 22, 2017, www.naacpldf.org/case/school-prison-pipeline.

[19]Kevin Gilbert, quoted in Flannery, "School-to-Prison Pipeline."

[20]"The School to Prison Pipeline: And the Pathways for LGBT Youth," 2011, Gay-Straight Alliance Network, www.gsanetwork.org/files/resources/STPPdiagram.pdf.

[21]"Civil Rights Data Snapshot: School Discipline," USDE Office for Civil Rights, Issue Brief 1, March 2014, www2.ed.gov/about/offices/list/ocr/docs/crdc-discipline-snapshot.pdf.

[22]"Alvin Ailey," Ancestry.com, accessed August 22, 2017, www.iloveancestry.net/post/75315812948/alvin-ailey-january-5-1931-december-1-1989-if.

[23]Susan Sturm, "Lawyers and the Practice of Workplace Equity," Columbia University Law School, WIS. L. REV., 2002, 277-81.

[24]"Implicit Bias in School Discipline," OSU Kirwan Institute for the Study of Race and Ethnicity, accessed August 22, 2017, www.kirwaninstitute.osu .edu/researchandstrategicinitiatives/school-discipline.

[25]Michelle Alexander, *The New Jim Crow: Mass Incarceration in the Age of Colorblindness* (New York: New Press, 2012), 197.

[26]USDE Civil Rights Data Collection, "Data Snapshot: School Discipline."

[27]The Annie E. Casey Foundation, "Youth in Incarceration in the United States," 2011, www.aecf.org/m/resourcedoc/aecf-YouthIncarcerationInfographic -2013.pdf (last accessed April 15, 2016).

[28]Carla Amurao, "Fact Sheet: How Bad Is the School-to-Prison Pipeline?," PBS, March 28, 2013, www.pbs.org/wnet/tavissmiley/tsr/education-under -arrest/school-to-prison-pipeline-fact-sheet.

[29]Caroline Wolf Harlow, "Education and Correctional Populations," U.S. Department of Justice, Office of Justice Programs, Bureau of Justice Statistics, January 2003, 1.

[30]Amurao, "How Bad Is the School-to-Prison Pipeline?"

[31]"California State Prison–Child Welfare Data Linkage Study," California Department of Social Services, April 8, 2014, 2, www.cdss.ca.gov/cdssweb /entres/pdf/CaliforniaStatePrison-ChildWelfareDataLinkageStudy .pdf.

[32]ACLU, "Locating the School-to-Prison Pipeline."

[33]David N. Figlio, "Testing, Crime and Punishment," *Journal of Public Economics* 90, nos. 4-5 (May 2006).

[34]Anya Kamenetz, "As the Number of Homeless Students Soars, How Schools Can Serve Them Better," NPR, June 13, 2016, www.npr.org/sections/ed /2016/06/13/481279226/as-the-number-of-homeless-students-soars -how-schools-can-serve-them-better.

[35]Melinda Anderson, "When Schooling Meets Policing," *Atlantic*, September 21, 2015, www.theatlantic.com/education/archive/2015/09/when-schooling -meets-policing/406348.

[36]Ibid.

[37]Amanda Petteruti, "Education Under Arrest: The Case Against Police in Schools," Justice Policy Institute Executive Summary, November 15, 2011, 2, www.justicepolicy.org/uploads/justicepolicy/documents/educationunder arrest_executivesummary.pdf.

[38]Anderson, "When Schooling Meets Policing."

[39]Lauren Pearle, "School Shootings Since Columbine: By the Numbers," ABC News, February 12, 2016, www.abcnews.go.com/US/school-shootings -columbine-numbers/story?id=36833245.

[40]Anderson, "When Schooling Meets Policing."

[41]Ibid.

[42]Ibid.

[43]Carol Cole-Frowe and Richard Fausset, "Jarring Image of Police's Use of Force at Texas Pool Party," *New York Times*, June 8, 2015, www.nytimes .com/2015/06/09/us/mckinney-tex-pool-party-dispute-leads-to-police -officer-suspension.html?mcubz=3.

[44]Ibid.

[45]Ibid.

[46]Mark Keierleber, "Why So Few School Cops Are Trained to Work with Kids," *Atlantic*, November 5, 2015, www.theatlantic.com/education/archive /2015/11/why-do-most-school-cops-have-no-student-training-require ments/414286.

[47]Ibid.

[48]Ibid.

[49]Artemis Moshtaghian, "Dallas School Police Use Handcuffs to Restrain 7-Year-Old Boy," CNN News, May 19, 2017, www.cnn.com/2017/05/16/us /boy-handcuffs-dallas-school-trnd.

[50]Keierleber, "Why So Few School Cops Are Trained to Work with Kids."

[51]Regarding Jasmine Darwin, see Holly Yan, "Video Shows North Carolina School Officer Slamming Girl, 15, to Floor," CNN, January 4, 2017, www .cnn.com/2017/01/04/us/north-carolina-officer-body-slams-student.

[52]Maria Guerrero, "Dallas ISD Police Officer Body Slams 12-Year-Old Girl During School Fight," NBCDFT.com, www.nbcdfw.com/news/local/Dallas -ISD-Police-Officer-Body-Slams-12-Year-Old-Girl-During-School-Fight -422397263.html.

[53]"School Resource Officer Accused of Having Sexual Relationship with Student," *The State* (South Carolina), February 8, 2017, www.thestate.com /news/state/south-carolina/article131491979.html.

[54]The following two paragraphs are based on my article "Juvenile Justice System," *Conformed to Be Transformed* (blog), April 17, 2015, www.ctobt.com /juvenile-justice-system.

[55]"Execution of Juveniles in the U.S. and Other Countries," Death Penalty Information Center, accessed August 22, 2017, www.deathpenaltyinfo.org /execution-juveniles-us-and-other-countries.

[56]Juan E. Méndez, "Report of the Special Rapporteur on Torture and Other Cruel, Inhuman or Degrading Treatment or Punishment," Human Rights Council, March 5, 2015, www.ohchr.org/EN/HRBodies/HRC/Regular Sessions/Session28/Documents/A_HRC_28_68_E.doc.

[57]"All Children Are Children: Challenging Abusive Punishment of Juveniles," Equal Justice Initiative, 2017, www.eji.org/sites/default/files /AllChildrenAre Children-2017-sm2.pdf.

[58]Ibid.

[59]Ibid.

[60]Jake Ziedenberg, "You're an Adult Now," National Institute of Corrections, Center for Juvenile Justice, December 2011, www.nicic.gov/Library /files/025555.pdf.

[61]Ibid.

[62]Laura Dimon, "How Solitary Confinement Hurts the Teenage Brain: Teens Isolated in Prison Can Suffer from Mental Health Consequences for Years," *Atlantic*, June 30, 2014.

[63]Lindsay M. Hayes, "Juvenile Suicide in Confinement: A National Survey," National Center on Institutions and Alternatives, February 2009, 24.

[64]"Growing Up Locked Down: Youth in Solitary Confinement in Jails and Prisons Across the United States," ACLU, October 2012, www.aclu.org/report /growing-locked-down-youth-solitary-confinement-jails-and-prisons -across-united-states.

[65]"Children Exposed to Violence," Attorney General's National Task Force, December 12, 2012, 190, www.justice.gov/defendingchildhood/cev-rpt-full.pdf.

[66]Dimon, "How Solitary Confinement Hurts the Teenage Brain."

[67]"Children Exposed to Violence," 190.

[68]Ibid., 177.

[69]Ibid.

[70]Ibid., 175.

[71]Ibid.

[72]"Defending Childhood: Protect, Heal, Thrive," Attorney General's National Task Force on Children Exposed to Violence, accessed August 23, 2017, 175, www.justice.gov/defendingchildhood/cev-rpt-full.pdf.

6 PROTESTANT REFORMERS

[1]Jerry L. Sumney, *Colossians: A Commentary,* The New Testament Library (Louisville: John Knox, 2008), 1.

[2]David E. Garland, *Colossians, Philemon,* NIV Application Commentary (Grand Rapids: Zondervan, 2009), 20-22.

[3]While some believe he might have passed through the city on his third missionary journey, the fact remains that he had no relationship with the congregation.

[4]Murray J. Harris, *Colossians and Philemon* (Nashville: B&H Academic, 2010), 4-5.

[5]Sumney, *Colossians*, 10-11.

[6]Douglass J. Moo, *The Letters to the Colossians and to Philemon* (Grand Rapids: Eerdmans, 2008), 47.

[7]Jennifer Graber, *The Furnace of Affliction: Prisons and Religion in Antebellum America* (Chapel Hill: University of North Carolina Press, 2014), 19.

[8]Ibid., 17.

[9]Ibid., 18.

[10]Ibid.

[11]Ibid., 9.

[12]Adolph Caso, *We, the People: Formative Documents of America's Democracy* (Wellesley, MA: Branden, 1995), 19.

[13]Graber, *Furnace of Affliction*, 20.

[14]"Some historians estimate that 15,000 had been imprisoned by 1689, when the Act of Toleration finally was passed." Margaret H. Bacon, *The Quiet Rebels: The Story of Quakers in America* (New York: Basic Books, 1969), 19.

[15]At that time, a woman's children typically accompanied her to prison.

[16]Bacon, *Quiet Rebels*, 19.

[17]Danny Day, "Prison Reform: Brutality Behind Bars," *Christian History* 57 (1997).

[18]Angela Y. Davis, *Are Prisons Obsolete?* (New York: Seven Stories, 2003), 68.

[19]Graber, *Furnace of Affliction*, 20.

[20]Thomas Eddy, quoted in ibid., 17.

[21]Thomas Eddy, *Account of the State Prison, or Penitentiary House, in the City of New York* (New York: Isaac Collins, 1801), 16.

[22]Ibid., 5.

[23]Graber, *Furnace of Affliction*, 15.

[24]Ibid., 28.

[25]Ibid., 5.

[26]Ibid., 44.

[27]Ibid., 5.

[28]Atonement is a theological term describing how reconciliation between the Creator and creation was manifested through Jesus.

[29]Graber, *Furnace of Affliction*, 12.

[30]Ibid., 13.

[31]Mark Noll, quoted in ibid., 12.

[32]Ibid., 6.

[33]Ibid., 48.

[34]Ibid., 47.

[35]"About Our Founder, Chuck Colson," Prison Fellowship, accessed August 23, 2017, www.prisonfellowship.org/about/chuckcolson.

[36]Morgan Lee, "How Churches Change the Equation for Life After Prison," *Christianity Today*, August 22, 2016.

[37]Aaron Griffith, "Reconsidering Evangelicals and 'Tough on Crime' Politics," Religion and Incarceration, January 23, 2015, www.religionandincarceration.com/2015/01/23/reconsidering-evangelicals-and-tough-on-crime-politics.

[38]"Celebrating Chuck Colson, 'Like I Am,'" YouTube, April 23, 2012, www.youtube.com/watch?v=rJMssRKkS8o&t=435s.

[39]Charles Colson, quoted in Winnifred Fallers Sullivan, *Prison Religion: Faith-Based Reform and the Constitution*, repr. ed. (Princeton, NJ: Princeton University Press, 2011), 104.

[40]Colson, "Celebrating Chuck Colson: 'Like I Am.'"

[41]"The Death Penalty," Prison Fellowship, accessed August 23, 2017, www.prisonfellowship.org/resources/advocacy/sentencing/the-death-penalty.

[42]Charles W. Colson, "Capital Punishment: A Personal Statement," Rutherford Institute, November 11, 2002, www.rutherford.org/publications_resources/oldspeak/capital_punishment_a_personal_statement.

[43]Ibid.

[44]Morgan Lee, "Adding Criminal Justice Reform to Prison Ministry," *Christianity Today*, August 22, 2016, www.christianitytoday.com/ct/2016/september/criminal-justice-reform-prison-ministry.html.

[45]Ibid.

[46]"Faith and Justice Fellowship," Prison Fellowship, accessed August 23, 2017, www.prisonfellowship.org/about/justicereform/landing-pages/faith-and-justice-fellowship.

[47]Sarah Nelson, "Time for Justice Reform Is Now, Leading Evagelicals Say," *Washington Times*, June 20, 2017, www.washingtontimes.com/news/2017/jun/20/evangelicals-say-justice-reform-should-be-a-top-co.

[48]Graber, *Furnace of Affliction*, 2.

[49]Sullivan, *Prison Religion*, 95.

[50]Prison Fellowship, "Responding to Crime and Incarceration: A Call to The Church," 3, www.prisonfellowship.org/site/wp-content/uploads/2017/08/Justice-Declaration-White-Paper_FINAL.pdf

[51]Aaron Griffith, "Prisoners and the Least of These in American Protestantism," *Christian Century*, April 30, 2014, www.christiancentury.org/blogs/archive/2014-04/prisoners-and-least-these-american-protestantism.

[52]Ibid.

[53]Ibid.

[54]Don Davis, "The Essence of TUMI," Urban Ministry Institute, October 7, 2014, youtu.be/s4QYnftRC5Y.

[55]Ibid.

[56]Ibid.

[57]Ibid.

7 THE PRISONERS' PASTOR

[1]"Religion in Prisons—A 50-State Survey of Prison Chaplains," Pew Research Center Religion & Public Life, March 22, 2012, www.pewforum.org/2012/03/22/prison-chaplains-exec.

[2]Maura Poston Zagrans, interview by Sean Salai, "Holistic Prison Ministry," *America: The Jesuit Review*, January 7, 2015, www.americamagazine.org/content/all-things/holistic-prison-ministry-author-qa-maura-poston-zagrans.

[3]Ibid.

[4]Maura Poston Zagrans and David T. Link, *Camerado, I Give You My Hand: How a Powerful Lawyer-Turned-Priest Is Changing the Lives of Men Behind Bars* (New York: Image, 2013), 168.

[5]Ibid., 161.

[6]Jennifer Graber, *The Furnace of Affliction: Prisons and Religion in Antebellum America* (Chapel Hill: University of North Carolina Press, 2014), 52-58.

[7]Ibid., 54.

[8]Seth Bliss, *A Brief History of the American Tract Society* (Boston: American Tract Society, 1857), 4.

[9]John Stanford, *Directory on the Scriptures for Those Under Confinement*, pamphlet 8.

[10]Graber, *Furnace of Affliction*, 106.

[11]Ibid., 113.

[12]Ibid.

[13]Ibid.

[14]Ibid., 114.

[15]James Brice, *Secrets of the Mount-Pleasant State Prison* (Albany, NY: Sabin Americana, 1839), 55.

[16]Graber, *Furnace of Affliction*, 88-91.

[17]Ibid., 88.

[18]Louis Dwight, quoted in Jenks, *A Memoir of the Rev. Louis Dwight* (Boston: T. R. Marvin, 1856), 22.

[19]Graber, *Furnace of Affliction*, 88-92.

[20]Ibid., 108.

[21]Ibid., 111-13.

[22]Levi Burr, *A Voice from Sing Sing: Giving a General Description of the State Prison* (Albany, NY: n.p., 1833), 15.

[23]Ibid., preface.

[24]Graber, *Furnace of Affliction*, 115.

[25]Prison Discipline Society of Boston, "Fifth Annual Report" (1830), 340-42.

[26]Graber, *Furnace of Affliction*, 117.

[27]Prison Discipline Society of Boston, "Fifth Annual Report," 345.

[28]Graber, *Furnace of Affliction*, 120.

[29]W. David Lewis, *From Newgate to Dannemora: The Rise of the Penitentiary in New York 1796–1848* (Ithaca, NY: Cornell University Press, 2009), 149-55.

[30]Graber, *Furnace of Affliction*, 121.

[31]Robert Wiltse, "Report of the Agent of the Mount-Pleasant State Prison," Assembly of the State of New York, March 24, 1834, 40.

[32]Graber, *Furnace of Affliction*, 132.

[33]Ibid., 123.

[34]Ibid.

[35]Ibid., 124.

[36]Kelly Raths, quoted in Emma Green, "What It's Like to Be a Prison Chaplain," *Atlantic*, August 17, 2015, www.theatlantic.com/national/archive /2015/08/helping-people-find-god-in-a-prison-cell/401414.

[37]"Religion in Prisons—A 50-State Survey."

[38]Ibid.

[39]Ibid.

[40]Ibid.

8 THE SPIRIT OF PUNISHMENT

[1]Martin Luther King Jr., "Advice for Living," Stanford University, November 1-30, 1957, kinginstitute.stanford.edu/king-papers/documents/advice -living-1.

[2]Martin Luther King Jr., *Where Do We Go from Here: Chaos or Community?* (Boston: Beacon, 2010), 62-63.

[3]Christopher Marshall, *Beyond Retribution: A New Testament Vision for Justice, Crime, and Punishment* (Grand Rapids: Eerdmans, 2001), 253.

[4]Christopher Marshall, "Divine Justice as Restorative Justice," Center for Christian Ethics, 2012, 12, www.baylor.edu/content/services/document.php /163072.pdf.

[5]Ibid., 14.

[6]Timothy Keller, *Generous Justice: How God's Grace Makes Us Just* (London: Penguin, 2012), 10.

[7]"Righteousness," Theopedia, accessed August 24, 2017, www.theopedia .com/righteousness.

[8]Jörg Jeremias, "Justice and Righteousness: The Message of the Prophets Amos and Isaiah," *Sacra Scripta* 14, no. 1 (2016): 21, 24.

[9]Marshall, "Divine Justice as Restorative Justice," 15.

[10]Ibid., 15, 16.

[11]This means anyone who commits the same violation should be given an equitable penalty, regardless of race, gender, national origin, social status, or sexual orientation. Thus the disproportionate sentencing for crack and powder cocaine would be a prime example of a blatant violation of *mishpat*.

[12]Elsa Tamez, *Bible of the Oppressed* (Maryknoll, NY: Orbis, 2007), 73.

[13]Keller, *Generous Justice*, 6.

[14]Donald Gowan, "Wealth and Poverty in the Old Testament: The Case of the Widow, the Orphan, and the Sojourner," *Interpretation* 41, no. 4 (October 1987): 341.

[15]Ibid., 342.

[16]Ibid., 5.

[17]Daniel Groody, *Globalization, Spirituality & Justice*, rev. ed. (Maryknoll, NY: Orbis, 2015), 34.

[18]Jeremias, "Justice and Righteousness," 21, 25.

[19]Ibid., 23.

[20]Ibid., 25.

[21]David Doty, *Eden's Bridge: The Marketplace in Creation and Mission* (Eugene, OR: Wipf & Stock, 2012), 82.

[22]*Dikaios, dikaioun*, and *dikaiosynē* are words for righteousness in the New Testament (Marshall, "Divine Justice as Restorative Justice," 14).

[23]Ibid.

[24]Ibid., 15.

[25]Doty, *Eden's Bridge*, 83.

[26]Jeremias, "Justice and Righteousness," 24.

[27]Keller, *Generous Justice*, 10.

[28]Ibid., 18.

[29]Doty, *Eden's Bridge*, 83.

[30]*Retribution* comes from the Latin word *retribuere*, meaning "repayment"— giving back what is deserved: reimbursement, reward, or reproof.

[31]Bryan Stevenson, *Just Mercy: A Story of Justice and Redemption*, repr. ed. (New York: Spiegel & Grau, 2015), 17-18.

[32]Ibid., 289-90.

[33]Michelle Alexander, *The New Jim Crow: Mass Incarceration in the Age of Color-blindness* (New York: New Press, 2012), 141.

[34]Marshall, "Divine Justice as Restorative Justice," 14.

[35]Ibid.

9 ATONEMENT AND SANCTIFYING RETRIBUTION

[1]Christology is the study of the person, nature, life, ministry, death, and resurrection of Jesus.

[2]See Scot McKnight, "The Wrath of God Satisfied," *Jesus Creed*, June 22, 2012, www.patheos.com/blogs/jesuscreed/2012/06/22/the-wrath-of-god -satisfied; Ron Sider, "The Cross: Divine Child Abuse, or Astounding Love?," Evangelicals for Social Action, March 26, 2013, www.evangelicals forsocial action.org/holistic-ministry/the-cross-divine-child-abuse-or-astounding -love; and Taylor S. Brown, "Michael Gungor and Misunderstanding

Atonement," March 5, 2017, www.patheos.com/blogs/thechristian revolution/2017/03/michael-gungor-misunderstanding-atonement.

[3]Augustine, quoted in Andrew Skotnicki, *Criminal Justice and the Catholic Church* (Lanham, MD: Rowman & Littlefield, 2007), 36.

[4]Anselm, quoted in Sidney L. Green, *Beating the Bounds: A Symphonic Approach to Orthodoxy in the Anglican Communion* (Eugene, OR: Wipf & Stock, 2013), 10.

[5]Thomas Aquinas, *Summa Theologica* 2.2.1 (New York: Cosimo, 2013).

[6]Ibid., 4.3.1, art. 1.

[7]Frederick Christian Bauerschmidt, *Holy Teaching: Introducing the Summa Theologiae of St. Thomas Aquinas* (Grand Rapids: Brazos, 2005), 242.

[8]"Satisfaction Theory of the Atonement," Theopedia, accessed August 24, 2017, www.theopedia.com/satisfaction-theory-of-the-atonement.

[9]John Calvin, quoted in David Coffey, *Deus Trinitas: The Doctrine of the Triune God* (Oxford: Oxford University Press, 1999), 106.

[10]C. Norman Kraus, *Jesus Christ Our Lord: Christology from a Disciple's Perspective* (Eugene, OR: Wipf & Stock, 1990), 155.

[11]Christopher Marshall, "Divine Justice as Restorative Justice," Baylor University, 2012, 14.

[12]C. S. Lewis, "The Humanitarian Theory of Punishment," Angelfire.com, accessed August 24, 2017, www.angelfire.com/pro/lewiscs/humanitarian .html.

[13]Ibid.

[14]Ibid.

[15]Winnifred Fallers Sullivan, *Prison Religion: Faith-Based Reform and the Constitution* (Princeton, NJ: Princeton University Press, 2011), 101.

[16]Christopher Marshall, *Beyond Retribution: A New Testament Vision for Justice, Crime, and Punishment* (Grand Rapids: Eerdmans, 2001), 65-66.

[17]Ibid., 199.

[18]John Heagle, *Justice Rising: The Emerging Biblical Vision* (Maryknoll, NY: Orbis, 2010), 52.

[19]Angela Y. Davis, *Abolition Democracy: Beyond Empire, Prisons, and Torture* (New York: Seven Stories, 2011), 41.

[20]Marshall, "Divine Justice as Restorative Justice," 18.

[21]Walter J. Burghardt, *Justice: A Global Adventure* (Maryknoll, NY: Orbis, 2004), 25.

[22]Christopher Marshall, *The Little Book of Biblical Justice: A Fresh Approach to the Bible's Teaching on Justice* (Intercourse, PA: Good Books, 2005), 45.

[23]Wrongdoers includes the community that incarcerates people who are innocent.

[24]Burghardt, *Justice*, 54.

[25]T. Richard Snyder, *The Protestant Ethic and the Spirit of Punishment* (Grand Rapids: Eerdmans, 2000), 75-76.

[26]Marshall, *Beyond Retribution*, 257.

[27]Ibid., 47.

[28]Bryan Stevenson, "We Need to Talk About an Injustice," TED Talk, March 2012, www.ted.com/talks/bryan_stevenson_we_need_to_talk_about_an_injustice.

[29]Bryan Stevenson, *Just Mercy: A Story of Justice and Redemption* (New York: Spiegel & Grau, 2015), 313.

[30]Ibid., 53-54.

[31]Rima Vesely-Flad, "The Social Covenant and Mass Incarceration: Theologies of Race and Punishment," *Anglican Theological Review* 93, no. 4 (Fall 2011): 544.

[32]Ibid., 545.

[33]Ibid., 552.

[34]Stevenson, *Just Mercy*, 142.

[35]Bryan Stevenson, "Talks to Oprah About Why We Need to Abolish the Death Penalty," Equal Justice Initiative, November 28, 2015, www.eji.org/news/bryan-stevenson-tells-oprah-winfrey-why-we-should-abolish-death-penalty.

[36]Ibid.

10 DIVINE JUSTICE IS INHERENTLY RESTORATIVE

[1]Michelle Ye Hee Lee, "Does the United States Really Have 5 Percent of the World's Population and One Quarter of the World's Prisoners? Fact Checker," *Washington Post*, April 30, 2015, www.washingtonpost.com/news/fact-checker/wp/2015/04/30/does-the-united-states-really-have-five-percent-of-worlds-population-and-one-quarter-of-the-worlds-prisoners/?utm_term=.f434a000fda8.

[2]Christopher Marshall, "Divine Justice as Restorative Justice," Center for Christian Ethics, 2012, 19, www.baylor.edu/content/services/document.php/163072.pdf.

[3]Ibid.

[4]Bryan Stevenson, *Just Mercy: A Story of Justice and Redemption* (New York: Spiegel & Grau, 2015), 6.

[5]Ibid., 18.

[6]Marshall, "Divine Justice as Restorative Justice," 19.

[7]The restorative justice movement started after philosopher Howard Zehr began to both write about and explore restorative justice in victim-offender conferencing, judicial reform, and criminal justice issues.

[8]These practices have been named by Restorative Justice Practices International. See www.rpiassn.org/practice-areas/rj-models.

[9]For more on the work of Dominic Barter in the favelas, see www.restorative circles.org.

[10]These practices are led by Margaret Burnham of the Civil Rights and Restorative Justice Project (CRRJ), based out of Northeastern School of Law (Boston).

[11]Pew Center on the States, *State of Recidivism: The Revolving Door of America's Prisons* (Washington, DC: Pew Charitable Trusts, 2011), 9. Bridges to Life is a restorative justice-based program that brings "healing to victims of crime, reduces recidivism among offender graduates of the program, and helps make our community a safer place." See more at the Bridges to Life website: www.bridgestolife.org.

[12]Sarah Anne Behtz, "Justice for All? Victim Satisfaction with Restorative Justice Conferences" (PhD diss., East Tennessee State University, December 2004), http://dc.etsu.edu/etd/974.

[13]Restorative circles bring key stakeholders together to honestly share the consequences of the offense and what is needed from each other to move forward together.

[14]Henrissa Bassey, Martha A. Brown, Sonia Jain, and Preety Kalra, *Restorative Justice in Oakland Schools: Implementation and Impacts Report* (Oakland, CA: Data in Action, 2014).

[15]Walter Burghardt, *Justice: A Global Adventure* (Maryknoll, NY: Orbis, 2004), 25.

[16]Christopher Marshall, *The Little Book of Biblical Justice* (Intercourse, PA: Good Books, 2005), 36.

[17]Ibid., 15

[18]Cush (Kush) was the territory south of Israel, in what constitutes Ethiopia today.

[19]Daniel Hays, *From Every People and Nation: A Biblical Theology of Race* (Downers Grove, IL: InterVarsity Press, 2003), 79.

[20]Committee on Causes and Consequences of High Rates of Incarceration and Committee on Law and Justice, *The Growth of Incarceration in the United States: Exploring Causes and Consequences* (Washington, DC: National Academies Press, 2014), 71.

[21]While SB 1070 is Arizona's law, similar bills have been passed into law in Alabama, Georgia, Indiana, South Carolina, and Utah.

[22]Pew Research Center, "America's New Drug Policy Landscape: Two-Thirds Favor Treatment, Not Jail, for Use of Heroin, Cocaine," *U.S. Politics & Policy*, April 2, 2014.

[23]Michael Botticelli, quoted in German Lopez, "The White House's Plan to Reform the War on Drugs," *Vox*, September 10, 2014.

11 HOLY INTERRUPTIONS

[1]Daniel Groody, *Globalization, Spirituality and Justice*, rev. ed. (Maryknoll, NY: Orbis, 2015), 34.

[2]Ibid., 50.

[3]Martin Luther King Jr., "Letter from a Birmingham Jail," April 16, 1963.

[4]Ibid.

[5]Michelle Alexander, quoted in Brentin Mock, "Life After 'The New Jim Crow,'" CityLab, September 30, 2016, www.citylab.com/equity/2016/09/life -after-the-new-jim-crow/502472.

[6]Dennis Gaddy, quoted in Morgan Lee, "How Churches Change the Equation for Life After Prison," *Christianity Today*, August 22, 2016, www.christianity today.com/ct/2016/september/life-after-prison.html.

[7]Michelle Clifton-Soderstrom, "Liberal Arts in Prison: Integrating Lives and Liberating Minds," TEDxNorthPark, June 12, 2017, www.youtube.com /watch?v=C6pf1dW9Bok.

[8]Michelle Clifton-Soderstrom, interview by author, May 31, 2017.

[9]"Certificate in Prison Studies," Duke Divinity School, accessed August 29, 2017, www.divinity.duke.edu/academics/certificates/prison.

[10]Erik Eckholm, "Bible College Helps Some at Louisiana Prison Find Peace," *New York Times*, October 5, 2013, www.nytimes.com/2013/10/06/us/bible -college-helps-some-at-louisiana-prison-find-peace.html.

[11]Burl Cain, quoted in Marilyn Stewart, "NOBTS Angola Prison Celebrates 20 Years of Changing Lives with New Facility," New Orleans Baptist Theological

Seminary, September 8, 2015, www.nobts.edu/gatekeeper/news/2015/nobts -angola-prison-celebrates-20-years-of-changing-lives-with-new-facility.html.

[12]Ibid.

[13]Eckholm, "Bible College Helps Some at Louisiana Prison Find Peace."

[14]Ibid.

[15]Charles S. Kelley Jr., quoted in "NOBTS Angola Prison Celebrates 20 Years of Changing Lives with New Facility."

[16]Yana Kunichoff, "Should Communities Have a Say in How Residents Are Punished for Crime?," *Atlantic*, May 2, 2017, www.theatlantic.com/politics /archive/2017/05/chicago-restorative-justice-court/524238.

[17]Ibid.

[18]Cliff Nellis, quoted in ibid.

[19]Ronal Serpas, quoted in Tracy Conner, "Police Leaders Join Forces to Reduce Mass Incarceration," NBC News, October 21, 2015, www.nbcnews.com/news /us-news/police-leaders-join-forces-reduce-mass-incarceration-n448531.

[20]Conner, "Police Leaders Join Forces to Reduce Mass Incarceration."

[21]Ibid.

[22]See the Old Skool Café website at www.oldskoolcafe.org.

[23]"Why We Do It," Homeboy Industries, accessed August 29, 2017, www .homeboyindustries.org/why-we-do-it.

[24]"What We Do," Homeboy Industries, accessed August 29, 2017, www .homeboyindustries.org/what-we-do/faq.

[25]Michael Carrion, email interview by author, June 1, 2017.

[26]Michelle Alexander, *The New Jim Crow: Mass Incarceration in the Age of Colorblindness* (New York: New Press, 2012), 176.

[27]Christopher Marshall, *Beyond Retribution: A New Testament Vision for Justice, Crime, and Punishment* (Grand Rapids: Eerdmans, 2001), 33.

C|C   CHRISTIAN COMMUNITY
D|A   DEVELOPMENT ASSOCIATION

The Christian Community Development Association (CCDA) is a network of Christians committed to engaging with people and communities in the process of transformation. For over twenty-five years, CCDA has aimed to inspire, train, and connect Christians who seek to bear witness to the Kingdom of God by reclaiming and restoring under-resourced communities. CCDA walks alongside local practitioners and partners as they live out Christian Community Development (CCD) by loving their neighbors.

CCDA was founded in 1989 under the leadership of Dr. John Perkins and several other key leaders who are engaged in the work of Christian Community Development still today. Since then, practitioners and partners engaged in the work of the Kingdom have taken ownership of the movement. Our diverse membership and the breadth of the CCDA family are integral to realizing the vision of restored communities.

The CCDA National Conference was birthed as an annual opportunity for practitioners and partners engaged in CCD to gather, sharing best practices and seeking encouragement, inspiration, and connection to other like-minded Christ-followers, committed to ministry in difficult places. For four days, the CCDA family, coming from across the country and around the world, is reunited around a common vision and heart.

Additionally, the CCDA Institute serves as the educational and training arm of the association, offering workshops and trainings in the philosophy of CCD. We have created a space for diverse groups of leaders to be steeped in the heart of CCD and forge lifelong friendships over the course of two years through CCDA's Leadership Cohort.

CCDA has a long-standing commitment to the confrontation of injustice. Our advocacy and organizing is rooted in Jesus' compassion and commitment to Kingdom justice. While we recognize there are many injustices to be fought, as an association we are strategically working on issues of immigration, mass incarceration, and education reform.

To learn more, visit www.ccda.org/ivp

TITLES FROM CCDA

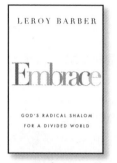

Embrace
978-0-8308-4471-5

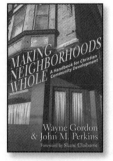

**Making
Neighborhoods Whole**
978-0-8308-3756-4

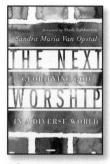

The Next Worship
978-0-8308-4129-5

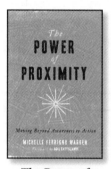

**The Power of
Proximity**
978-0-8308-4390-9

**Rethinking
Incarceration**
978-0-8308-4529-3

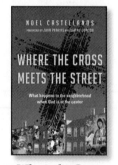

**Where the Cross
Meets the Street**
978-0-8308-3691-8

White Awake
978-0-8308-4393-0